CIVIL SERVICE OR BUREAUCRACY?

By the same author

Civil Service Staff Relationships (1943)

The Civil Service: Its Problems and Future (1945)

Second Edition (1948)

An Introduction to Public Administration (1949)

Second Edition (1952)

The Essentials of Public Administration (1953)

CIVIL SERVICE OR BUREAUCRACY?

E. N. Gladden

M.SC.(Econ.) PH.D.(Public Admin.)

STAPLES PRESS LIMITED
LONDON

FIRST PUBLISHED 1956

This book is set in the 'Monotype' Times New Roman series

Made and printed in England by
STAPLES PRINTERS LIMITED
at their Rochester, Kent, establishment.

'It is the purpose of an organization to "make common men do uncommon things" – this phrasing is Lord Beveridge's. No organization can depend on genius; the supply is always scarce and always unpredictable. But it is the test of an organization that it make ordinary human beings perform better than they are capable of, that it bring out whatever strength there is in its members and use it to make all other members perform more and better. It is the test of an organization that it neutralize the weaknesses of its members.'

PETER F. DRUCKER in *The Practice of Management*
William Heinemann, 1955

INTRODUCTION

My aim in writing this book is (i) to provide an up-to-date description of the British Civil Service as a developing institution, with special reference to its problems as a working body, and (ii) to examine critically the present situation and suggest lines for future development. The book is therefore divided into two parts. Part I – Inquest, while it does not attempt to suppress the writer's viewpoint, is designed primarily to provide an objective picture of the Civil Service as it was and is. Part II – Discussion proffers the writer's personal views which a lifetime's experience as an official, coupled with many years' study of public administration, may perhaps with due modesty justify.

If any justification is needed for yet another book on the Civil Service it is surely that we have reached a watershed in administrative history when it is more important than ever that as much information as possible should be available to assist the citizen in reaching constructive decisions. For this reason the increasing interest in the Civil Service, as indicated by the recent appearance of a number of informative studies on the subject, is to be welcomed. It is a vast and intricate field which existing literature does not even yet completely cover and which in any case cannot be covered in one book of normal dimensions.

In this book I do not hide my view that we have reached a moment of crisis at which complacent acceptance of past successes and virtues, as an excuse to continue on similar lines with the least possible change, may well lead us to irrevocable decline. Apart from the existing urgency, this particular moment, when a new Royal Commission (Priestley) has just reported and the vast portent of automation is casting its challenging shadows before, seems to be a very suitable one for a stocktaking of the type that I have attempted here. Indeed, I have been fortunate in being able to bring the text up to the time of the recent agreement between the Government and the Civil Service on the Royal Commission's findings.

A glance at the Contents sheet will suffice to show the reader what the book is all about. A few words on what it is *not* may save some misconceptions. In the first place, it is not a new edition of my *The Civil Service: Its Problems and Future* which was first published, by the Staples Press, in 1945. That book gives a picture of the pre-war Civil Service, as modified by wartime events. There are inevitable parallels in the design of the two works, but the present book has been completely re-written from a mid-century standpoint. In the second place, the present book is confined to the administrative sectors of the Civil Service (using the term in the broadest sense to cover the office branches). Limitation of space has made it necessary to pay only occasional attention to wide and important sectors of the Civil Service, e.g. the Foreign Service and other specialist branches, the technical and professional sectors, the manipulative grades, the industrial side. It is usual to restrict the scope of Civil Service studies in this way, though all writers do not make it clear that they are doing so. In my view the necessity for this is to be deplored, but writers, more today than ever, are conditioned by economics. A post-war attempt on my own part to cover the wider field, in a work running to at least twice the length of the present book, was doomed to be stillborn. As a further consequence of the vastness of the subject, it should also be emphasized that the present work does not deal, except incidentally, with the functions and organization of the Central Departments. To attempt in a book of normal size to perform a task that calls for separate treatises would be to ensure the maximum of dissatisfaction on the reader's part.

With the general reader's interests in view I have embodied as much information as possible in the text, using footnotes sparingly only when further information seemed essential. With the student's interest in view – and I should consider my efforts more than justified if my writings served to increase the academic interest in this subject – I have appended an annotated bibliography, the judicious use of which will, I hope, enable the interested reader to follow up ideas only broadly outlined in the text.

Let me now state categorically that this study has been written without financial aid of any sort. It is my entire responsibility. If there are mistakes – and I hope I have succeeded in cutting these down to the minimum – the blame is mine alone. I shall be more than grateful if the reader who is sufficiently interested will drop me a line on the subject. While I have been given official permission for the publication of the work, in accordance with the usual practice in the case of writings of this nature by State servants, I must emphasize that the book does not in any way present an official viewpoint, nor does permission to publish in any way endorse the factual accuracy of the text itself.

I would like to take this opportunity to place on record my gratitude to Mr Ronald Staples, of Staples Press Ltd., for the great interest he has shown both in this present work and in previous studies in public administration. Without his live interest and the willingness of the publishers to take the inevitable financial risks of producing works in this field, in which demand is painfully restricted, these studies could not have been pursued.

Acknowledgment is also due to the Controller of Her Majesty's

Stationery Office for information quoted from various official publications, and to the Staff Side of the Civil Service National Whitley Council for information quoted from *The Whitley Bulletin*.

In conclusion, I would like to thank very sincerely Mr W. H. A. Sutton, B.A.(Oxon.), an experienced colleague in another Government Department, for his trouble in going through the typescript and for his constructive and very illuminating comments in our subsequent conversations. My gratitude is also due to my wife for her creative silences and domestic forbearance when the work was being thought out and written, and for participating in the arduous task of reading through the proofs.

E. N. GLADDEN.

Birmingham, *July* 1956.

CONTENTS

Part I - INQUEST

Part II – DISCUSSION

TABLES, DIAGRAMS, ETC.

PART I

INQUEST

CHAPTER I

THE MEANING OF CIVIL SERVICE

'Civil Service' is the name of an important government institution, comprising the staffs of the central administration of the State. It is more, for it stands for a spirit essential to the success of modern democracy, an ideal of vocation in public officials who devote their lives to the service of the community. Such a spiritual driving force was needed to replace the traditions of aristocratic public service, peculiar to more oligarchic types of government, that modern developments have to such a great extent rendered ineffectual.

As an institution the Civil Service in Britain is well known and highly regarded. Its high professional integrity and absence of personal scandal are accepted without question by a nation that rarely stops to consider what it has done to deserve so much. For it is widely understood that in other climes similar levels of public service, prestige and official morality are, even today, too frequently the exception rather than the rule. To the no less essential spirit of civil service much less attention is given. It is taken for granted where it is understood at all. But such a spirit needs understanding and appreciation on the part of those served and unfortunately much misplaced antagonism tends seriously to undermine the confidence that the citizen in his own interest should be eager to conserve. It is, however, true that the most critical reactions are against the individual official rather than the institution itself. For even in an age when almost everyone expects to receive some service from the State, the civil servant is habitually regarded as a nuisance, a bureaucrat, or even a drone, employed non-productively at the instance of some Lord High Inventor of Useless Posts.

No doubt there was a better excuse for such attitudes in the past than in this age of the Social Service or Welfare State which calls for the ministrations of such a large band of public officials. Throughout the ages officials have been reviled as the agents of the strong in oppressing the weak, agents not usually averse from turning the public business to their own advantage. The official was ubiquitous and his services essential from a very early age. On the mountains and the plains, and especially in the river hinterlands, of the Middle East extensive evidence has been unearthed of an advanced administrative system that already existed over four thousand years ago. Incised stones, baked clay tablets marked in cuneiform characters, hieroglyphics on temple walls and, later, papyrus rolls, all of which were the stock-in-trade of the recorders of government activities, have as if by a miracle survived in abundance. When it all first began we do not know, but that it has continued since the beginnings of civilization in many forms and continues today, in increasing volume, we are too well aware. Not only in the magnificent realms of Babylon, Egypt, China, Greece, Rome and Byzantium, but in every petty realm throughout the world the official has been industriously occupied. As the household of the ruler acquired new public functions the demand for the educated official grew. There has been a regular pattern in this development which has persisted right up to the modern age. From among the growing band of personal servants around the leader, confided with the task of minding the goods and monies, accounting for the supplies, transmitting the ruler's authority, taking care of his authenticating seals, individuals stood out as functionaries with administrative duties. In good periods positions of trust were given to those who were both competent and trustworthy. In Britain this pattern could still be discerned in the times of the Stuarts and the first Hanoverians. It was not indeed until the end of the eighteenth century that the true ideal of civil service began to emerge – a new idea for a new era.

It was in relation to the East India Company that the term 'Civil Service' was first used, mainly to distinguish between the military and civil sectors of the Company's personnel. The Oxford English Dictionary gives the date of its emergence as 1785. This was an important distinction at the time, though we are today less bothered by the confusion between the civil and the other branches of government. In all those early empires, which we have just mentioned, the distinction was only occasionally clearly drawn and so long as war was the habitual means of governing this was bound to be so, as indeed it still is today when war supervenes. Civil Service, therefore, is a child of peace rather than war, however important its efficiency may be in organizing the State for armed conflict. During the nineteenth century a further differentiation, namely between the politician and the official which had been under way for some time, was considerably accelerated, but it was not until the defeat of patronage and the introduction of impartial selection by means of open competition that the idea of a professional, impartial and devoted service of the State, irrespective of the political colour of the Government, took on its modern shape. A true Civil Service had at last emerged.

Legal definitions are to be found in the Superannuation Acts of 1859 and 1887, depending upon the holding of the Civil Service Commissioners' certificate, but these confined the term 'civil servant' to permanent officers. It would, however, be unrealistic to exclude the large fringe of temporary officials who are at all times to be found in the central departments. As good and as authoritative a description as any was provided in the Treasury's submission[1] to the Royal Commission (Tomlin) on the Civil Service of 1929–31, which ran: 'Broadly, therefore, a civil servant may be defined as a servant of the Crown (not being the holder of a political or judicial office) who is employed in a civil capacity and whose remuneration is wholly paid out of monies provided by Parliament.' Even this definition excludes the staffs of certain quasi-civil service organizations such as the Crown Agents for Oversea Governments and Administrations, the Church Commissioners, and Trinity House, whose status and conditions of service are practically indistinguishable from those of the Civil Service, except that these departments do not subsist upon Parliamentary monies. It is also usual to exclude the industrial workers of the dockyards, ordnance factories, Post Office and certain other departments and to confine the term to the non-industrial grades who deal with the administrative rather than the productive functions of the central departments. The field with which we are concerned is broadly covered by the Civil Service National Whitley Council.[2] In order to keep this book to reasonable limits the discussion will be confined to the non-industrial Civil Service, although it will be as well to remember that similar considerations and principles often apply also to the industrial sphere.

The Civil Service comprises broadly the civilian employees of the central government. The staffs of the numerous local government authorities and of the public corporations, while sharing both public virtues and public vices with the Civil Service, do not share the label, and by reason of their different constitutional positions may very well be less subject than the central government official to the slings and arrows of public opinion. Even so the distinction is sometimes very narrow. Local government officials, acting as agents of the central departments, may differ very little from, say, the minions of a central department sharing a contiguous office. In some countries indeed members of the Civil Service operate in the local government departments. It is a matter of history rather than logic whether the railway official is a State servant like his opposite number in the Post Office, and of constitutional custom whether the policeman or the schoolteacher are civil servants. In Britain they are not. But with the growth of socialization the boundaries cannot be defined and it would perhaps be as well to keep an open mind on where precisely the lines of demarcation should be drawn.

Some writers, even in official publications, have used Civil Service as a synonym for the central departments in the broadest sense. This may

[1] *Introductory Memorandum relating to the Civil Service* (1930), see p. 2.

[2] But this includes certain Post Office engineering and allied grades which are industrial and excludes the Foreign Service, which is independently organized.

confuse and is to be avoided. It is true that the central departments are mainly staffed by the Civil Service, but the wider term must also include the political leaders as well as such non-Civil Service elements as the professional members of the armed forces in the Defence departments. In this book Civil Service refers only to the personnel of the central administration so defined. The departments and their work are a separate consideration, even though the Civil Service is the very essence of their being.

The broad categories of the non-industrial Civil Service are shown in Table I, on page 20.

TABLE I

Non-Industrial Civil Servants in Britain, 1939, 1947 and 1955

Official classification	1939 April 1st	1947[1] April 1st	1955 April 1st
Administrative	2,100	4,200	3,500
Executive (general service and departmental)	19,300	50,600	67,300
Clerical and sub-clerical (general service and departmental)	112,900	260,500	184,800
Typing	15,300	30,400	26,800
Inspectorate	5,800	5,600	2,800
Professional, scientific and technical[2]	11,000	37,400	72,600
Ancillary technical, etc.[2]	25,900	54,600	38,600
Minor and Manipulative[2]	162,600	195,100	190,600
Messengers, porters, etc.	19,400	45,600	29,700
Total whole-time officials	374,300	684,000	616,700
Add part-time (two counted as one)	13,100	21,500	19,000
Grand Total	387,400	705,500	635,700
Males	289,000	434,400	434,000
Females	98,400	271,100	201,700

[1] 1947 was the peak year for whole-time staff.

[2] These groups were re-defined between 1946 and 1947; the second and third columns are not therefore comparable with the first.

THE WORK OF THE CIVIL SERVICE

Despite certain popular prejudices the civil servant has a considerable job of work to do. He is not employed for the good of his health; the day of the sinecure post has passed and although 'empire building', or the creation of unnecessary posts for prestige purposes, is always a possibility this is one of the dangers that a wider understanding of the Civil Service's true function will help to counter. The tasks of the Civil Service are indeed multifarious and not easy therefore briefly to describe.

Broadly speaking the Civil Service carries out the work of the Executive branch of the Government. The Executive has grown out of the Royal Household and developed since the day when the King himself was the Executive. As his work extended it became necessary to delegate functions to assistants or ministers. Gradually a system of departments emerged, each branch more or less specializing in work of a particular type. The extension of the scope of the Executive has been due partly to the action of Parliament in confiding it with new tasks, and partly to the changing nature of the modern social and economic community for which the Government acts. Today we are confronted by a vast array of immensely powerful and all-pervading central departments whose function it is to serve us, although many feel as children in their impressive embrace. Table II on page 22, which classifies the staffs covered by Table I[1], according to the departmental pattern, will serve to indicate the size of these larger departments.

It is in the nature of this development of the offices of the State that each minister, the king's specialist in his own particular sphere, is assisted by the permanent members of his department, who virtually form his collective secretary. The permanent head is still usually known as the Secretary, assisted indeed by a band of Deputy, Under and Assistant Secretaries. He is in fact the historical descendant of the Minister of State's secretary, whose job it was to keep his master's records and act as his general factotum. Today the department, with its vast number of civil servants in many grades, is still the minister's administrative factotum, who enables him to carry out the State functions for which he has been made responsible. The department is the store of administrative experience ever at hand to inform the minister and assist him in making up his mind or to warn him against attempting the impossible. In other words the department is the minister's secretary that keeps his records in their infinite complexity and enables him to render an account of his stewardship almost at a moment's notice: it is also his executive arm, expert in carrying out his particular specialism in governing, possibly in a merely regulatory way as in the more traditional type of government, possibly by the provision of actual services, as the State becomes more and more the nation's Universal Provider.

TABLE II

Non-Industrial Civil Servants, Distributed according to Departments, on April 1st, 1955

Post Office		247,800
Service and Supply Departments		
Admiralty	33,700	
War Office	39,200	
Air Ministry	26,600	
Supply	34,000	
Smaller departments[1]	800	
		134,300
Social Services		
Education	2,900	
Health	5,800	
Housing and Local Government	3,000	
National Assistance Board	10,300	
Pensions and National Insurance	37,800	
Smaller departments[1]	6,200	
		66,000
Revenue Departments		
Inland Revenue	50,500	
Customs and Excise	14,900	
		65,400
Trade, Industry and Transport		
Agriculture and Fisheries	12,400	
Food	5,600	
Forestry Commission	2,300	
Fuel and Power	2,100	
Labour and National Service	22,900	
Scientific and Industrial Research	3,200	
Board of Trade	7,300	
Transport and Civil Aviation	10,700	
Smaller departments[1]	2,600	
		69,100
Agency Services		
Ordnance Survey	4,000	
Stationery Office	3,000	
Works	13,100	
Smaller departments[1]	700	
		20,800
Central Government, Home and Legal Departments		
County Courts	2,000	
Home Office	3,300	
Prison Commission	6,700	
Smaller departments[1]	11,900	
		23,900
Foreign and Imperial Services		
Foreign Office	5,700	
Smaller departments[1]	2,700	
		8,400
	Grand Total	635,700

[1] These entries cover all departments with Staffs numbering less than 2,000.

The central departments are no longer confined within the once regal precincts of Whitehall, nor is the individual civil servant of today so inevitably a man of the desk. Yet the idea of the Civil Service as an essentially clerical occupation still persists and, despite the recent additions to the vast central administrative structure, it is to be admitted that there is still good logic in this. The Civil Service is predominantly an administrative profession. The one activity that most of its members invariably undertake at one time or another is penmanship and the keeping of records. It is in the very nature of this universal activity, the main means to administering, that the special problems of the Civil Service are to be found.

It might be possible in a book of the present length to provide a reasonably adequate outline of the multifarious tasks of the Civil Service in Britain, but there would be little room for anything else. Thus we indicate here only a few of the general aspects of this varied field of activity.

As we have seen the most characteristic activity of the civil servant is administration, meaning the whole gamut of office work from mechanical copying and recording of the routine clerk or machinist, through the various shades of clerical work, and office supervision and management to the higher policy-making tasks of administration. It is difficult to draw a line between clerical work and administration, and in fact the best definition will permit the greater to include the lesser. It is true that the leaders will be concerned with policy formulation, together with organization, direction and control, but in this they do not differ from leaders in other fields of activity, except that their field is administration, not as a by-product, but as a major activity. They, too, are concerned with records, with correspondence and particularly with the manipulation of files, with committee meetings and personal consultations. Their work is still essentially of a literary nature.

The leading civil servants are the administrators whose function is to advise the political ministers and to run the administrative organization which is essential to the fulfilment of the tasks that Parliament and the Government have delegated to the ministers. They are the recipients of the store of experience of the department, able without acting politically to understand the political assumptions of the particular field of activity and to manipulate the administrative means needed to achieve the ends determined by the minister, as well as to make him aware of the administrative limits within which the policies he may be inclined to choose are workable. Below the administrators are the middle grades responsible for running the administrative machine, often in offices distributed throughout the country: management is one of their important functions. Below them are the clerks in various grades, the machinists, the office-keepers and the messengers who carry out the ordinary routines of the offices. There is indeed a wide variety in this office work and, especially today when the State provides many services directly to the people, these clerks have contacts with the public which call for capacities that were rarely needed by the office worker in the past. There is throughout these various departments work of a specialized type which is the same in each department and is carried out by members of the general classes, e.g. personnel or establishment work, finance work, instruction work.

These general administrative processes are universal, not only throughout the government departments, but wherever administration goes on. This means almost everywhere in the modern world, which is increasingly becoming an Administrative Society. The main difference is that in the public sphere administration is still usually the major activity and is subject to special rules and conditions that are prescribed by the peculiar nature of State activity.

In addition, the staffs of the several departments have to be expert in the specialized work of their own department. Each minister is at the centre of a specialist world and the functions of the departments vary considerably. The main departments are well known, ranging as they do over financial affairs and tax collection, defence measures, Commonwealth and foreign contacts, internal domestic affairs, social services, industry, employment and general supplies, but a reference to Table II on page 22 will suffice to refresh the reader's knowledge of the great variety of work of the central departments. Some departments have work of a regulatory nature, others actually provide services direct to the public. There is a great difference between the work of the defence departments and that of the revenue and taxation departments, between trade and communications departments and the social service departments. In some cases the civil servants, down to the most junior office grades, need to study the law and regulations on which their work is based: in some cases expert gradings have been introduced or special departmental classes have been recruited instead of the general classes.

Experts of all kinds act sometimes in an advisory capacity, sometimes as executives. They are usually specially recruited. Members of most of the professions are required, particularly legal experts who are needed in all departments to advise on legal matters and possibly to handle legal proceedings in which the department is concerned. Medical officers are widely needed, as well as qualified accountants, where the examination of outside accounts is in question. Scientists are widely employed, especially in the defence and supply departments and scientific research branches. A vast organization like the Post Office not only has a large complement of the ordinary Civil Service grades to carry out the administrative work, but also needs a host of competent engineers to design and service the large communications machine on which the Post Office's main activities depend, as well as a number of specialist grades peculiar to its own line of activity, such as postmen, sorters, telegraphists and telephonists, who are usually classified as the manipulative grades. The Stationery Office needs printers; the Ministry of Works, architects and builders; the Prison Commission, warders and governors of prisons. Nor must we overlook the specially appointed inspectors of schools and of factories, and the rest, whose responsible duties are a characteristic of public administration.

The modern state has need of the services of specialists galore and to define the functions of the Civil Service becomes increasingly difficult. If, however, we remember that, despite their legal status as civil servants, members of the professions and other distinct occupations, which have a wider sphere outside the government service, are ultimately conditioned by the occupational requirements of their own particular vocations; and if we remember that certain almost purely public activities – such as posts, telecommunications, prison administration – present specialized fields of activity calling for independent study, it will be clear that there remains a reasonably homogeneous core of more purely administrative workers about whom the traditional and characteristic problems of the Civil Service arise and to whom the attention of this book can be rationally confined. Moreover, this restriction of focus is justified by the common conception of the Civil Service which does not usually bring to mind the more specialist sectors to which very broad reference has just been made. Our main concern, therefore, is with the office workers with whom more than anyone else the essential characteristics of the Civil Service can correctly be associated. But in adopting this standpoint it would be misleading to overlook the possibility of a radical disturbance of the relative importance of the different groups taking place in the not distant future. The present situation in this respect is certainly dynamic. The increasing importance of technology in the national economy and the advance of automation are portents of change.

THE CIVIL SERVICE OUTLOOK

During the last two hundred years there has been a radical change in the outlook of the official in Britain, a change exemplified by the gradual emergence of the Social Service or Welfare State out of the Aristocratic Police State. In the earlier phase the Government was concerned mainly with preserving the peace, defending the realm from foreign enemies and obtaining the supplies necessary for achieving these objectives, a broadened version of the original function of the ruler and his household. There was, of course, always an element of social service, but it was necessarily limited by the resources available and was usually confined to local operation. Religious and voluntary organizations bore the main burden, while the initiating energies were associated with the free services of the leisured class. It is only during the last hundred years or so that the advances of science and invention have provided the means for administering effectively country-wide services.

The concept of a Civil Service, a professional body of neutral experts in administration dedicated to serve the nation irrespective of their own gain and without reference to party political views or class interests, is thus a modern one. It is interesting to note that during the same period most of the restrictions on office-holding based upon religious belief have disappeared, but sad to relate that in the most recent phase the holding of views of a certain religio-political nature have had to be prescribed to holders of certain posts of trust.

It is characteristic of the idea of Civil Service that the individual official is known as a 'servant'. This is not a usual designation for the member of a service and it deserves consideration. The truth is that the civil servant, although basically his service is to the Crown, whose servant he still is, is habitually conscious of his duty to serve the community, albeit through his master, the Government, which is indeed the people's instrument. In this, indeed, the Civil Service differs fundamentally from Bureaucracy, which is self-seeking and self-controlled or the instrument of a narrow oligarchy. There is a tendency to use the term 'bureaucracy' to mean an organization of offices on a large scale, usually with an implication of inefficiency through the use of roundabout or red tape methods, but in truth the mention of Bureaucracy rarely fails to conjure up the vast brute figure of one of the giants against which the ordinary man must ever be prepared to contend. There is nothing of the essence of Civil Service about this. The Civil Service is the people's service, set up to do nothing more than the people's will.

Much criticism of the Civil Service is misinformed and, it is to be feared, misguided. Even high-minded authorities allow themselves to nod when confusing Civil Service with Bureaucracy. Much of the late Lord Chief Justice, Lord Hewart's famous tirade against the Civil Service represented a natural personal reaction against what he considered to be Parliament's attrition of the Judiciary's historic prerogatives. Lord Hewart, in making his case in *The New Despotism* (1929), accused the Civil Service of grasping for power through the exercise of subordinate legislation and delegated adjudication; developments which were in fact the legislature's way of ensuring the efficient execution of technical matters no longer, for reasons of time and complexity, effectively within its own competence. But the delegation is made according to the conscious sovereign will of Parliament and the criticism, if it was to be made at all, should have been directed to the right quarter. It is an unfair, as well as a misguided, form of attack, not only because the Civil Service is constitutionally incapable of defending itself, but because it panders to the ignorant, if understandable, reactions of many citizens. For this reason it is not likely to cease to be effectively used by publicists who prefer to mask their rooted dislike for all State activity under a more popular cloak. They may be fully justified in their dislike of the policy adopted by the legislature yet dishonest in insisting upon beating the wrong horse in the name of justice. Certain, less responsible, members of the Press, well aware of the popular dislike of the official even among avowed socialists, take every opportunity to stigmatize the civil servant as 'bureaucrat', and to magnify his every failing while ignoring even the most obvious virtue. Thus one of the most popular dailies rejoiced over an announcement by the Civil Service Commissioners in November 1953 that they were unable to attract sufficient competent clerks to the examinations. They allowed their dislike of the Civil Service to obscure the obvious truth that a loss of official efficiency is to nobody's advantage.

Even a well-wisher such as the late Professor Laski, who knew the Civil Service very well, suggested in his *Democracy in Crisis* (1933) that, with the advent of a leftish government, the Civil Service was likely to show partiality for the *status quo* and obstruct the introduction of necessary social changes. The wrongheadedness of this suggestion, adopted no doubt at the time to add point to the Marxist thesis which the writer supported, was amply proved with the implementation of the radical policies of the post-war Labour Government of 1945. Possibly it is unwise to take such pronouncements too seriously, particularly as Professor Laski himself had earlier[1] made a special point of the essential neutrality of the British Civil Service in serving whatever political party might be chosen by the people. It is a vital characteristic of Civil Service that it shall be professionally inspired and politically neutral. Its job is to administer and a citizen who is not prepared to serve loyally any government chosen by the people, whatever its political colour, should never think of entering the Civil Service.

Much current criticism, it must be insisted, rests upon ignorance, not merely of the Civil Service and its function, a sufficiently obscure field of knowledge it must be confessed, but of the very form and scope of our government and of the duties and rights of citizenship. As the attainment and maintenance of democracy itself depends upon the wide dissemination of positive knowledge any excuse for this citizen ignorance is virtually a plea for some form of oligarchy or dictatorship.

All this is not to suggest that the Civil Service is above criticism. This is indeed far from being the case, as later chapters of this book will most certainly show. Our plea is that all criticism should be based upon understanding, for only in this way can the people participate constructively in reshaping their own instrument. The Civil Service itself loses from a lack of understanding and suffers irreparably if it

[1] Introduction to Henry Taylor's *The Statesman* (1927 reprint).

cannot call upon the considered views of those, outside its ranks, whose minds are not biased through being too close to the official grindstone.

FROM THE WIDER STANDPOINT

It is not an uncommon habit of other administrators piously to pray that they will not act in the roundabout or procrastinating way to which civil servants are supposed to be inherently addicted or of the outside critic to suggest that what the Civil Service needs is an inflow of persons brought up in the school of business. There is both truth and misconception in such attitudes. If, however, the civil servant is habitually non-committal and inclined to get everything down in black and white, with somewhat dilatory results, this is surely attributable to the system he serves and not necessarily to his own ineradicable nature. It is true, of course, that the circumspect and the unenterprising are more likely to feel at home, to settle down as it were, in the Civil Service: it is equally true that lifelong service in the cautious atmosphere of a government department is calculated to damp down any inclination to experiment, but it is the public nature of the system itself that moulds the Civil Service and not vice versa. Responsibility to the political head means that the Civil Service must be anonymous and objective. Responsibility to the public at large through the machinery of parliamentary government means that the civil servant must place on record much that is inessential to the ordinary administrative purposes of his department.

On the other hand it is easy to overemphasize the failings of red tape and 'bureaucracy', so called, in the Civil Service. Critics often speak from hearsay. Some civil servants undoubtedly press caution too far – but these are matters to consider at the end rather than the beginning of this survey. There is certainly a tendency to exaggerate the influence of red tape on the administration of the central departments, and to underestimate its effects elsewhere. It will, for example, be a much more important factor in the working of a department of the older regulatory type than in a technical department like the Post Office where much of the detailed day-to-day working of the system will have no shadow of interest to the ordinary citizen, or, at the opposite extreme, in a social service ministry which in its numerous daily contacts with individual citizens carries out many public relations activities that depend upon effective human understanding and not necessarily upon the keeping of records.

There is also, on a somewhat different plane, the suggestion that the State alone is the inspirer of bureaucratic methods, as exemplified by the proliferation of offices, the inordinate use of forms and the lack of the personal touch. It seems, however, that these trends towards technical bureaucracy can be attributed just as much to the large-scale element in State activity as to its governmental aspect. In a world in which the large-scale element tends more and more to abound traits common in the Civil Service are encountered more and more in other spheres of activity. The Organizational Revolution[1] touches all branches of human activity, and it is arguable that the growth of hierarchy which has always characterized governmental organization, both military and civil, and created special problems of relationship within the public structure, is now spreading far and wide, wherever large-scale organization becomes necessary.

The expansion of public administration is a phenomenon that cannot be ignored. Yet it is easy to take it for granted and to evade the problems that the change of emphasis between the private and the public sectors of the economy has been effecting, particularly during the last fifty years. It is easy enough to condemn it out of hand on the lines adopted by the critics already mentioned or of equally stimulating writings exemplified by Ludwig von Mises in *Bureaucracy* (1945), C. K. Allen in *Law and Orders* (1945) and G. W. Keeton in *The Passing of Parliament* (1952), but the cure, if there be one, will be found only in a wider understanding of the basic reasons for these developments. It is certainly unfortunate that democracy, whose success ultimately depends upon such understanding, displays a frightening lack of interest in such matters.

It is as part of this wider sphere of public administration, which encompasses not only the activities of the State, but also those of the numerous local authorities and the growing band of public corporations and other semi-autonomous public bodies, that the Civil Service needs to be understood, unless the people are to wash their hands of all responsibility for its shaping. To be understood the Civil Service must be studied and it is as an aid to such study that this present volume is offered. In the course of generalization much detailed information will have to be omitted, for the pattern is so infinitely varied that only a long treatise could adequately convey the precise shape and varied essence of the Civil Service as it really is today. Within the vast machine, and despite its general rules, practices vary so infinitely that almost everything that can be generally denied in relation to the Civil Service will be found to be true in relation to some small part of it.

In a democracy the Civil Service belongs to the people, and really to belong a thing must be understood. Such understanding in the present instance depends to a high degree upon an appreciation that the Civil Service differs in no way from other political institutions in being the product of an historical development which is exemplified in its living structure. Accounts that do not recognize this, attempting to describe and analyse the Civil Service as though it were a dead butterfly on a

[1] See particularly K. E. Boulding in *The Organizational Revolution* (U.S.A., 1953).

setting board, fail inevitably to convey a true picture of it in its dynamic significance.

The next chapter will explain briefly how the present organization of the British Civil Service has emerged and sketch out its general structure.

CHAPTER II

THE MODERN PATTERN EMERGES

The beginnings of the British Civil Service are to be discovered in the courts of the Anglo-Saxon kings, when for the first time administration had emerged as a distinct activity and clerks were beginning to be employed on a whole time basis. An administration profession had been born in Britain for the first time since the Roman withdrawal. We do not know precisely when or at which court this happened, but the distinction of being the first named civil servant appears to be due to a certain Ælfwine, to whom, when making him a grant of land in 993, King Æthelred II referred as 'his faithful writer'. Stenton suggests that the history of the Civil Service actually begins in the reign of Æthelstan (A.D. 925–39) when it is known that a staff of clerks was available to accompany the king in his progresses through his realm.[1]

To trace this development for the next thousand years would take more space and, indeed, more research than this present work demands. It is only occasionally, in the interstices of general history, as it were, that the activities can be discerned of these servants, whom we can justly dub, to use a modern expression, the back-room boys of court and government. The whole interesting story would take us along with the struggle of the monarchy with the nobles, the conjuncture of Church and State, the rise of the Tudors, the struggle between Crown and Parliament, and, finally, the achievement of supremacy by the latter in the name of the people. We should watch the Exchequer Court in session; see the tallies being notched, the royal seals being impressed, the Pipe Rolls being laboriously copied. We should note how the Chamber and the Wardrobe gradually gave place to new offices; as the Royal Household became departmentalized, and witness the early emergence of the Treasury, the Secretaryship of State and the Board of Admiralty. We should travel with Chaucer to Canterbury, with Samuel Pepys to Chatham, and with Henry Fielding to the Fleet Prison. On February 11th, 1780, in the House of Commons, we should be listening to an impassioned appeal by Edmund Burke for retrenchment under the submission of 'A plan of reform in the constitution of several parts of the public economy'.

It is not in fact necessary to go back further than the year 1853, which has as good a claim as any to be designated the birth-date of the modern Civil Service. It is true that a good deal had already been done to build

[1] F. M. Stenton *Anglo-Saxon England* (1943), p. 349.

up a coherent State administrative service. Sinecures had been considerably reduced, the Treasury had already gained the right to lay down general conditions of service and many of the evils castigated by Burke, if not completely eliminated, had been considerably restricted. But the administrative staffs of the central government were still, though legally servants of the Crown, subject to the ministerial heads of the several departments. They formed a service in their ultimate allegiance, but otherwise were within the patronage of a number of separate political authorities. Only with regard to their superannuation had Parliament claimed the right to lay down the terms to which they should be subjected.

The history of the Civil Service during the next hundred years is most clearly recorded in the reports of the various committees of investigation set up to inquire into its structure and working. Therefore the story may perhaps be most helpfully condensed through a brief review of the most important of these inquiries.

THE TREVELYAN-NORTHCOTE PROPOSALS[1], 1853–4

The most notable of these reports, which was signed on November 23rd, 1853, and subsequently published under the title 'Report on the Organization of the Permanent Civil Service', was the work of two outstanding men, Sir Charles Edward Trevelyan and Sir Stafford Northcote. The former was at the time Assistant Secretary at H.M. Treasury, or virtually head of the permanent staff of that department, a post he held for nineteen years. He had come to this position after a distinguished early career in the Indian Civil Service, to which he was later to return. Northcote had been legal assistant at the Board of Trade, as well as private secretary to Gladstone when he was President of that Board: he subsequently transferred his main activities to the political sphere. These investigators had had the advantage of participating in a series of inquiries into the public offices which had begun with the Treasury itself in 1848 and was still in progress. Although the ideas in the Report were by no means new they amounted to a charter for the modern Civil Service, of which Trevelyan can justly be singled out as the father.

[1] 1854 has recently been officially recognized as the year of the Report but, in so far as the inquiry was authorized by Treasury Minute during 1853 and the Report itself was both drafted and signed during the same year there appears to be little excuse for this post-dating. Further, the proposals are now officially labelled 'Northcote-Trevelyan' but as Trevelyan was undoubtedly the driving force in this matter the previous common practice of using the description 'Trevelyan-Northcote' seems preferable. Already the present author has noted, both in a reliable recent book about the Civil Service and in an article in a Civil Service journal by a noted writer on social topics, the attribution of the entire reform to Northcote. Even among a galaxy of notables in a brilliant age C. E. Trevelyan's light is excessively subdued by historians, whose interests are usually not in administration.

The main objective was the destruction of patronage, upon the evils of which the Report dilated in no unmeasured terms. This was to be achieved by the introduction of competitive recruitment through a system of examinations of a literary type, controlled by an independent board of examiners. Broadly the work of the central departments was to be classified into two types – mechanical and intellectual – and performed by two grades of official. These were to be recruited from candidates, in the case of the former, between the ages of 17 and 21, in the case of the latter, between the ages of 19 and 25. The higher positions were to be mainly recruited from inside the Service, by promotion based upon merit rather than seniority. An important outcome of this system was to be the welding of a number of distinct departmental staffs into a real general Service with a high degree of interchangeability.

The patronage-mongers were immediately up in arms to defend their perquisites and they were aided by many who honestly felt that the disadvantages of the new system would outweigh the advantages. Opinion was at first fairly evenly divided. This is clearly demonstrated by the views of the numerous band of notabilities and administrators to whom the Report was specially circulated by the Treasury and whose replies were subsequently published, an interesting essay in public relations that speaks well for the authorities at the time. Opinion in Parliament reflected the general situation.

In view of this situation the Government decided to hurry slowly. The proposal to introduce reform by statute was dropped, after being mooted in the Queen's Speech at the opening of Parliament early in 1854. The only immediate reform was introduced by the Order in Council of May 21st, 1855, which authorized the establishment of a Civil Service Commission, with powers 'to examine young men proposed to be appointed to any of the junior situations in the Civil Service Establishments'. This enabled a system of pass examinations to be introduced, but nomination still rested with heads of departments and it was not difficult, by throwing in some obviously inferior nominees, to ensure the selection of a favoured candidate. However, some sort of minimum standard was thus introduced and it was no longer possible for nominees who could hardly read or write to obtain Civil Service posts. The Civil Service Commissioners' first reports disclose clearly the inferior nature of the candidates with whom they had to deal.

SELECT COMMITTEE OF 1860

Although by 1857 opinion in the House of Commons had definitely swayed in favour of open competition, the movement for reform still hung fire. Early in 1860 the House set up a Select Committee to inquire into the existing system of recruitment and its possible improvement.

This Committee, under the chairmanship of Lord Stanley, included Sir Stafford Northcote in its distinguished membership. Although they endorsed the principle of open competition the Select Committee's report was disappointing. Recognizing the power of the vested interests and the dangers of retrogression if things were pushed too far too quickly, they concentrated upon improving the existing examination system by radically reducing the scope for evasion. A wider pooling of vacancies was recommended and it was proposed that there should be as many as five and at least three candidates for each vacancy. These proposals were accepted. During the next decade an effective system of limited competitions was built up by the Civil Service Commission. One or two departments even introduced open competition on their own.

At last, following the advent of Gladstone's first ministry in 1868 with Robert Lowe, an avowed reformer, as Chancellor of the Exchequer, an Order in Council, dated June 4th, 1870, made open competition obligatory, with certain authorized exceptions. This was a red letter event in the history of the Civil Service. The Civil Service Commissioners could now go ahead, not only in perfecting a system of open competitive examinations of a general educational type similar to those already introduced for the Indian Civil Service, but also under Treasury inspiration in rationalizing the pattern of staff gradings on an all-Service basis: although in practice the varying needs of the work were to prevent the elimination of all departmental gradings. The Order in Council also confirmed and extended the Treasury's powers and responsibilities in staff control.

THE PLAYFAIR 'COMMISSION', 1874–5

Within a year or two it was found necessary to make a further investigation into the situation and a committee of eight, consisting of heads of departments and Members of Parliament was set up in 1874 under the chairmanship of Mr Lyon Playfair, to inquire, *inter alia*, into recruitment, transfers and general grading. In its three reports the Playfair 'Commission', as it is usually called, presented a comprehensive review. It found that the principle of organization proposed by the joint investigators of 1853, based upon a horizontal all-Service general division of labour, had been disregarded in favour of a vertical division between departments. The results had been wasteful and had led to further discontent inside the departments.

The Playfair Commission's plan covered four types of post: (i) a top class of Administrative or Staff Officers, chosen by merit from inside the Service or from outside if there were no satisfactory internal candidates; (ii) a small Higher Division, so remunerated as to attract men of liberal education recruited by a preliminary test examination at the age of 17, which was to be followed by a further, but more specialized, competitive examination between the ages 18 and 23 at the completion of their education: successful candidates were to remain eligible for appointment by heads of departments only until their 25th birthday; (iii) a Lower Division recruited by a competitive examination in 'subjects included in an ordinary commercial education', from candidates between the ages of 17 and 20; and (iv) Boy Clerks recruited between the ages of 15 and 17, who would have opportunities to compete for the Lower Division, but would be discharged at the age of 19 if they failed to pass a further examination.

The proposals with regard to the Higher Division were retrogressive: in any case they were ignored. A reorganization covered by Order in Council of February 12th, 1876, related only to the Lower Division and the Boy Clerks. As a result the Lower Division began to emerge as an all-Service class and a blind alley grade of Boy Clerks began to replace the previous nondescript class of writers.

THE RIDLEY COMMISSION, 1886–90

The next comprehensive survey was confided to a Royal Commission under Sir Matthew White Ridley in 1886. It presented four reports, the last of which appeared in July 1890. On the question of the division of labour the Ridley Commission were of opinion that this was still defective, because the line of demarcation between the two general levels had been drawn too low. They proposed a reorganization into First and Second Divisions, the former to be a small class in three distinct grades recruited between the ages of 20 and 24, by open competitive examination in subjects grouped similarly to the honours examinations at the universities, and the latter to continue substantially on the lines of the existing Lower Division. Outside these two divisions there was to be provision for special professional appointments and for a class of Boy Clerks or Copyists to carry out the mechanical copying work. The issue of general regulations for the grades covering the whole Service was advocated.

These proposals led to a consolidation of the Second Division as an all-Service class and to a considerable advance in the regulation of the Civil Service as a whole, but again the Upper Division, or Class I posts as they were officially called, was left to develop without formal regulation.

A period of considerable administrative activity lay ahead, during which the State's central administration was to expand in order to cope with the many new functions confided to it by Parliament. The general grades grew and new departmental grades were introduced. Women and girl clerks were employed in increasing numbers, particularly in the Post Office, and typing staff was more widely introduced. Under the policy of segregation these female office workers were separately graded. A new general class began to appear between the Second and First Divisions to deal with work of a higher quality than that of the Second Division, but less important than the policy work of the top class. The new class, which was mainly concerned with accounting, auditing and stores control, was given the appropriate title of 'Intermediate'. At the base of the pyramid, under the Second Division, another general class also appeared; namely, the Assistant Clerks to provide permanent posts for Boy Clerks of a satisfactory standard who could not all be absorbed into the somewhat limited field of the Second Division. They were recruited by competitive examinations of a limited specialized type confined to Boy Clerks.

Thus, many developments, both social and administrative, were occurring to remodel the simple scheme of the 1853 reforms, whose principles, however, were pursued consistently by the Treasury and the Civil Service Commissioners. But these authorities had, at the same time, to contend with a powerful trend in favour of departmental autonomy, reinforced by the principle of ministerial responsibility for administration and the consequent practice of leaving the appointing power in the hands of heads of departments. In any case the personnel solution had to be sufficiently flexible to meet the new administrative situations that were emerging with the coming of the twentieth century. A hidebound scheme would have acted as a strait jacket and led inevitably to breakdown. As examples of the need for a flexible approach the recruitment of the Labour Exchange Service in 1910 and of the National Insurance Commissions' staffs in 1911 were important. In these instances it was necessary to recruit older staff with appropriate outside experience: only a nucleus of civil servants was transferred from existing departments. The normal competitions were considered unsuitable for selecting older experienced non-official candidates. To preserve the competitive element and counter patronage, interview panels were set up, with the Civil Service Commission represented in their membership, and selection by competitive interview was thus introduced.

MACDONNELL COMMISSION, 1912–15

Obviously, with so many changes going on and in light of the understandable dissatisfaction inside the Service, due to chaotic developments, the time was ripe in 1912 for the commissioning of a new full-scale inquiry into the Civil Service. Under the chairmanship of Lord MacDonnell a royal commission was appointed which included Philip Snowden and Graham Wallas among its nineteen members. A thorough survey was ordered and its six reports, published between 1912 and 1915, covered not only the organization of the departments and working of the Civil Service, but also the specialist branches of the Foreign and Legal Departments. Only the non-clerical officials of the Post Office were left to a select committee, usually known as the Holt Committee, which had been appointed concurrently to investigate this field.

The MacDonnell Commission made a thorough survey and their reports deal with many administrative matters of outstanding importance. They were much concerned to discover lingering pockets of patronage. They also found that the general organization had become somewhat confused and in need of reform. Their Fourth Report (1914), which dealt with the administrative-clerical field, contained in addition to Majority proposals, a Minority Report signed by three of the nineteen members.

The Majority, adhering to the principles laid down in 1853, proposed that the general Civil Service should be reorganized into (i) a Junior Clerical Class, recruited from boys of 16 who had completed the intermediate stage of secondary education (to replace the existing Boy Clerks and Assistant Clerks); (ii) a Senior Clerical Class, recruited at 18 on the completion of a full secondary education (to replace the existing Second Division and Intermediate Classes); and (iii) an Administrative Class, in place of the existing Class I, with conditions standardized throughout the Service. The Minority proposed that the five main existing classes should be similarly reclassified as (i) Second Grade Clerks; (ii) First Grade Clerks and (iii) Junior Secretariat Officers, the main difference being that (ii) was to replace only the existing Intermediate and (i) accordingly to include the Second Division as well as the other two subordinate grades and to be divided into an Upper and a Lower Section, the former being selected from among the latter.

Neither solution was to be adopted, although both were to have an important influence on the future of the Civil Service. In 1914 war came to put a stop to any planned reform for the time being. The war itself, by bringing in experienced temporaries from business and the professions, and inexperienced temporary clerks of all sorts, including many women who had never undertaken paid work before, and by making the Civil Service responsible for many tasks it had never previously undertaken, altered the whole situation overnight, as it were; but in the main only temporarily with regard to the structure and fundamental principles of the Civil Service, as subsequent events were to show.

During the war the shape of things to come was never lost sight of. Our institutions were kept under review and the Civil Service was no exception. In 1917 the Minister of Reconstruction appointed a

Machinery of Government Committee under the chairmanship of Viscount Haldane of Cloan. The Haldane Report (Cmd. 9230), which appeared in 1918, is one of the most notable state documents in the field of public administration. It is concerned primarily with the principles and structure of cabinet government and the functions of the departments, and only incidentally with the Civil Service, to which, nevertheless, its findings are of outstanding importance.

An expert committee under Viscount Gladstone, appointed by Treasury Minute of January 2nd, 1918, was given the task of considering the Recruitment of the Civil Service after the war, special reference being made to the MacDonnell proposals with regard to revising the structure of the class covering 'the inferior clerical work in the Public Departments'. In their findings they favoured the solution offered in the MacDonnell Minority Report, emphasizing the importance of leaving it to the individual departments to decide whether they should employ First Grade or Second Grade Clerks. This committee also made recommendations on recruitment during the reconstruction period, upon which in fact immediate post-war policy was to be based. Another important Committee on Staffs under Sir John Bradbury, appointed by Treasury Minute of February 13th, 1917, issued five reports which contained important proposals on post-war Civil Service organization and working.

THE REORGANIZATION COMMITTEE, 1919–20

Shortly after the war there occurred the only truly revolutionary change in this field since 1870, namely the application of the system of joint Whitley councils to the Civil Service. Chapter VII is devoted to this development. For the moment it is sufficient to note that the next important report on Civil Service structure was issued by a Reorganization Committee of the new Civil Service National Whitley Council, consisting of representatives of both Official and Staff interests. It is upon the scheme propounded by this committee of officials that the present organization of the Civil Service is based, and it is a matter of considerable interest that a plan proposed by the interested parties should have stood up so well to the stresses and buffets of the ensuing thirty years. However, it should not be overlooked that this new committee had little research to undertake. Apart from the invaluable working knowledge of its individual members the Reorganization Committee had for its briefing the up-to-date recommendations of committees referred to in the preceding section.

The Reorganization Committee's main Report of February 1920 proposed a new Civil Service structure, which bore the imprint of the recent investigations. The solution can best be conveyed in the Committee's own words:

'The administrative and clerical work of the Civil Service may be said broadly, to fall into two main categories. In one category may be placed all such work as either is of a simple mechanical kind or consists in the application of well-defined regulations, decisions and practice to particular cases; in the other category, the work which is concerned with the formation of policy, with the revision of existing practice or current regulations and decisions, and with the organization and direction of the business of Government.

'For work so different in kind it is clearly necessary to secure more than one type of agent. Qualifications adapted to the performance of the simplest kind of work would be unequal to the discharge of the highest kind of work; and it would be impossible to justify the employment on simple mechanical duties of persons capable of performing the highest duties. After the most careful consideration we have agreed that, in order properly to provide for the work falling within two main categories, it will be necessary to employ not less than four different classes, viz.:

(*a*) A Writing Assistant Class for simple mechanical work.
(*b*) A Clerical Class for the better sort of work included in the first main category defined above.

<table>
<tr><td>(c) An Executive Class; and
(d) An Administrative Class</td><td>}</td><td>for the work included in the second main category defined above.'</td></tr>
</table>

The effect of these proposals was to reclassify the office work of the departments into three broad types, namely Clerical, Executive and Administrative, each of which was to be performed by a specially recruited class drawn at school leaving stages from young persons of either sex with an appropriate educational background. Each class was to be divided into grades, recruited successively from the grade below, and it was to be left to the departments to decide which grades would be most suitable for their work. In theory, if not in practice, the classes were to form separate hierarchies and there was no suggestion that members of each of the three main classes should be employed in every department.

The Clerical Class, recruited by open competitive written examinations of intermediate secondary standard from boys of 16 to 17 and girls of $16\frac{1}{2}$ to $17\frac{1}{2}$ (subsequently brought into line with the boys) was to have duties which were defined as 'dealing with particular cases in accordance with well-defined regulations, instructions and general practice; scrutinizing, checking and cross-checking straightforward accounts, claims, returns, etc., under well-defined instructions; preparation of material for returns, accounts, and statistics in prescribed forms; simple drafting and précis work; collection of material on which judgments can be formed; supervision of the work of Writing Assistants.'

The Writing Assistants, although officially regarded as a separate class were to work inside the clerical sphere in close co-operation with the Clerical Class. They were to be recruited by similar examinations of higher elementary standard from among girls between the ages of 16 and 17, and they were to be employed on the more mechanical clerical practices, including machine operation, but not typewriting, which was to be assigned to a separately recruited class.

The Executive Class was also to be recruited by open competitive written examinations, of full secondary standard, from young persons between the ages of 18 and 19 (except that for the time being special conditions were to apply to the recruitment of young women). The Report states that the work of this class 'covers a wide field, and requires in different degrees qualities of judgment, initiative and resource. In the junior ranks it comprises the critical examination of particular cases of lesser importance not clearly within the scope of approved regulations or general decisions, initial investigations into matters of higher importance, and the immediate direction of small blocks of business. In its upper ranges it is concerned with matters of internal organization and control, with the settlement of broad questions arising out of business in hand or in contemplation, and with the responsible conduct of important operations.' It was originally intended that the junior grade of this class should be a training grade, but for practical reasons this was a condition that was never to materialize.

The Administrative Class, which for the first time was to become a true all-Service class, was to be recruited between the ages of 22 and 24,[1] by an open competitive examination in subjects embraced by the various honours courses of the universities. Although the examination was to be mainly written it was to include a *viva voce* which was to constitute a test of personality and character, the marks for which were to be added in with those of the written papers. This was an innovation at the time justified in view of the class's leadership function. On the duties of this class the Report was brief, but to the point. It said that these duties would comprise 'those concerned with the formation of policy, with the co-ordination and improvement of Government machinery, and with the general administration and control of the Departments of the Public Service.'

Recruits of this class were to be regarded as a cadet corps from which selection would be made to higher administrative posts, and this is how the Assistant Principal grade has in fact since been regarded, namely, as a training grade of a purely transitory character whose members have to graduate within a few years to higher duties.

[1] Later, the conditions for men and women were assimilated, and from 1937 the age limits for both sexes were altered to 21 and 24.

The Reorganization plan was adopted and gradually applied by the departments. The new general service, or 'Treasury', classes as they were to be called, were not however adopted by all departments, some of which regarded it as essential that they should continue to recruit their own special grades; for example, the Ministry of Labour and the Boards of Customs and Excise and of Inland Revenue. The specialized nature of the department's work was generally adduced as the reason for this deviation. Elsewhere different patterns of Treasury class groupings emerged. Thus some departments chose a Clerical-Administrative pattern, others a Clerical-Executive pattern. In some the directing class was of the technical or professional type; in others all three Treasury classes appeared. The assimilation of members of existing grades to the new classes was a difficult operation with which there is not space to deal here. Guidance on the subject was provided in a later report of the Whitley Reorganization Committee.

THE TOMLIN COMMISSION, 1929–31

The next comprehensive survey was held too soon and in unpropitious circumstances. Unless a Royal Commission is in a position to study its problem in its long-term aspects it is bound to be at least partially frustrated. This was the situation in which the Tomlin Commission found itself when it was appointed in July 1929 to inquire into, and report upon, the structure and organization of the Civil Service, as well as its conditions of service. The financial crisis was at its height and the new investigations could not avoid being unduly affected by this serious turn in the nation's affairs. Moreover, since the war the situation within the public service had never really returned to normal and in 1929 the Reorganization scheme could hardly be said yet to have been properly tested. The difficult problems created by the special post-war recruitment of ex-Service men were still in course of settlement, while the return to normal recruitment methods, on which the Reorganization scheme was ultimately to have rested, had only recently taken place. In the dire national situation which seemed at the time destined to continue from bad to worse, the call for economy, an admirable enough precept for any investigatory committee if taken in moderation, was too insistent not to colour adversely the whole of the Commission's findings.

The Report, when published in 1931[1], was received with disappointment, especially by the Civil Service itself, which nevertheless in all the circumstances could hardly have expected anything better. In fact much criticism of the Tomlin Report was misdirected and failed apparently

[1] Cmd. 3909.

to appreciate the measured truth of its diagnosis in light of the existing situation. The chief fault is to be found less in the results than in doubts raised by the investigatory methods adopted by the Commission, which while normal to this type of body pose the question whether in the modern world with its complex structure and procedures the examination of a series of *ex parte* statements, however thorough, is likely to search deeply enough into the fundamentals of the situation. The Tomlin Commission's investigations were certainly thorough, but from an examination of the evidence submitted in the best faith both by official and by staff interests, and which indeed formed the bulk of the information before the Commission, it is obvious that the protagonists were concerned primarily with making a case and not in providing an objective analysis of the situation. It would seem that in future to be really successful such a commission will need the assistance of a competent survey team.

As far as the theme of this present chapter goes the Royal Commission had little to suggest. It generally endorsed the grading structure laid down in the Reorganization Report, subject to two suggested readjustments: one of which was eventually adopted and the other rejected. The first was a proposal to extend the range of duties of the Writing Assistants, a class that had attracted a higher educational type than had been originally visualized and whose members were therefore capable of a wider range of simpler clerical work. The new class, rechristened Clerical Assistants, was thus to overlap the Clerical Officer grade at the lower levels. This modification was introduced officially in 1936. The other organizational proposal, largely inspired by complaints of stagnation and lack of promotion prospects in the Clerical Officer grade at the time, was that a new grade should be fitted in between the Clerical Officer and Higher Clerical Officer grades, to which suitable members of the existing junior grade should be promoted. This redivision of the Clerical Class by the insertion of an overlapping grade, as it was called, did not commend itself to the staff nor was it welcomed sufficiently by the official interests to lead to its implementation by administrative action.

With the levelling out of the financial crisis and the change in the political outlook in the 'thirties the situation in the Civil Service gradually changed. Following a period of contraction a mild expansion now began, as the Government, almost against its will, gradually participated more and more in economic control and social amelioration. In the later 'thirties the drive to rearm, again forced upon a government and a nation that had put off the evil day longer than was compatible with public safety, caused this expansion to accelerate. Although the British Civil Service is essentially a pacific body, its professional interest gained considerably from this phase of defence preparation.

Between 1929 and 1939 the total of the non-industrial staffs of the central departments rose from 259,000 to 371,000[1].

THE PRESENT ORGANIZATION

On the organization of the general office, or Treasury, classes the Second World War, which began on September 3rd, 1939, had little effect. The structure stands today very much as it has just been described, although in many ways other conditions have radically changed, as the following chapter will show. During the war, which was much more totalitarian than the previous one, an even more radical expansion of official posts took place and this time, with the cessation of hostilities in 1945, the expected rapid shrinkage back to normal failed to be realized. This was due to a complexity of reasons: firstly, the world itself was in greater chaos and reconstruction meant much more conscious planning: secondly, in this country a new approach to social welfare and nationalization of industry led to the change over from a war economy to a Welfare State, which presupposed little or no diminution in state activity; and thirdly, the continued threat of war, due to the division of the victors into two camps, entailed a higher level of defence preparation than had been normal before the recent hostilities. Not only did many of the older government departments continue to maintain much larger staffs than hitherto, but new wartime and post-war ministries continued to operate: for example, the Ministries of Supply and of Food, the Ministries of Fuel and Power and of National Insurance. Numerous other new branches were found to be necessary to cope with the new administrative tasks and conditions. The machinery of government, both at the centre and the periphery, was greatly expanded and rendered more complex.

Some structural changes were made which had the effect of narrowing the gap between the three main classes – Administrative, Executive and Clerical – and reducing their separateness. The Clerical Class today consists only of two grades, namely Clerical Officer and Higher Clerical Officer, all of the previous Staff Clerk grades having been assimilated to the equivalent levels of the Executive Class. An inclination towards a similar tying up of the upper levels of the Executive Class with equivalent levels of the Administrative Class, tentatively proposed in 1945[2], has seemed to mark time. The structure of the Administrative Class itself has been simplified by the elimination of the Principal Assistant Secretary grade which previously stood between the Assistant Secretary and Under Secretary grades. There were also further moves in the Treasury's campaign to replace the equivalent departmental classes by structures similar to that of the Treasury classes. For example, the

[1] These figures exclude part-time workers (mainly in the Post Office).
[2] Cmd. 6680.

National Assistance Board, which had its own departmental gradings, went over to the standard pattern and the new Ministry of National Insurance adopted the Treasury gradings, although its work was of the management-specialist type for which departmental gradings would previously have been considered most appropriate. The Ministry of Labour and National Service, although still maintaining its own gradings approached so close to the general pattern that the main difference is now little more than one of nomenclature. The Inland Revenue and Customs and Excise Departments, on the other hand, while introducing their own modifications to meet changing times, continued to maintain their own patterns of staff organization. The present grading pattern of the main classes is indicated in Diagram I opposite.

There are two important developments, however, that call for comment before this brief description of the emergence of the present Civil Service structure is concluded, developments which are bound to have a great influence on future changes in the Civil Service pattern and which already affect in one way or another all the problems that are to be discussed in later chapters. The first is the definite shift of the centre of gravity of the Civil Service from Whitehall to the provinces[1]: the second is the emergence of nation-wide Civil Service classes in the professional and scientific spheres.

During the Second World War a pattern of regional government that had already emerged in the previous war and indeed much earlier, was given a definite shape for defence purposes. This specific governmental need never in effect materialized, but a regional administrative structure took shape for war purposes and continued afterwards. Based largely on the administrative pattern already worked out on a divisional basis for the pre-war Ministry of Labour, the new regional scheme, subject to modification for technical reasons in such branches as the Post Office and later in the Ministry of Health's hospital organization, was well-designed to meet the needs of an administration that required to have offices in close contact with the local communities throughout the country. In these offices the provision of social services brought the civil servant more closely into touch with the public and modified both his outlook and his methods. Indeed, the Employment Exchanges and the National Assistance Board's Offices had already introduced[2] this new element before the Second World War. At the same time the spread of the management function, necessitated by the existence of numerous small offices, which had at one time been largely confined to the Post Office and the tax departments, further extended this sector of the Civil Service's responsibilities.

[1] On July 1st, 1955, of the total established staffs, 165,000 were stationed in London and 325,000 elsewhere.
[2] In 1910 and 1934 respectively.

DIAGRAM II

The Administrative and four other Hierarchies of the British Civil Service Compared, January 1st, 1956

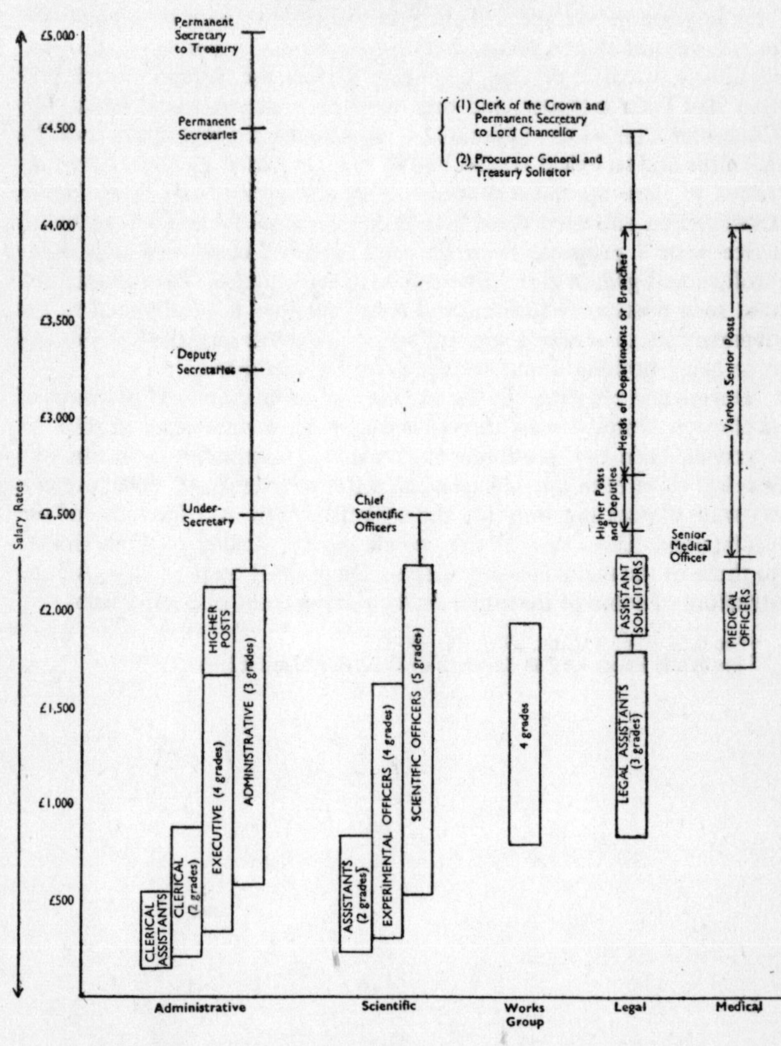

N.B. This diagram is based on information supplied to the Royal Commission on the Civil Service, as modified by subsequent salary adjustments.

The division of each hierarchy into Classes, Grades and Individual Posts is shown on a salary basis as at January 1st, 1956, and does not embody the changes, as from April 1st, 1956, arising from the agreement on the Royal Commission's proposals.

Progress between the grades of a class is usually difficult and subject to promotion selection. The grade structure of the Administrative hierarchy is shown in greater detail in Diagram I, facing page 44.

It should be emphasized that there is a number of other hierarchies, large and small, constructed on similar principles, e.g. Post Office Engineering and Manipulative Classes, Tax Inspectorate of the Inland Revenue, Factory Inspectorate of the Ministry of Labour and National Service, Officers of Customs and Excise and the Waterguard Service of the same Department, Accountants, Statisticians, etc., etc., and the Foreign Service.

The other development, in the extension of the technical sphere, is also very important. Members of the professions have long been employed in the central departments, but usually in small numbers – lawyers, architects, medical officers, engineers. Before the Second World War they had been recruited and organized on a departmental basis. The Carpenter Committee, appointed to investigate the organization of the scientific and technical grades, had in 1930 proposed a general reorganization of these specialist officials on an all-Service basis. The Tomlin Commission endorsed these findings[1], but found themselves unable to agree with a proposal from the staff interests concerned that other professional groups should be similarly reorganized. They considered that such posts were too few and their functions too individual to the departments to render a general service structure practicable. For the time being nothing was done, even for the scientists.

During and after the war the numbers of technicians and members of professions employed by the Government have risen considerably. As a consequence the development considered impracticable before the war has since been introduced as a matter of course and there are now separate classes not only for the scientists[2], but also for most of the professions. These new all-Service classes are graded on lines similar to those of the main Treasury classes. Diagram II on page 45 shows the structure of some of these classes for the purposes of comparison.

[1] See their Report (Cmd. 3909), pp. 49–57.
[2] See White Paper on *The Scientific Civil Service* (Cmd. 6679).

CHAPTER III

CONDITIONS OF SERVICE

The general tone and standards of a public service are ultimately determined by the official's conditions of service. In those countries where the official is allowed, and indeed compelled by circumstances beyond his own control, to take bribes low standards of public service have to be accepted as inevitable. The methods of recruitment[1] are, of course, of first importance and the offer made at that stage is embodied in existing conditions of service, usually embellished by promises of later advancement. It is on the other hand not possible adequately to assess the offer made without taking into account the past history and present prestige of the particular service. A civil service may continue for some time to live upon past reputations or be dragged back by past inefficiencies, at any rate to the limits of the working life of the present incumbents of public office. The actual conditions offered are the outcome partly of history and custom, but mainly of public policy put into operation by the controlling authority: in the case of Britain, by Her Majesty's Treasury.[2] The general social and economic situation of the country is a non-evadable limiting factor and the degree to which the existing staffs are able to participate in the revisionary process, through normal or modified trade union channels, is also important.[3] It is proposed in this present chapter to consider some of the more weighty factors in the Civil Service's conditions of service.

LIFE CAREER

In an economically unstable world the offer of a secure pensionable employment has undoubtedly exerted a great influence upon the recruit to the Service. Parents exert considerable pressure upon their children to compete for jobs that are sheltered from the normal economic uncertainties of life, and competitors are willing to accept less favourable monetary prospects on this account. It is often alleged that this particular circumstance has attracted to the Civil Service profession a larger proportion than usual of persons of unenterprising character. No one would choose public service as a field for adventure: yet there is scope therein today more than ever before for the adventurous spirit and it is no longer just to overstress this characteristic. Most men seek security,

[1] See Chapter IV.
[2] See Chapter VIII.
[3] See Chapter VII.

if few find it: there are other valid reasons for the civil servant's lack of enterprise and these originate in the very nature of public administration.

Today the civil servant's security is no doubt less prized than in the past, partly because the Civil Service no longer stands as one of the few careers in which pensionable employment exists, partly because the fear of unemployment has been greatly mitigated by the advent of a State system of social security. There is unfortunately the overriding change in the general attitude to life, brought about by the scientific advance in humanity's power to destroy itself, that inevitably colours youth's whole attitude to the future and vitiates appreciably the attractiveness to them of security of employment. There is also the insidious menace of inflation that constantly threatens any standards that may have been laid up for the future.

The State, when recruiting a permanent official, usually asks for a lifetime's allegiance. Even in the days of patronage official posts were regarded as very much the perquisites of the occupant and there was no question of officials being sacked, as under spoils systems, to make way for the clients of new political leaders. Permanency is certainly an important characteristic of our Civil Service pattern, and even if historical reasons partly account for it the resultant system is not less valid on that account: quite the contrary in fact. It is important to the efficiency of Cabinet government that it should be able to call upon the resources of a skilled professional administration. Permanency means a gradual accumulation of skill and the maximum return from training and experience inside the Service. There is also the important point that, other things being equal, permanency maximizes loyalty and reduces the dissemination of confidential official information that inevitably follows upon the flow away from the Service of experienced officers.

Security of tenure is therefore offered to the Civil Service recruit as a matter of course. Without doubt those who adopt public service as a life career are more likely to be faithful servants of the nation than those who regard it as a stepping stone to some other sphere of activity. With increasing service they become more valuable to the State, while on the other hand their abilities become less and less likely to find a market outside the public field. This factor has certainly been modified by the growth of public administration in recent decades and arrangements that have latterly been introduced to facilitate the flow out of the Civil Service into other public fields.

Until October 1946, when the marriage bar was abolished, security of tenure for women civil servants was assured only so long as they remained single. Subject to a minimum of six years' established service they were entitled to receive as compensation a gratuity based upon length of service, but it was possible, where the interests of the Service were considered to justify it, for married women to continue in employment on an unestablished basis, although this rule was only exceptionally applied. With the removal of the bar, as a matter of government policy in face of the national manpower shortage[1], married women may compete for and continue in Civil Service employment on an equality with men. They retain the right to the marriage gratuity on voluntary retirement and provision has been made for the granting of maternity leave.

This change, which is of course in line with general social developments, was bound to have a considerable effect on the Civil Service. In the past young girls were administratively acceptable for routine machine and clerical work because of their high rate of outflow, on account of marriage, which rendered it unnecessary to keep them too long on soul-destroying work. In an age when there is a definite shortage of this kind of labour this factor is no longer of great importance, although it still leaves the problem of the routine worker to be solved. On the other hand, despite their subjection to the same conditions of employment as men, married women are obviously less mobile than other workers and naturally more liable to absences through domestic pressures. This is an inefficiency factor that no responsible executive is likely to underrate.

So long as the established civil servant continues to perform his duties with reasonable efficiency and to conduct himself with rectitude he is assured of security of employment. But all civil servants are not established. There is an extensive temporary fringe to which these conditions do not apply.[2]

Recruited temporarily, usually by the departments and not as the result of a stringent examination imposed centrally, such officers are needed to deal with emergency conditions which are likely to disappear within a reasonable time. In wartime such temporary recruitments take place on a large scale. At all times some departments need a fringe of temporary staffs to cope with work of a seasonal and fluctuating nature. Their services will be relinquished as soon as the emergency disappears. That indeed is the theory, and there is an understanding with the staff representatives that temporary officials will be employed only to fill temporary posts, but in fact there is a steady tendency for such posts to become semi-permanent, to exist for long periods and for some temporary officers to be temporary in status only. They continue in State employment without receiving the advantages of permanency. They soon form a pressure group inside the Service whose one object is to

[1] A recent Whitley enquiry had shown the staffs to be divided on the question; see *The Marriage Bar in the Civil Service* (Cmd. 6885), 1946.

[2] On April 1st, 1955, there were approx. 146,000 temporary non-industrial civil servants.

obtain permanancy of tenure. The permanent officials are concerned at the threat which large bodies of temporaries exert upon their own standards of employment; and the problem has the unfortunate effect of deflecting the activities of the staff associations from more important questions, as well as diminishing the importance of maintaining standards of competence. The mere holding of a temporary post for some time is offered as proving the competence of the holder.

The size of the temporary corps needed by the Administration is not easy to determine. In view of the fluctuating needs of departments the solution of dispensing with temporary employment altogether, a solution that would have obvious advantages from the public's point of view, would create its own administrative difficulties whenever a contraction or shift of work led to large-scale redundancy.

The grave defect of this form of recruitment is the effect it has upon the efficiency of the Civil Service. It has to be operated locally, varying standards of competence are inevitable and personal nomination is almost unavoidable. When permanency is offered, competency on the job is one of the tests imposed, but it is very difficult to ensure this in public employment and the general efficiency levels of such recruits are usually much below those of the normal competition recruits to the same positions. Persons are thus able to side-step into the Civil Service without being subjected to the sieve of the open competitive examination. In times of national upheaval, such as have operated almost continuously since 1914, it is impossible to eliminate completely from the most carefully and justly regulated Civil Service the influences of chance and high favour.

It is not possible to separate the condition of security of tenure from the problem of superannuation, but as this is also virtually part of the key-problem of remuneration its discussion will be delayed until this vital question has been considered.

CAREER PROSPECTS

The entrant to the Civil Service will most certainly be influenced not only by the immediate conditions of employment, but also by the career prospects of the particular branch which he proposes to enter. Advancement has been provided for by the system of grades within the classes which has been gradually evolved to meet this requirement. But the qualifications and qualities required for the different classes may restrict the scope for interflow between classes, and the entrant to the Civil Service cannot normally expect his career to lead outside the class he chooses to enter. This is not strictly true in all cases and does to some extent depend upon competence in the expertise required for the specific class. In the case of the Treasury classes, for example, the promotion avenue of the Clerical Officer entrant now leads into the Executive Class (although before the war there was a separate Clerical hierarchy). Despite official pronouncements equality of opportunity cannot yet be said to exist for all entrants of these several office classes. In their information booklets the Civil Service Commissioners give some indication to would-be competitors of the career prospects at the various entry points, suggesting the grade to which a normally successful officer may expect to rise, but in practice this is a matter still dependent very much upon opportunities occurring in the particular department to which the new entrant is assigned, opportunities inevitably determined by the unforeseeable future developments of the department's work, and it is quite impossible to give more than a rough and ready forecast at such an early stage. The separateness of the government departments in determining such prospects is not easily appreciated by those who believe the theoretical assumption of the unity of the Service. Having decided to avoid the incalculable element of chance in the field of outside employment the civil servant soon finds himself subjected to a quite different but equally disconcerting chance situation inside the official sphere. As we shall see when considering the promotion arrangements, steps have been taken, constructively but not with complete success, to eliminate some of these faults of the official career system. But we are still a long way from achieving a structure in which the individual is able to contribute much to his own personal success.

REMUNERATION

The size of the weekly wage packet, or more appropriately the monthly salary, for many permanent civil servants are paid monthly[1], is the most important of the conditions of service of the civil servant as of all workers. It determines not only the short-term supply of new entrants, but the long-term efficiency of the Service. Poorly paid public services are always inefficient and, although this is not necessarily the only inefficiency factor, little improvement can be hoped for so long as it subsists.

In this, as in all occupations, the complex conditions of supply and demand in the general labour market have a determining influence which is not easy to analyse, but public policy and social context have significant importance in the case of the Civil Service. An expensive civil service may not constitute an undue burden so long as it is small in size. A service with a high prestige and a high sense of public service in an aristocratic community may for long obtain its leading officials for a comparatively modest salary rate. This was undoubtedly the position in Britain up to 1939. At that period the competitions attracted many

[1] On the basis of one twelfth of the annual salary, paid in arrear.

more suitable candidates than were needed and the examining body could pick and choose. Supply was in the ascendant. Today it is quite otherwise. In the main rather than improve the salary offer the State has preferred to lower the standards called for. But the new situation cannot be wholly attributed to the change in the standards of remuneration (although these are very important and the present Royal Commission has been asked to concentrate upon them) or to other conditions of service, for there have been revolutionary changes in the national social and economic context, not least of which may well be the heightened general demand for talents of an administrative type.

Before the First World War the prevailing view was that the Government as employer should set an example, should lead as a good employer in a situation when the bad employer predominated. This principle of the Government as a 'model employer' was accepted by the MacDonnell Commission in 1914[1] and more or less endorsed by a Treasury spokesman in 1922.[2] But the Geddes Axe[3] was already operating over the whole field of government expenditure and with post-war economic stringency a different attitude was bound to grow. The Anderson Committee on the Pay of State Servants (1923) set up in accordance with a recommendation of the Geddes Committee, stated categorically, 'In our view there is only one principle in which all the factors of responsibility, cost of living, marriage, children, social position, etc., are included – the employer should pay what is necessary to recruit and to retain an efficient staff.'[4] The Tomlin Commission, which reported in 1931, discarded the model employer doctrine as too variable and contradictory and laid it down that Civil Service remuneration should be based upon broad general comparisons with the remuneration of equivalent outside employments, considered on a long-term basis. This so-called 'Tomlin formula' was adopted as official policy, but there are so many varying factors to be taken into account and so many differences in technical operation between public and private enterprise that strict comparisons have never been easy to make. Since the Second World War the standards of remuneration in the Civil Service have tended to drag behind and the Treasury have been satisfied to suggest that the appropriate offer should be based upon fair market rates. They have called upon the Royal Commission to lay down a sort of revised Tomlin principle for general application and we shall return to this matter later.

In the face of hard fact there seems to be little to be argued against the conclusion of the Anderson Committee that the proper level of remuneration for the Civil Service is that needed to recruit and retain an efficient

[1] Cmd. 7338, Chap. IX, para. 87.

[2] Sir Russell Scott, Controller of Establishments, to Select Committee on Estimates, on July 24th, 1922.

[3] Cmd. 1561, 1582 and 1589 (1922).

[4] See p. 4 of *Reports of Committee on Pay, etc., of State Servants* (1923).

staff. But it all depends upon what is meant by an efficient staff, upon how the long-term trend is interpreted and upon what values are assigned to the other conditions of service that have to be weighed in the balance. The decision is then a matter for a Solomon rather than for a harassed governmental agency impelled by expediency rather than far-sighted statesmanship. At one time H.M. Treasury could be depended upon doing justice to the Service, albeit in its guise of strict parent, without losing sight of its main task as watchdog of the public purse: recent history suggests that it has allowed public policy in the direction of economy to obscure the Civil Service aspect, which is left in the normal trade union manner to the staffs themselves to protect.

Fluctuating living costs and money values have always had a serious disintegrating effect upon salary scales devised for career services. During and after the First World War the situation was met by the application of a bonus to the basic salary, on a sliding scale basis so devised as to give a proportionate increase only to the lowest paid officials and one tapering off steeply at higher salary levels. This system was not liked very much, particularly during the period of deflation when prices were dropping. It is psychologically less satisfactory to lose money income when prices are falling than to lose purchasing power when prices are rising, and after the Second World War the staff representatives of the Civil Service, expecting history to repeat itself, were not inclined to press for a cost of living bonus system. To date costs have continued to rise and salaries inevitably to drag behind. The staff associations and the Whitley councils have had to campaign continuously against the Treasury, whose offers have usually been considered unsatisfactory, with the result that the Arbitration Tribunal has often been given the task of deciding the issue.

In one direction an attempt has been made to change the general salary levels inside the Civil Service, namely for the top grades. Top civil servants during the modern period have never been overpaid. Devotion to public service has been counted upon to attract and retain persons of outstanding capacity for salaries much lower than they could have obtained in outside employment. After the war the worsening of conditions inside the Service was emphasized at the top levels by increased competition from outside: for example, from the newly constituted public corporations. There is also the fact that the Civil Service's need for scientists and members of other professions has made it necessary to offer competitive salaries to them and that the remuneration of the senior administrative officers has tended to fall behind. As a result of a special enquiry and proposals made by the Chorley Committee in 1949[1] substantial improvement in top-level salaries was introduced.

[1] *Report of the Committee on Higher Civil Service Remuneration* (1949), Cmd. 7635.

Except for certain specialist and top-level posts, to which a specific salary is attached, Civil Service remuneration usually involves a system of salary scales whereby regular annual increments are awarded to the individual until the maximum of the scale is reached. In the basic grades the lower steps on the scale are often assigned according to the new entrant's age: this is usually known as the weight-for-age principle. Subsequent advances are made subject to the individual's continuing efficiency on his work, and in light of the natural increase of knowledge and experience that a worker may be expected to accumulate there can be no doubt that the system of increments is a reasonable one. There is, however, an automatic element in the award of such increments and in a large-scale organization there can be no question of paying each individual strictly according to his performance. The civil servant is paid not on a precise assessment of his personal merit, but upon the standardized salary conditions of the grade to which he belongs. This is a point that has an important bearing upon the limits of Civil Service efficiency and one that is too frequently overlooked when Civil Service remuneration is discussed.

Civil Service salary scales usually relate to male officers working in London and are subject to modification for those working elsewhere, and for women, though since the agreement with the Staff Side to implement the policy of equal pay the latter type of variation will shortly disappear. Provincial differentiation is adopted on account of the differences between the cost of living in the Metropolis and elsewhere. At one time some mobile classes subject to constant transfer from one part of the country to another were conditioned to London rates throughout, but since the war provincial differentiation has been pressed by the Treasury to cover most of the Civil Service. The system has its administrative disadvantages since it adversely affects the willingness of officers to transfer away from London. The Staff Side challenge the assumptions on which the relative costs of living are assessed and want the system to be abolished. There appears to be a tendency for costs to level up throughout the country and there can be little doubt that in some of the large industrialized areas, like Birmingham and Manchester, the differences are not easily assessed. There is also the point, often overlooked and when recognized certainly deplored by many, that the inflated Metropolis has undoubted amenities that make many people willing to work in and live near it even at some financial sacrifice.

The campaign for equal pay for women has been waged by the staff since the recognition of equality between the sexes following the First World War. The Tomlin Commission recommended the principle of 'a fair field and no favour'[1] and this was generally adopted although

[1] Cmd. 3909, p. 115, para. 398.

pay differences were only tidied up by the general acceptance of the rule that women's salaries should approximate to 80 per cent of the male scale, in place of existing widespread variations. The Government continued to accept the general principle, but to delay its implementation on the plea of economy (a recurrent excuse for not making changes in the Civil Service) and of difficulties in implementation. The staff associations pressed strongly for the acceptance of equal pay and there was little vocal opposition from inside the Service. Some women and many men may have had doubts, for rather different reasons, but it was not popular to challenge such an eminently fair principle as equal pay for equal work, although one might cynically ask whether there could be a more difficult principle to apply to the existing Civil Service system. At last the weight of opinion prevailed, supported by competition between the two political parties and an inclination on the part of the Government to use the Civil Service as an example to outside employers. The long-term effect, of course, is to give unmarried women as a class a larger share of the national income, but whether the equating of a married man who has a non-wage-earning wife with a single unit is altogether equitable or socially desirable is another matter. These afterthoughts may be still to come! Unless the principle becomes universal the long run effect on the Civil Service may be to reduce its pay standards to that of the single woman. The agreement of 1955 involved the gradual approach to equal pay over a period of six years. Obviously this particular arrangement was a compromise based upon financial expediency rather than equity, but it was generally welcomed in the Civil Service.

SUPERANNUATION

An important part of remuneration is the superannuation payment which in the case of the Civil Service has been subject to a series of Acts of Parliament extending from 1834 to the present day.[1]

It is a peculiarity of these statutes that they do not confer a right to a pension: they lay down the terms on which a pension may be granted by the Crown, a function that is performed by H.M. Treasury. Should a pension be withheld the official would have no legal remedy. It never is in fact withheld where the conditions laid down in the statutes are satisfied. These conditions include the attainment of the normal retirement age of sixty or breakdown of health, and the receipt of the full award depends upon satisfactory service. An allowance may also be granted for retirement on abolition of office, a not very usual occurrence

[1] See H.M. Treasury's comprehensive *Digest of Pensions Law and Regulations o, the Civil Service* (1952).

today since there would normally be no difficulty in finding the occupant of such a post equivalent employment in another branch of the Service. Similarly, an officer retired for inefficiency may be granted a proportionate allowance[1].

Eligibility for pension depends upon appointment to an established post and the tests for this, laid down in Superannuation Act, 1859, are sufficiently interesting to deserve quotation. Section 17 of that Act reads as follows:

> 'For the purposes of this Act, no person hereafter to be appointed shall be deemed to have served in the permanent Civil Service of the State unless such person holds his appointment directly from the Crown or has been admitted into the Civil Service with a certificate from the Civil Service Commissioners; nor shall any person, already appointed to any office, be held to have served in the permanent Civil Service as aforesaid, unless such person belong to a class which is already entitled to superannuation allowance, or to a class in which, if he had been appointed thereto subsequently to the passing of this Act, he would, as holding his appointment directly from the Crown, or as having been admitted into the Civil Service with such certificate as aforesaid, have become entitled to such allowance; and no person shall be entitled to any superannuation allowance under this Act, unless his salary or remuneration has been provided out of the Consolidated Fund of the United Kingdom of Great Britain and Ireland, or out of monies voted by Parliament.'

An important characteristic of Civil Service superannuation is that it is non-contributory. Some earlier superannuation acts did provide for contributions, but the system was finally abolished in 1857.[2] Superficially this may appear as an advantage of Civil Service employment but, coupled with the fact that the pension cannot be claimed as a right, a condition that could not very well exist under a contributory system, it has the effect of making the life contract a reality by rendering withdrawal to another sphere of activity too expensive an expedient for the civil servant to contemplate unless he takes the plunge at an early stage of his career. Nevertheless, pension has usually been considered as deferred pay which should be taken into account when fixing the scales of salary appropriate to the different classes. The Tomlin Commission's recommendations included the introduction of contributory pensions[3], but the Superannuation Act of 1935, which improved the

[1] These allowances, which are known as compensatory and retiring allowances respectively, must not exceed the amount that would have been granted on retirement for ill-health.

[2] Contributory pensions were introduced in an Act of 1822, and repealed two years later. The principle was re-introduced in 1829 and confirmed in the Act of 1834.

[3] See Tomlin Report, Chap. XVII, pp. 201–216.

existing system on certain lines proposed by the Commission, did not include this innovation.

Under the present Superannuation Acts benefit is granted at the rate of 1/80th of a civil servant's emoluments[1] for each completed year of service, with a maximum of 40/80ths for forty or more years of service, which thus allows an entrant to the Civil Service whose age is not more than twenty to earn a full pension amounting to half salary by the time he reaches his sixtieth birthday. He also receives at the time of retirement a lump sum based upon 3/80ths of his emoluments for each completed year of service.[2]

Until 1935 these pensions did not provide for the civil servant's family except in so far as a death grant, based upon 1/30th of his salary for each completed year of service, could be paid to his next of kin if he died while in harness and subject to a minimum period of five years' established service. In the Superannuation Act of that year, however, provision was made for the allocation by the retiring officer of a proportion of his pension to a dependant. This arrangement, which is worked out on a strict actuarial basis, involves the definite assignment to a dependant of right to a part of the pension actually awarded and depends on proof of good health on the part of the pensioner.

Since the war a further important advance has been made. Under the Superannuation Act, 1949, pensions on a contributory basis are now provided for the widow and dependants of an established civil servant. In addition, a civil servant resigning after his fiftieth birthday may now retain accrued pension rights, which will become payable on his reaching his sixtieth birthday, although on compassionate grounds the Treasury may grant such a pension immediately. The authorities also have the power to place on pension immediately an officer of over fifty whose services no longer reach a reasonable standard of competence. There is little evidence yet that this option is being very widely used to improve the efficiency of the Service. New regulations also permit the retention of superannuation rights by civil servants transferring to other public services, including teaching, and vice versa.

Until July 5th, 1948, established civil servants were excluded from National Insurance, except as voluntary contributors under the Widows, Orphans and Old Age Pensions scheme. With the introduction of the new comprehensive scheme the Civil Service, together *inter alia* with all other employed persons, became compulsorily insured. This means

[1] These emoluments are assessed by averaging remuneration during the last three years of service.

[2] This lump sum allowance was introduced in the Superannuation Act of 1909 which changed the basis for assessment of the pension from 40/60ths to 40/80ths. It is also averaged over the salary received during the last three years of service. It is now possible for the pension of officers retained beyond their sixtieth birthday to exceed 40/80ths, but only for completed years beyond that date.

that existing rights are modified accordingly, National Insurance sickness benefit being deducted from full Civil Service sick pay and pensions of future entrants[1] being reduced by the amount of the National Insurance retirement pension.

HOURS AND LEAVE

N.B.–*The conditions under this and the following heading have been radically altered, as from July* 1*st*, 1956, *by the agreement reached on the Priestley Commission's proposals,* *see page* 210.

The hours of attendance of civil servants have usually been favourable and annual leave arrangements since 1920 have in the main been generous. These were undoubtedly among the factors that made employment in the Civil Service attractive. During the early Victorian period a six-hour day (usually from 10 a.m. to 4 p.m.) was quite common. A minimum day of seven hours for the office staffs was laid down by the Order in Council of 1910, an arrangement which was confirmed at Reorganization, 1920, with provision for a half day's holiday each week. In London the Saturday half-holiday was allowed as a privilege, reducing the 42 hour week to 38½ hours net. In the provinces a week of 44 hours net was applied.[2] Hours in excess of the gross standard week were, except in the case of supervisory and executive grades, paid for as overtime. Longer hours were worked by the manipulative and industrial staffs.

During the wartime emergency these and other conditions of service were suspended by mutual agreement and very long, frequently excessively long, hours were worked by all officials. After the war a standard week of 45½ hours was applied to the office staffs, the excess over 42 hours in London and 44 in the provinces being paid for as overtime. The standard week for the manipulative and industrial staffs remained at 48 hours. To a limited extent the five-day week was granted, namely, in those instances where the office staffs were employed in industrial establishments to which, in accordance with outside practice, a five-day week had been applied since the war. The major part of the non-industrial Civil Service, however, still attended on Saturday mornings.

The annual leave allowance ranges from three weeks for the more junior grades in the clerical sphere up to six weeks for all Administrative and Executive officers. Senior officers of the two major classes are entitled to as much as eight weeks annually, but since the war this privilege has not been restored. In addition short periods of special leave, with or without pay according to circumstances, may be granted in cases of domestic urgency and sick absences on full pay may be

[1] As from March 1st, 1948.
[2] In both cases these totals included a lunch break of 45 minutes.

allowed up to six months, subject to the deduction of National Insurance benefits.

Before the war the Civil Service, especially in London, was very well placed with regard to the length of its working day, but with its present longer hours and in the light of improvements in other spheres it is doubtful whether it still holds any real attractions on this score, particularly when the general application of the five-day week or the granting of additional Saturday absences, which are now common outside, are taken into account. In the matter of annual leave the Civil Service is still in a favoured position. The allowance of six weeks to the senior grades is certainly generous, but there are many factors to be taken into account before coming to a final conclusion on the matter.

In the first place many senior officers do not take all their leave (and there is no compensation for not doing so). But this is not necessarily a net advantage to the community. Leave is given for recuperative and refreshment purposes and it can be justly argued that an official who profits fully from his annual leave allowance is likely to be a more efficient worker during the remainder of the year. Some officials, particularly at the top, do not take their full allowance because they are hard pressed. This is a bad thing and relief should be given on grounds of efficiency. It may be true that some of these officials do not take all their leave because they find their work so interesting that they do not feel the need for it. This of course depends very much on the nature of the work. There is also the other type of official who cannot bear to leave his job to anyone else. He often, by giving up leave, obtains a reputation for zeal, when the real reason is more likely to stem from lack of confidence in his assistants and an inability to delegate responsibility.

Before condemning the apparently generous leave allowances of civil servants the factor of recuperation needs to be taken very seriously into account. In a sedentary occupation the wise use of leave periods can contribute appreciably to increasing the general efficiency of the Service. Moreover, it must not be forgotten that any time off required by a civil servant (except under those circumstances that justify the granting of special leave) must be taken out of the annual leave allowance and most civil servants take a good number of odd days in this way. Personal privileges that are usual in the private and professional sectors of the economy cannot be granted in a public service.

The Staff and Official Sides were not able to agree on the full restoration of pre-war conditions of hours and leave as was embodied in the wartime promise of the Government to return to pre-war practices after the emergency had passed. The Staff Side naturally pressed for a complete return to the previous conditions, but at the same time it has wanted a five-day week to be generally applied to the Civil Service. The compromise offer by the Treasury in 1949 of a 10½-day fortnight of 83 working hours in London, and 88 hours outside, with proportionate reductions in annual leave, received only partial support from the staff associations and was not therefore acceptable to the Staff Side as a whole. This arrangement would have allowed one Saturday off in two, it being arranged with reason that service to the public precludes the Civil Service from switching to a full five-day week.

TEMPORARY SERVICE

Apart from being excluded from superannuation, temporary civil servants have often received less favourable rates of pay and other conditions of service than their permanent colleagues. The tendency since the war has been for the gap to be narrowed and on the grounds of justice and equality the staff associations are usually in favour of complete assimilation. However, it does not necessarily follow that there is any injustice in granting more favourable conditions to those who have been subject to more severe entrance tests and have longer experience behind them in a permanent capacity. It perhaps throws a significant light on the decline in general standards that persons recruited outside the normal course can vie sufficiently well with their long-serving colleagues to give an air of reasonableness to a claim to equality of treatment!

PRESTIGE, CIVIL RIGHTS AND RULES OF CONDUCT

As a condition of service the prestige of an occupation is an imponderable factor, yet none the less important on that account. In the past many, particularly among the highly educated, have been willing to devote themselves to public service as a vocation and to sacrifice the normal opportunities of advancement in economic and social standards that they might have achieved elsewhere. The civil servant's position was held in high esteem and strenuously competed for. Once obtained it was felt to be both a trust and a privilege to be held on to at all costs. This endowed it with an attractiveness that offset a number of manifest disadvantages. One of these is that the civil servant has but one employer, the State: if he is dissatisfied there is usually no alternative market for his wares.[1] He is restricted in his participation in public affairs and subject to special rules of personal conduct, which to some extent involve a sacrifice of some of his citizenship rights. These important matters, which are discussed in Chapter IX, must be taken fully into account when assessing the conditions of Civil Service employment. By some they may be considered to more than offset the accepted advantages of the Service. The completely efficient Civil Service calls for a high degree of self-sacrifice and dedication from its members.

[1] The recent loosening of this condition by permitting transfers to other branches of public service with the retention of superannuation rights applies only to a limited range of civil servants and in any case the civil servant seeking such a transfer is dependent upon his one employer for a 'character'.

WELFARE

An aspect of the Civil Service that deserves brief mention is the increased attention now given to the welfare of the staff. Much is being done to improve working conditions in government offices[1], the past policy of using unsuitable buildings for public offices, coupled with the perennial difficulty of coping with the housing of an expanding administration having led to the use of many buildings totally unsuitable for office purposes, or the gross overcrowding of buildings that would otherwise have been suitable. The policy is to continue such improvements, but there is still much leeway to be made up.

In addition the personal difficulties of individual members of the Civil Service have been placed under the specialist care of officials designated as welfare officers, to whom any member of the staff may go for advice without following the normal official routine of passing the problem up the line. This service was to some extent introduced as an example to the private sectors of the nation when the Government during the war were pressing outside firms to introduce welfare facilities. It has since become an established part of Civil Service staff management, but unfortunately its retention seems mainly to be justified by the deterioration in staff standards, which presupposes that recruits will have welfare problems that are beyond the capacity of their immediate supervisors to solve as part of the normal function of management. This was not the position before the war and indicates a worsening of the conditions of service rather than a social advance, as is sometimes claimed. A properly constituted Civil Service should not generate welfare problems that the leaders normally have not the capacity or the time adequately to deal with. As things are, however, the welfare services of the departments are valuable from the staff's standpoint.

IMPACT OF A CHANGING WORLD

The war years of the early 'forties accelerated a social revolution that had long been marking time. The situation by which a rapidly ageing Civil Service had been confronted in 1939 was vastly changed at the end of the war, although few administrators yet appeared to realize it. The general opinion, on the basis of post-1919 experience, was that there would be a strong ebb tide towards the *status quo*. As it was, the emerging situation was destined to render the civil servant's conditions of service ever so much more important than hitherto. The laws of supply and demand were soon to demonstrate the inadequacy of the traditional policies of both the Treasury and the Staff Side.

With the increase in the social and economic status of the working class it was inevitable that the Civil Service, as a predominantly middle

[1] See *Working Conditions in the Civil Service* (H.M. Treasury, 1947).

class organization, should suffer a decline in relative importance. At first the special reconstruction recruitment situation effectively masked this change and the demand for Civil Service posts remained high. But the expanding Welfare State is also an Administrative State calling for a larger and larger proportion of clerical, professional and technical workers; to such a degree that a developing democratic educational system has been quite unable to increase the supply of the required skills proportionately to expanding demand. The candidate who normally would have looked to the Civil Service as the number one career now had an extending range of interesting alternatives from which to choose.

At the same time the demands of the official job upon the individual civil servant were increasing, partly in response to the growing complexity of the administrative functions of the State, partly on account of changing relationships inside the Service which reflect the march of time. For example, the decline in the value of security of employment – brought about partly by the success of the full employment policy, partly by the diminished value of personal security in face of a widespread sense of general insecurity introduced by the international ideological division of power and the invention of means of destruction that threaten the roots of our present civilization – renders the maintenance of discipline more difficult, especially in the public services. The task of the Civil Service supervisor calls for more skill, at a time when a decline of skills inside the Civil Service, inevitable to some extent in a period of staff inflation, is too widespread to be denied. There can be no doubt that the civil servant of today is faced by a much more considerable task than any of his forebears were called upon to grapple with. Without any other changes this might well justify a relative improvement in the civil servant's terms of employment in order to maintain the Civil Service's efficiency. However, changes have been so revolutionary that it would be hopelessly unrealistic to place too much emphasis on this one point.

A further adverse factor has been the decreased esteem of the public for the Civil Service, due not to any failure of the Service to do its job, but to an increase of officialdom's interference with the individual citizen's daily life, which even if usually benevolent in intention and fully in accordance with social policies supported by the majority of the community, inevitably engenders a sense of exasperation which is easily traded upon by unscrupulous publicists in search of copy or by political opponents of social reform. The success of the Press in furthering this trend presents an example of shortsightedness upon which history is likely to place the highest censure.

At the same time the general policy of the Treasury in pursuing its public duty of enforcing financial economy on the Civil Service, coupled with the Government's continuance of the wartime policy of using the

Service as an example to the rest of the community, acted as further brakes upon the relative attractiveness of a Civil Service career.

THE PRIESTLEY COMMISSION, 1953–5

Recognizing that the situation of the Civil Service was becoming a major problem the Government announced in July 1953 the setting up of a Royal Commission under the chairmanship of Sir Raymond Priestley. Although this was heralded as one of the periodical major reviews of the Civil Service that had been conducted at more or less twenty year intervals the Commission's somewhat restricted terms of reference fail to support this notion. Its inquiries were to be restricted to the principles that govern pay, changes in current rates of pay as well as in hours of work, overtime and annual leave allowances, and also in the existing superannuation scheme. These important matters are so completely within the scope of the present chapter that it will not be irrelevant to consider here the general trend of the evidence placed before the Commission. It will be noted that the vital subjects of structure, classification and personnel management – the major problems of previous Royal Commissions – were outside the scope of the new commission. Whether the underlying assumption that these matters called for no major adjustment is justified will become clearer as the themes of our later chapters are developed.

If the latest Royal Commission's task was a restricted one compared with that of its most famous predecessors, in a rapidly changing situation it was sufficiently complex and difficult to call upon the Commissioners' fullest energies. Apart from the printed materials placed at its disposal it took oral evidence on twenty-eight days, extending from February 1954 to March 1955.[1] The bulk of this evidence was presented by the Treasury and the departments, the Staff Side of the Civil Service National Whitley Council and the separate staff associations. In view of the great importance to them of the Royal Commission's verdict the Report was awaited by the Civil Service with a mixture of impatience and trepidation.

On the major subject of pay the Treasury called for an authoritative restatement of principle and indicated the general lines which they hoped would be followed. They considered that Civil Service remuneration should be based upon comparisons with the amounts paid to similar outside employments, taking differences in other conditions of service fully into account and having regard to the maintenance of internal relativities between the Civil Service classes. They agreed that in the existing fluid economic situation it was unreasonable to insist upon the

[1] *Introductory Factual Memoranda on the Civil Service* (H.M. Treasury, 1954). *Minutes of Evidence* 1–28 (1954–5). *Appendix I and Appendix II to the Minutes of Evidence. Supplement to Introductory Factual Memorandum* (1954).

long term basis for such adjustments to which the Tomlin formula had been anchored. The staffs also wanted a modification of the Tomlin formula in the direction of fluidity, but had been unable to agree upon a general policy on this vital subject. Varying viewpoints were put to the Commission by different staff groups and the Staff Side were in no position to give an authoritative lead in the matter. Some of the main difficulties arose on the question of internal relativities: the manipulative staffs in particular wanting further to reduce and in fact to abolish the gap between themselves and the clerical sectors, an endorsement of outside trends; while the supervisory grades in all classes wanted to reverse the movement that had for some time narrowed the differentials for skill. Indeed on this point Treasury witnesses agreed that the 'concertina' had been closed rather too much in determining post-war rates for the middle grades of the Service. The professional classes were concerned to improve their position *vis-à-vis* the Administrative Class and, both here and in making comparisons between the Administrative and Executive Classes, witnesses came perilously near to infringing upon the territories of function and structure which the Commission were barred from exploring.

In general the Staff Side pressed for the restitution of all pre-war practices that were still in abeyance. On matters of superannuation, hours and leave, they were able to present agreed views. The Staff Side wanted a five-day week and considered that minimum services to the public on Saturdays could often be met by the attendance of skeleton staffs. They were understandably critical of a Treasury proposal to combine a 10½-day fortnight with reduced annual leave on a basis inferior to the previous official offer of 1949, on which the staffs had then been unable to agree. The Staff Side were not in favour of maintaining different conditions of pay and hours between London and the rest of the country. In face of the improvements that had taken place in the superannuation scheme since the war it is hardly surprising that under this heading only matters of detail were at issue.

However just and common sense one might consider the determination of civil servants' conditions of service in accordance with comparable outside employments it is clear, from an examination both of the evidence submitted to the Commission and of the actual situation, that the propounding of a formula applicable to such a large and varied occupational field is infinitely difficult and that the result is likely to be too generalized to be of much practical value in specific cases. The real difficulty is to assess the market value of those conditions of service which on the one hand add to the attractiveness of a Civil Service career and on the other have quite the opposite effect. There was, for example, a good deal of discussion before the Commission by representatives of the higher grades on the question of the alleged perquisites common outside the Civil Service, and of the senior civil servant's inferior position with regard to entertainment expenses. Little was said about the amount of monetary compensation due for the restriction of the civil servant's citizenship, both political and occupational, and particularly about the fact that he works for a monopoly employer and cannot easily take his wares to another market.

The evidence is that the laws of supply and demand will beggar any formula that ignores them. There was no disagreement before the Royal Commission about the changed relationship between the Civil Service and the rest of the economy on the lines already discussed above. On the evidence of the Civil Service Commissioners it was becoming increasingly difficult to obtain sufficient competent recruits, even at the reduced standards that were having to be accepted in some directions. It was agreed that various special expedients were failing to obtain an adequate inflow of clerical and sub-clerical gradings and that the margin of acceptable Administrative Class recruits was dwindling seriously. Even while the Royal Commission was sitting the position had so deteriorated that the hitherto relatively good Executive Class inflow had ceased to be satisfactory, while the latest Administrative competition had failed to obtain sufficient satisfactory recruits.

It is obvious that the nation will not in the future get a better Civil Service than its conditions of service attract and that if it pays less than the true market rate for its officials (whatever that may mean in terms of formulae) it will have to put up with a greater margin of inefficiency at a time when an improvement in this direction may well be vital to the ultimate success of the Welfare State, and much else.

CHAPTER IV

CHOOSING THE OFFICIAL

The efficiency and morale of the Civil Service depend ultimately upon the standards prescribed and the methods adopted at the recruitment stage. It is an immemorial characteristic of public employment that it should be regarded as a bounty to be conferred upon the adherents of the governing power, a return for services rendered rather than a creative opportunity to promote the public weal. Throughout history administrative offices have been in the gift of the ruler; sometimes by mere whim to retainers about the court; sometimes in accordance with hereditary precedence; sometimes even by sale to the highest bidder, a practice not rare in English experience and habitual in France under the *ancien régime* that fell with the Revolution. The degree to which the competence of the candidate was taken into account would depend upon the selector's assessment of current necessities. Too frequently the meeting of an irksome obligation or a chance to replenish the coffers of the state would overshadow any thought for day-to-day administrative efficiency, and the loss as time went on would be cumulative. Sometimes, of course, the right man was chosen for the job. Self-interest could be counted upon to ensure that none but the most incompetent of rulers should completely ignore the immediate needs of the situation. Where specific qualifications were laid down special arrangements might be made; as in Rome where the magistracies were subject to a scale of precedences, in Greece where election rather than lot might be preferred for filling technical posts, and in medieval England where churchmen for long monopolized the Household positions in virtue of being practically the only competent clerks in the community. Even where the power of appointment was delegated to lesser authorities some form of patronage was almost bound to operate. It is natural that the responsible minister should fill vacancies from among those with whom he is acquainted or on whose behalf the pressures of relations and friends have been exerted.

THE CIVIL SERVICE COMMISSION AND ITS TASK

With the advent of the modern state the need for more efficient methods of selection became apparent. Even the patronage wielders sometimes found entrance examinations desirable, but they were usually loath to give up privileges which seemed to be an essential perquisite of their office. We have already seen how, at the birth of the modern Civil Service in the middle of the nineteenth century, the storming of the citadel of patronage was the reformers' first and most difficult task. In seeking an objective method of selection to substitute for the subjective ways of patronage, open competition was chosen as the most satisfactory solution. But before any such objective tests could be imposed an independent recruiting agency had to be established. Thus, in 1855, the Civil Service Commission was first set up.

The Commissioners[1] are appointed by the Crown and hold office during the sovereign's good pleasure. They are responsible only for recruitment. The general conditions of candidature for the various posts and rules for the examinations are settled by the Treasury and Heads of Departments, and the latter continue to make the actual appointments after the requirements of the Commissioners have been satisfied. The Civil Service Commissioners' sphere of responsibility is therefore a restricted one, but within that sphere they act quasi-judicially and are not subject to outside interference, even from the Treasury. Assisted by a normal Civil Service staff they are indeed one of the smaller central departments. Their headquarters at Burlington House, just off Piccadilly, London, is well known to numerous examinees.

Except for appointments by the Crown and temporary posts, and a few special cases,[2] the holding of a Civil Service post is dependent upon the issue of a certificate by the Commissioners. The Commissioners have first to satisfy themselves on the candidate's age, health, character, nationality, and knowledge and ability. Certified evidence of the first four of these conditions can be readily obtained, and it is with regard to the testing of knowledge and ability that the main difficulties arise.

From the first the Commissioners have built up a high reputation for the effectiveness and impartiality of the tests which they impose. Various types of test have been adopted, but for open competitions to the 'Treasury' classes the written literary type of examination, based upon a general educational pattern, was for long favoured to the exclusion of other methods. It is only since 1919 that the variety of tests has been extended. By basing the syllabus of the examinations for the Administrative Class on the curricula of the universities, particularly of Oxford and Cambridge, it was possible to ensure not only that these universities should supply the majority of the cadets to the leadership group, but also that the Commission's examinations and the standards and methods of the educational establishments should keep in step. Similar principles were applied at lower levels, although before the First World War some steps were taken to include appropriate clerkship subjects in

[1] Originally there were three; today there are six.
[2] The exceptions are scheduled in the principal Order in Council.

TABLE III

University and Degree Class of Successful Candidates to the Administrative Class of the Home Civil Service

University	Class	A. Period 1934–38					Total five years	B. Period 1949–54					Total five years
		1934	1935	1936	1937	1938		49–50	50–51	51–52	52–53	53–54	
REDBRICK													
Aberdeen	1st	—	—	—	1	—	1	½	—	—	—	1	2½
	2nd	—	—	—	—	—		—	—	—	—	1	
Belfast	2nd	—	—	—	—	—	—	—	1	—	—	—	1
Birmingham	1st	—	½	—	—	—	½	—	—	—	—	—	—
Bristol	1st	—	—	1	—	—	1	—	—	—	—	—	—
Durham	1st	—	—	—	—	—	—	—	1	—	—	—	1
Edinburgh	1st	1	½	2	—	2½	6½	1	1	1	1	1	7
	2nd	—	—	—	½	—		1	—	1	—	—	
Glasgow	1st	1	1	2	1	—	5	1	1	—	2½	1	10½
	2nd	—	—	—	—	—		—	2	2	1	—	
Liverpool	1st	—	—	—	—	—	—	—	—	—	1	—	1
London	1st	—	4½	3	3	—	18½	2	2	2	1	2½	33½
	2nd	—	1	—	2	4		6	10	3	2	3	
	Pass	—	—	1	—	—		—	—	—	—	—	
Manchester	1st	—	—	—	—	—	—	—	1	1	—	—	2

Nottingham	2nd	—	—	—	—	—	—	—	—	—	—	1	1
St. Andrews	1st	—	1	—	—	—	1	1	—	—	—	—	4
	2nd	—	—	—	—	—		—	—	1	1	1	
Wales	1st	—	1	—	—	—	1	—	1	—	—	—	3
	2nd	—	—	—	—	—		1	1	—	—	—	
Dublin	1st	—	—	1	—	—	1	—	1	—	—	—	2
	2nd	—	—	—	—	—		—	1	—	—	—	
Totals (a)		2	9½	10	7½	6½	35½=*14·6%*	13½	23	11	9½	11½	68½=*25·2%*
OXBRIDGE													
Oxford	1st	10	8	13½	13	10½		2½	8	15	13	8½	
	2nd	6	5	4	9	9		8	15	23	19½	15	
Totals (b)		16	13	17½	22	19½	88 =*36·2%*	10½	23	38	32½	23½	127½=*46·9%*
Cambridge	1st	18	20½	25½	20½	24		10	8	9	10	8	
	2nd	—	3	1	4	3		6	7	7	5	6	
Totals (c)		18	23½	26½	24½	27	119½=*49·2%*	16	15	16	15	14	76 =*27·9%*
Grand Totals (a+b+c)		36	46	54	54	53	243	40	61	65	57	49	272
Total Firsts		*30*	*37*	*48*	*38½*	*37*	*190½*	*18*	*24*	*28*	*28½*	*22*	*120½*
„ Seconds		*6*	*9*	*5*	*15½*	*16*	*51½*	*22*	*37*	*37*	*28½*	*27*	*151½*
„ Other		—	—	*1*	—	—	*1*	—	—	—	—	—	

Note. '½' indicates candidates shared by two universities.

the examinations for certain of the subordinate grades.[1] Examinations for certain departmental classes, e.g. the Customs and Excise Officerships, included subjects that were considered helpful in the performance of the department's work, but even in these cases the examinations remained predominantly of the general literary type. One point should be specially emphasized: for the purest type of open competition a specific educational experience or qualification was not laid down. Anyone satisfying the general regulations as regards age, health, character, etc., could compete, but in practice success came overwhelmingly to those who had undergone the type of education to which the examination syllabus was so closely related. Occasionally, it is true, a brilliant privately tutored candidate passed the examinations, but the advantages of having had the right type of schooling were so great that even the new universities made a poor showing beside Oxford and Cambridge.[2] In practice this pure form of open competition has never been appropriate except for a limited range of office posts. After 1919 a *viva voce* test was introduced for the Administrative Class with the object of assessing personality and the use of this method has since been extended in accordance with modern thought on the subject.

Technical and professional posts need vocational qualifications, which are laid down as the minimum requirement for candidature: formal selection is then usually settled by means of competitive interview. For many subordinate posts, and also for the allocation of a proportion of vacancies to a particular type of candidate, limited competitions have also been widely adopted. For example, a special limited competition has for long been available to members of the manipulative classes in the Post Office who aspire to transfer to the Clerical Class.

The examination system, built up during the later decades of the nineteenth century, probably had its heyday in the period immediately preceding the First World War. Relatively to the rest of the community the Civil Service from top to bottom was a highly educated vocation built in a strictly hierarchic form. Already, however, the expansion of the Post Office into the telecommunications sphere and the recent extension of government participation in the social service spheres of employment and health had led to the absorption into the Civil Service of older persons with special outside experience. Following the war recruitment from among school-leaving candidates was delayed by the need to absorb large numbers of ex-Servicemen. This again radically altered the normal age grouping of the Civil Service and was not effected without gravely lowering the entrance standards hitherto con-

[1] E.g. such subjects as précis writing, copying manuscripts, book-keeping and shorthand in the Second Division examinations.

[2] See Table III on pp. 68–9 based upon information extracted from the Civil Service Commissioners' *Annual Reports*.

sidered as the minimum essential to efficiency. A similar situation arose after the Second World War, but in this case, profiting by previous experience, a carefully devised Reconstruction scheme of recruitment[1] ensured that tests which were both fair and effective should be applied in the recruitment of the ex-Service men and women. These tests did involve the suspension for the time being of the general principle of open competition and the prescription of a specific educational experience as one of the conditions determining eligibility to compete. In the main, however, it is changes of a more general and radical nature that have created special recruitment difficulties, but it is proposed to leave the consideration of these matters until the present system of recruitment has been briefly examined.

THE EXAMINATIONS TODAY

The Administrative Class is recruited from candidates between the ages of 20½ and 24 by two types of competition known officially as Methods I and II. Four-fifths of the total vacancies are distributed between the two Methods in the proportion 3:1. There is also a limited competition for established civil servants between the ages of 21 and 28 to which the remaining fifth of the vacancies is allocated.

Method I is virtually the pre-war type of competition, based upon a wide range of school subjects at university honours degree level, to which a preliminary interview by a single interviewer has now been added. An university education is not prescribed, but only those who have had the advantage of such have much chance of success. The preliminary interview is not a weeding out test, but is designed to obtain information about the candidate that will be of assistance to the Final Interview Board. As in the case of the pre-war interview the marks awarded by the present board, based upon the interview and the candidate's record, are added to the marks for the written papers to determine the candidate's relative position in the final list. The final interview may modify, but does not determine the candidate's success.

Method II, a modern innovation designed to place special emphasis upon personality and quickwittedness as opposed to sheer intellectual ability, is based upon the so-called house party scheme, adopted during the war for the selection of army officers and by the Civil Service Commission for recruitment to the Administrative Class in the Reconstruction examinations. These examinations were devised for candidates whose career had been affected by war services. Under the original scheme candidates attended the Civil Service Selection Board at Stoke D'Abernon, Cobham, Surrey, organized on a residential basis for two

[1] See *Recruitment to Established Posts in the Civil Service During the Reconstruction Period* (Statement of Government Policy and Civil Service National Whitley Council Report, 1944), Cmd. 6567.

or three days: for reasons of economy the Board now sits in London and candidates attend daily, apparently without any distinguishable falling off in efficiency.[1] The procedures adopted allow for a friendly but searching review of the candidate's personal qualities and intelligence to be undertaken by the staff of the Board. There is a minimum qualification under this Method of a second class honours degree. All candidates appear before the Final Interview Board, which in this instance actually determines the result. The scheme for the competition limited to serving civil servants was similar to Method II, except that nomination by the candidate's department was substituted for the university qualification. For 1956 and 1957 the rules are being changed (i) to include examination by Method I, referred to above, as well as Method II and (ii) to omit nomination by the candidate's department. The results of these more liberal regulations will be watched with interest.

The Executive Class examinations now fall into five different categories, but a large proportion of the vacancies is filled by open competition from among young people between the ages of 17½ and 19, by a written examination of the pre-war type set in a wide range of subjects at the advanced level of the General Certificate of Education. An interview test has been introduced which, in conjunction with the written papers, helps to determine the aggregate marks: in other words it is not an eliminating test. In addition, three different open competitions are held regularly for (i) university graduates, (ii) young men who have completed their National Service, and (iii) for ex-Regular members of the armed forces. Finally, there is a limited competition, in substitution for normal promotion, for members of the clerical grades between the ages of 21 and 28. This test consists of a written examination of a general nature and an interview.

The open competitions for entry to the Clerical Class of young people between the ages of 16 and 18, are similar to those of the Executive Class, but at the ordinary level of the General Certificate of Education: there is no interview test. There are also separate open competitions for National Service and ex-Regular candidates, as well as a special limited competition for members of the minor and manipulative grades between the ages of 25 and 60. Owing to the failure of the ordinary competitions to obtain a sufficient flow of qualified candidates it was decided in 1953 to adopt two special expedients. The first, which involved the offer of vacancies to unsuccessful candidates in the ordinary Executive competition who were within the required age limits and had only just failed to

[1] See *Ninth Report from the Select Committee on Estimates* (*Session* 1947–8) *on the Civil Service Commission* (H.M.S.O. 1948), and *Memorandum by the Civil Service Commission on the use of the Civil Service Selection Board in the Reconstruction Examination* (H.M.S.O. 1951).

reach the executive standard, did not discard the open competitive principle: but the other certainly did. Under the second scheme recruits were to be selected from young people between the ages of 16 and 18 who had passed the General Certificate of Education at the ordinary or advanced level in certain stipulated subjects, including English Language. Originally this scheme was confined to London recruitments, but it has now been extended to the provinces.

Recruitment to the Clerical Assistant and Typing grades has been so difficult since the war that open competition has been virtually discarded for filling vacancies outside London. It has been impossible, for various reasons, to obtain a sufficient supply of young girls, who normally provide the best type of agent for this kind of work, and the field has been widened to take in older entrants.

For the Clerical Assistants simpler examination tests have been substituted for the earlier full-scale written examinations, which had at one time been effective in recruiting girls with a good secondary education and, except in London, where competition on the earlier basis continued to be held, recruitment has been carried out by limited competition from among temporary clerks after a period of approved service. The standards have often been mediocre compared with before the war. Men as well as women have become eligible and the whole nature of the class has been changed. However, the situation is clearly very fluid. Open competitions of a scholastic nature for Clerical Assistant posts are being restored during 1956 for recruitment in London and a number of large city areas.

Age limits for the recruitment of typists had been virtually abolished in 1949 and, while open competitions with a simple written examination were continued for London recruitment, elsewhere appointments have been made locally on a temporary basis, selection for permanent posts being subsequently made from among these temporary officers by means of limited competitions. Successful candidates are graded according to their technical skill in typing, which is determined by practical tests at the official typing schools.

During 1955 it was decided to recruit adults between the ages of 40 and 60 by competition on a permanent basis to both the Clerical Officer and the Clerical Assistant grades. This was announced as part of the national policy to provide work for the older employment groups. The Staff Side of the Civil Service National Whitley Council accepted this as a temporary expedient, holding with good reason that this is a further step towards reducing the standards of the Clerical sectors (and eventually the Executive sectors) of the Civil Service. It seems hardly likely that entrants so late in life, who normally will have already tackled some other type of work with only modest success, will measure up to the quality of the school leaving recruits. It is significant that this innovation had a good general press, showing how little outsiders appreciate the growing danger to the nation's well-being that falling standards in the Civil Service bring in train.

In addition to the examinations for the Treasury classes, which have been briefly described, there are similar competitions for departmental classes in the administrative field, such as the Foreign Service (Branch A of which is recruited by Method II of the Administrative Class examination), the Special Departmental Classes[1] (for which both Methods and the same papers are used as for the Administrative Class) and Officers of Customs and Excise.

The general educational type of examination is most suitable for recruitment for administrative work at various levels. Where specialist knowledge is a prerequisite for entry into official employment other methods have usually been found more appropriate. Proof of specialist knowledge depends upon the holding of prescribed professional qualifications: selection is then made from among qualified candidates by means of competitive interview. The selection boards for this purpose usually include representatives of the departments concerned, the universities and industry, under the chairmanship of a member appointed by the Civil Service Commission. Since the war the reorganization of the scientific and other professional classes on an all-Service basis has greatly expanded the Civil Service Commission's responsibilities in these fields.

For various reasons, some already discussed and others still to be touched upon, the task of recruitment has become much more difficult since the war. Following the Reconstruction phase there has been no question of a return to the pre-war situation. For a time sufficient candidates were forthcoming for the Administrative and Executive Classes[2] but, as we have seen, various expedients had to be introduced to obtain sufficient candidates at the Clerical and Sub-clerical levels. In the process the sphere of open competition has been inevitably narrowed. Although the effects of this restriction cannot be regarded with equanimity it must be remembered that open competition has never covered the whole Civil Service. Nomination appointments have always formed a large proportion of recruitments; subject of course to the normal safeguards conscientiously applied by the Civil Service Commission.

In some instances the competitive interview is competitive in little more than in name: for to have true competition there must be an excess of suitable candidates and often for professional posts this has

[1] These comprise Inspectors of Taxes in the Inland Revenue Dept., the Cadet Grade in the Departmental Class of the Ministry of Labour and National Service, Probationary Assistant Postal Controllers in the Post Office and Research Assistants in the Joint Intelligence Bureaux, Ministry of Defence.

[2] Latterly there has been a falling away in competition for these senior classes.

not been the position. For example, since 1949 it has been the practice for candidates for the Senior Scientific Officer and Scientific Officer competitions to be informed straight away by the selection board whether they are successful. This has had the advantage of making the competition more attractive to the prospective candidate who was probably considering alternative appointments for which an immediate decision was essential, but this more businesslike procedure is nevertheless incompatible with real open competition.

The Table IV, on page 76, divides recruitment to the Civil Service between Open Competition, Limited Competition and Nomination, for periods preceding and following the Second World War.

On the relative quality of pre-war and post-war appointees little can yet be said, except of course in those instances where examination standards have had to be lowered or even dispensed with. That the quality of recruits to the Clerical and Sub-clerical fields has been appreciably lowered is not open to challenge. The future effect on the efficiency of the Civil Service may well be serious. For the Administrative and Executive Classes competition was until recently keen,[1] but this is not necessarily conclusive evidence that quality levels are as high as previously. Changes in supply due to national causes and changes in examination methods can have an important effect one way or another. The Civil Service Commissioners have set up a Research Unit, one of whose tasks is to follow up the record of new appointees by means of periodical reports. It is doubtful, however, in view of the general tendency for reporting officers to be forbearing to newcomers and for their reports to lack true objectivity whether these enquiries will lead to definite conclusions, at least until more objective methods of assessment have been worked out.

One factor of great importance is the educational experience of the recruits to the leadership group. Before the war the public schools and universities naturally, in view of the examination requirements, predominated in the pass lists, but the outstanding characteristic was the practical monopoly of these successes by the Universities of Oxford and Cambridge, and by candidates from the literary rather than from the scientific schools. There has been some change since the war, but less than might have been expected. Table III, on pages 68–9, sets out the position with regard to the Administrative Class.

From this it will be seen that Oxford has replaced Cambridge as the dominant source of the senior ranks of the Civil Service. An even more significant change is the overwhelming increase in the proportion of the second class honours group among the successful candidates.[2] What-

[1] Royal Commission on the Civil Service: Minutes of Evidence: Days 3–4. Tables II, p. 53 and III, p. 54 (1954).
[2] The figures for 1954–5 indicate a continuance of the same trends.

TABLE IV

Types of Recruitment to Civil Service Posts by the Civil Service Commissioners in Pre-war and Post-war Periods

Pre-War

Type	1934	1935	1936	1937	1938
Open competition	4,216	6,539	10,396	10,883	13,865
Limited competition	1,055	1,444	1,904	1,736	1,579
Nomination	8,878	8,657	13,675	18,701	18,387
Yearly Totals	14,149	16,640	25,975	31,320	33,831

Post-war

Type	1949–50	1950–1	1951–2	1952–3	1953–4	1954–5
Open competition	12,497	6,905	8,480	6,218	6,446	5,378
Limited competition	6,918	14,189	4,494	11,203	2,984	4,225
Nomination	112,984	53,070	59,572	38,117	37,519	57,274
Yearly Totals	132,399	74,164	72,546	55,538	46,949	66,877

These totals, quoted from the Civil Service Commissioners' *Annual Reports* (H.M.S.O.), relate to candidates actually certified by the Commissioners for appointment.

ever may be the explanation in terms of supply and demand in the national employment market this trend suggests that the leadership group will find it less easy in the future to maintain its predominance over the rest of the Civil Service on the basis of outstanding intellectual brilliance.

THE CHANGING SITUATION

Following the Second World War various situations arose and changes occurred to affect the normal development of Civil Service recruitment. Before the end of the war arrangements had been agreed on the National Whitley Council[1] for the recruitment during the Reconstruction period of persons whose service with the armed and auxiliary Forces of the Crown had deprived them of the normal opportunities to compete for posts in the Civil Service. Every effort was made to avoid the somewhat haphazard approach of the previous 'Reconstruction' period.

[1] See *Recruitment of Established Posts in the Civil Service during the Reconstruction Period*, Cmd. 6567 (1944).

The new 'Reconstruction' examinations usually consisted of a written part which was of a general nature, suitable for persons who had got out of the habit of formal study, followed by an interview. In the case of the highest posts the so called 'house-party' system was adopted, as previously mentioned. Age limits were extended to allow for the candidate's period with the Forces and a prerequisite for entering the competitions was an educational experience suitable to the level of the normal competitions for the particular class. Thus for the Clerical Class the requirement was full-time education to the age of 16 or the holding of a School Certificate. This was a new principle for examinations for this type of post and the competitions were therefore limited and not open even within the restricted field of recruitment. Generally speaking these competitions presented a fair compromise in a difficult situation and seem to have worked effectively.

The adoption since the war of the security regulations has placed an unwelcome duty on the Civil Service Commission, who must now call upon new entrants to disclose membership of Communist or Fascist organizations. This does not of course affect selection, but it influences assignment after selection. If an unavoidable precaution in the present state of the world, it is yet one sincerely to be regretted, since any questioning of political beliefs must tend to weaken the principle of political neutrality with which membership of the British Civil Service has been associated since the defeat of patronage.

The maintenance of the size of the Civil Service in order to cope with the new post-war policy of economic planning and social reform prevented any serious redundancy problem from arising – at least immediately. Numbers of temporary civil servants left of their own accord, but for a time the outflow was restricted by the Control of Employment Order (Civil Servants) which operated from 1945 to early 1947. Some permanent posts were given to suitable temporaries, who were selected by interview boards. But the temporary element continued to be large and inevitably pressure began to be exerted through the staff associations for establishment to be offered to suitable temporary officers in the lower grades, e.g. Clerical and Sub-clerical. Naturally the general shortage of normal recruits at this level disposed the authorities to look at these proposals more favourably than they might otherwise have done and schemes were agreed from time to time for limited competitions to be held. Despite the modest educational levels of these competitions it was never easy to fill up the quotas agreed with the Staff Side, without lowering standards below any reasonable level. In any case it is obvious that the majority of recruits through these channels have not been up to the minimum standards normally required by the Civil Service.

The unanticipated continuance of certain wartime ministries, such as those of Food and Supply, meant the assimilation of numbers of older entrants with a limited Civil Service background, but an even more important development of this type followed the passing of the National Insurance Act of 1944, which authorized the establishment of the Ministry of National Insurance[1] to administer a comprehensive social security scheme. In the staffing of this new central department, whose main function was to be the implementation of the Beveridge proposals, not only were the Civil Service staffs of the different government departments already concerned with this work brought together under one control, but large blocks of non-Civil Service workers were assimilated from the Approved Societies, the Public Assistance Departments of the Local Authorities and certain private insurance offices concerned with Workmen's Compensation. These groups included many experts whose experience and skills were invaluable to the new ministry, but there were many others, particularly at lower levels who inevitably fell below the normal standards of the Civil Service. Their new grading was settled in terms of their previous status which was bound to have varied between one outside organization and another. They included many middle-aged workers who were too old to be completely assimilated to the Civil Service outlook and traditions. The cynic may suggest that that might have been a good thing. In some ways perhaps, but it must be remembered that civil servants are still expected to have certain virtues that outside organizations are less insistent upon. One interesting deviation from existing Civil Service practice was the provision that certain of these outside entrants should retain the right to work on till the age of sixty-five, instead of the normal Civil Service sixty. The object of this was to preserve the value of their previous superannuation rights.

It may be thought that developments peculiar to the post-war period having once been dealt with, the Civil Service, repeating the experience of the previous post-war era, would gradually return to normality, but apart from the general factors in the market situation briefly touched upon in Chapter III there are other extra-Civil Service developments that are bound to have a long run effect on recruitment. These are specifically the encouragement of employment of married women and of extending the active working age, both advocated nationally as essential ingredients of the full employment policy, as well as the conceding of equal pay to women civil servants, largely to meet the pressure of staff groups inside the Service. The lifting of the marriage bar in October 1946, although decided upon as a matter of national policy and despite divided opinion inside the Civil Service,[2] can be adjudged a logical outcome of the failure of the Service to recruit sufficient numbers of young

[1] Now the Ministry of Pensions and National Insurance.
[2] See *The Marriage Bar in the Civil Service*, Cmd. 6885 (1946).

girls for routine work. The tentative extension of the normal retiring age is to be supplemented by the recruitment of clerical staff from the over-40 age groups. It is too early to discern the effect of this, though some of the possibilities are both obvious and disturbing, or of the effect of equal pay, which should make the Civil Service relatively a more attractive field of employment to members of the fair sex, for the principle involved was finally accepted only in 1954 and its practical implementation is still in process.

SOME GENERAL CONCLUSIONS

Largely for historical reasons the extent to which the principle of open competition has been applied to the recruitment of the present Civil Service has been very much restricted, and as we approach nearer to normality it is certain that the scope for this form of recruitment will again be considerably extended. Yet there are factors that seem likely to weaken its full application in future, namely the introduction of selection on the basis of the General Educational Certificate for the Clerical Class and the continuing appointment of persons on the strength of minimum professional qualifications in certain specialist spheres. Further, the greater weight given in the open competitions to the interview in its various forms inevitably means that a subjective element has entered into the competition process and that the accepted impartiality of the competitions may be in danger of serious challenge. There is, of course, no suggestion that the appointing authorities will not approach their responsible task with the strictest impartiality, but as the late Sir Stanley Leathes, an expert on the interview procedure as then applied by the Civil Service Commission, stated in 1926,[1] 'If jobbery is suspected, it is almost as bad as if jobbery exists'. When personality meets personality across even the friendliest table it is possible for all sorts of class and social prejudices to enter into the picture without the participants themselves being aware of what is happening, and even when they are aware the very effort called forth to ensure strict impartiality may well lead to overemphasis in the opposite direction.

It is argued, with truth, that the written examination fails to eliminate candidates who are obviously unsuitable on the score of personality. This is a more valid objection where personality is an important factor in the actual job to be performed, but usually there is such a wide variety of tasks open to an entrant to a general grade in the Civil Service that there should be little difficulty in finding an effective niche for any generally suitable candidate. Even in an age when the social contacts of the Civil Service have grown so much more important than in the days before the Welfare State, efficiency in the back-room positions

[1] See *Public Administration*, Volume I, p. 356.

is still vital. One of the difficulties of attempting to pick and choose on the basis of personality is the lack of any generally accepted measure by which administrative ability can be assessed, particularly for younger people in whom such ability can be little more than potential.

The quality of Civil Service recruitment must be inevitably affected by the extended demand throughout the community for administrative talents. From a period when the Civil Service had access to a surplus of talents of the type required, we have moved rapidly into a situation when such talents are being spread more widely to meet the increased demands of many large-scale services in both the government and the non-government spheres. Despite the rapid advances in general education it is doubtful whether the national pool of clerical abilities is keeping pace with the vast new demands that have been created. Thus a restoration of the relative attractiveness of the Civil Service as a career, as discussed in Chapter III, would not be likely to bring back the favourable situation that existed before 1939. In this complex modern world the community has need of all its human capacities.

Although patronage, as a system presenting opportunities for personal advantage in the allocation of official posts, can be eliminated by a wise recruitment policy and was indeed so eliminated in principle in Britain in 1870, political policy may still have the effect of granting privileges to particular groups in the recruitment of the Civil Service. Pressures may be exerted through Parliament to this end. For example, after the First World War numerous ex-Servicemen were absorbed into the Civil Service, against the better advice of both the Treasury and the Civil Service Commission, as the result of political decisions. True, limited competitions were set, but as no minimum educational standards had been imposed at the original recruitment of these temporary officers their general educational standard was bound to be substantially below that of the ordinary open competitive recruits. Despite more carefully planned Reconstruction recruitment after the Second World War similar pressures have been at work, mainly through the staff associations, who had recruited the new temporaries to their membership and were therefore in honour bound to advocate the absorption of all who could be considered fit. But here again the competitive tests imposed have not been such as would ensure the educational standards that are normally required for this type of work. The abolition of the marriage bar and the policy of recruiting older persons to the Clerical and Sub-clerical grades – both adopted by the Government in pursuance of the full employment policy – are further instances of policy affecting the recruitment of the Civil Service and substituting political for administrative tests of effectiveness. The increasing tendency of the State to use the Civil Service as an example to the rest of the community has already been touched upon. It is not necessarily to be inferred that this sort of thing is avoidable or even undesirable, but it is an important factor that must be taken into account when considering the position of the Civil Service in the modern State.

It is difficult to compare the quality of one age with another. Older people, among whom writers are mainly to be found, almost invariably suffer under the delusion that things spiritual and intellectual have declined since the days of their youth. Mr H. E. Dale in his authoritative work on *The Higher Civil Service of Great Britain* (1941) suggested that the Administrative Class was not quite what it had been. There are today certainly good reasons for agreeing that the Civil Service, man for man, is not up to the standards of its predecessors, but much of this is due to special historical circumstances and make-shift expedients in recruitment that could have had no other effect. Whether a sustained period of normal recruitment will gradually restore the situation remains to be seen. Clearly no effort should be spared in the public interest to achieve this end. It will then be time seriously to compare the new Service with the old.

On one subject there certainly is general agreement, namely the widespread decline in the general literary ability of school leavers at all levels, a situation that is reflected in the widely recognized inadequacy of performance in this sphere of entrants to the universities. The ability to write lucid reports is an essential prerequisite to academic study. It is an even more important prerequisite to all administrative work. The poor general standards of official correspondence has been widely remarked upon and the two official publications of Sir Ernest Gowers, referred to in the next chapter, were commissioned with a view to rectifying this failing. Even in a mechanized age ability to use the pen is a basic skill of every office worker and we should not be far wrong in hazarding a guess that there are more civil servants today whose competence in this direction is mediocre than at any time since the modern Civil Service was shaped by the reformers.

In the meantime there is one factor that is adding steadily and to some extent unconsciously to the recruitment problem, namely the growing complexity of the administrative process. The men of the old Civil Service had much simpler tasks to perform. With the growth in scale of organization and the extension of the functions of the State over an expanding community the art of public administration has become more and more involved. The law to be administered is inevitably more complicated; new techniques have to be acquired and constantly modified; the processes of co-ordination require more forethought and conscious planning; supervision and management are expanding activities in the public field. This changing situation presents a challenge to the new officials beyond anything that the older civil servants had to contend with. The truth is that the old standards are no longer good enough and all the problems of yesterday have to be thought out afresh.

The State can no longer expect to recruit even its clerical workers fully skilled from the schools. To read and write are still of first importance, but certainly not enough. The problems of training call for a separate chapter.

CHAPTER V

FITTING THE OFFICIAL TO THE JOB

When the civil servant has been selected by the Civil Service Commission and accepted by one of the central departments the problem of his assimilation immediately faces the establishment branch of the department. He has to be made aware as soon as possible of the general rules of the Service as well as of the special needs of the work of the particular department, and a suitable job has to be found for him. This problem of assimilating a new member to a team, which is of course common to all recruitment systems, is complicated in the British Civil Service by two important factors: namely (i) the general educational nature of the entrance examinations and (ii) the general grading of posts, which means that a wide range of different jobs is included within the scope of each class. The functions of the Clerical, Executive and Administrative Classes are broadly defined, as we have seen, but their actual work itself varies considerably, not only as between the State departments, but also as between the branches and sections of the same department. This does not apply to the comparatively few specific posts and it is less true where definite manipulative, technical or professional skills are a prerequisite to selection by the Civil Service Commission. On the other hand, although the Treasury classes are largely in mind in this discussion, many of the problems of assimilation inevitably arise in connection with appointments to more specialized posts.

The staffs of the departments are strictly limited to needs, and appointments are made to fill existing vacancies. Newcomers will therefore be assigned to those branches in which vacancies exist and at this stage the question of geography is important, especially today when it is not easy to move officials about freely in order to create vacancies in the most suitable positions for new entrants. The task therefore of choosing posts that are both suitable for the new entrant's training and likely to be particularly suited to his temperament and potential qualities is not easily achieved. All that can be said is that the establishment branches do their best, but that the accidental incidence of vacancies is bound to have a good deal to do with the new entrant's initial allocation.

PROBATION

The rules of the Service impose a period of probation, lasting a year or two, during which confirmation of the recruit's appointment is withheld pending satisfactory reports on his progress. All the investigatory committees on the Civil Service have emphasized the importance of the probationary period. Indeed it is particularly important in a system depending upon selection by a general educational test, which if effective in assessing the potential suitability of a sample group for Civil Service work does not presume to certify that a particular individual will not only be suitable, but will take to his new occupation and derive full satisfaction from it.

It is one thing, however, to recognize the importance of probation, quite another to ensure its effective accomplishment, as each succeeding investigation has had to admit. The tendency inside the Civil Service is to give the newcomer the benefit of the doubt, if there is any. After all, he has much to learn and should improve. Only the obvious misfits are rejected at this stage, and once the appointment has been confirmed on the evidence of a favourable report the time for reassessment has passed, unless the new officer's incompetence is too blatant to be ignored. Should a recruit fail to pass his probation his rejection is by the department to which he has been initially assigned and the Civil Service Commission may still offer him to another department, without disclosing his initial failure.

It is a weakness of State employment that no one is likely to suffer personally if an unsuitable official is recruited. The individual chief will be content to attribute the main responsibility for selection to the examining authority; the individual supervisor will see no good reason to be hard on a newcomer who may well improve: especially when an adverse report may bring his own judgment under immediate scrutiny. It is much easier to take the line of least resistance.

Since the war new regulations have been issued by H.M. Treasury with the object of improving the operation of probationary reviews. Heads of departments are enjoined to ensure that suitable tests are imposed to assess the conduct and capacity of the recruit, with the general aim of making probation a more positive stage. In view of the importance of the Administrative Class a Central Probation Board has been established under the control of the Civil Service Commission to consider the personal representations of new Assistant Principals upon whom an adverse probation report has been made. The Establishment Officer of the probationer's department is a member of the Board. It is of course of particular importance to the Civil Service that an unsuitable person should not be confirmed in the top class.

The importance of probation is generally recognized and the existence of a real problem is not challenged. One point in favour of a more rigorous attitude is often overlooked: namely, that it is not a kindness to allow a young person to become rooted in a life employment for which he is not fitted and in which he is never likely to find real satisfaction. It is important that a right decision should be reached while alternative avocations are readily accessible.

TRAINING BEFORE THE WAR

A civil servant has to be trained for his work. Under some systems this training may commence before he enters the Service, particularly where special skills and qualifications are called for as a prerequisite to entry. Thus the shorthand typist may be expected already to have acquired a minimum skill in the appropriate techniques and recruits to the technical and professional classes are required to hold suitable qualifications, which presuppose university study or professional experience, or both. For the general Treasury classes, however, the policy of recruiting juniors with the widest possible range of academic experience has been justified in practice and the presupposition of special studies at this stage would narrow inadvisably the scope of the competitions.

All new entrants, however highly qualified, have to learn the ways and attitudes of their new occupation, and various means are adopted to speed up their initiation. It was for long assumed, rightly in the circumstances, that for the general office work of the Civil Service no other initial instruction was required. The successful candidate's educational abilities – his proved capacity to write and to cypher – were all that were needed to enable him to get on with the job. The open competitions not only precluded the need for professional pre-entry training, but the nature of the work to be performed also reduced the need for initial training to little more than a formality. Not only was it sufficient to learn the job by doing it, as dogs learn to swim, but it was unnecessary to encourage the recruit to do anything more to broaden his professional knowledge.[1]

With the steady development of administrative techniques and the extension of the work of the central departments into new fields the pattern of work assigned to the general classes became more and more varied, until today the simple assumptions of the older Civil Service no longer apply. Open competition is still effective in selecting the right sort of human raw material for the Civil Service, but the competent official can no longer be said to spring fully fledged from the schools. He has to learn his profession's techniques and his task is by no means a light one. Unlike almost every other profession the public official has to accept practical responsibilities while fitting himself to his work. This difficulty is to some extent met in the important Administrative Class by making the lowest grade, namely the Assistant Principals, mainly a

[1] Some special exceptions to this are mentioned below. Furthermore the system encourages entrants at lower levels to compete in the open competitions for more senior classes. Such efforts normally absorb any surplus energies of officers in their early years of service.

cadet or training grade. It was originally the intention of the Reorganization Committee of 1919–20 that the basic grade of the Executive Class should also be a training grade, but that idea was never implemented.

Between the two wars the central departments were feeling their way towards new methods of training. Although there was little formal training more thought was given to desk training, for example, by way of preliminary explanations and planned tours of the office and allied branches. Some departments recognized the importance of planning a young officer's tour of duties, so that he was given, by means of periodical transfers from one branch to another, an opportunity to learn different aspects of the department's work. This scheme might extend over a number of years during the young officer's early service. Some attention too was given to the dissemination of information, which had often been carried out, if at all, in a somewhat haphazard way. For example, the Post Office in the 'thirties issued a valuable series of *Green Papers* explaining the department's work and also introduced a house journal, *The Post Office Magazine*, which still maintains the highest standards and has been emulated by other departments.[1]

Formal training at special schools was not generally considered necessary, although here the Post Office, largely on account of its special problems and needs, had led the way in setting up separate schools for teaching Counter, Telephone, and Engineering work. These schools are so equipped as to reproduce the actual work situations and thus to enable students to exercise manipulative skills, to face up to practical problems and to gain confidence before actually entering upon their new duties.

Little encouragement was given to officers to undertake sparetime studies either in subjects having a close bearing upon their work or in others having a general relationship to the Civil Service's broader activities. As advancement within the Service did not depend upon such professional studies there was little urge within the Service to improve its quality in this way. To this situation there were a few interesting exceptions. In the Inland Revenue Department, for example, Tax Officers were required to study for an internal examination in income tax law and procedure as a minimum qualification for promotion, which did not, however, follow automatically upon success in the examination. Instructional courses were organized by the officers' association, the Inland Revenue Staff Federation.[2]

[1] Notably *Minlabour* by the Ministry of Labour and National Service and *The Window* by the Ministry of Pensions and National Insurance.

[2] For further details see E. N. Gladden *Civil Service Staff Relationships* (1943), pp. 128–32. This excellent scheme has since been absorbed into a comprehensive official staff training programme.

Examples of other interesting deviations from general Civil Service practice were afforded by the three specialist groups, recruited as Executive Officers who were required to obtain professional qualifications by spare time study after entry: namely, (1) Actuaries in the Government Actuary's Department, required to obtain the Fellowship of the Institute of Actuaries or the Faculty of Actuaries; (2) Examiners in the Estate Duty Office of the Inland Revenue Department, required to secure the Bachelor of Laws degree of the University of London or be called to the Bar; and (3) District Audit Staff appointed by the Ministry of Health[1] who had to qualify under a special departmental training scheme.[2] There was also the instance of the Assistant Inspectors of Taxes, in the Inland Revenue Department who were required to take two departmental examinations to qualify for a 'Commission'.

THE WAR AND THE ASSHETON REPORT

With the onset of the Second World War the objectives of training were immediately switched to the briefing of officers in new work and the inducting, as quickly as possible, of temporary officers to the ways of the Civil Service. Under the exceptional impact of war conditions existing training schemes closed up and the resources, so far as they were tangible, were switched to more urgent work. Whether this strictly empirical approach was wise is another matter. One would have thought that the special wartime conditions would have called for a special and prolonged training effort. Be that as it may, the practical, and therefore essentially English, tendency to regard all training and education as something of a luxury invariably attracts the economy axe to this sphere of activity as soon as emergency conditions begin to appear.

The war itself was soon to teach the lesson, applicable in many fields, that the old haphazard rule of thumb methods would no longer do. The easy thinking of active, and oftimes blundering, practical men was clearly not enough for the complex administering of the sort of war effort that the nation was being called upon, rather reluctantly, to undertake. In 1942 the Select Committee on National Expenditure issued, as its Sixteenth Report for the Session 1941–2, a paper dealing with the *Organization and Control of the Civil Service*. This important document contained recommendations which led to the present notable development of Organization and Methods work in the central departments and the setting up of a committee, under the Chairmanship of the Financial Secretary to the Treasury,[3]

[1] Now by the Ministry of Housing and Local Government.
[2] These three schemes continue today.
[3] The Rt. Hon. Ralph Assheton, M.P., who was assisted by three senior civil servants, three administrators from outside the Civil Service and two representatives of the Staff Side of the Civil Service National Whitley Council.

'To examine the general question of the training of civil servants, including the question whether a Staff College should be established, and if so, the particular form and character which that College should take.'

The Report of the Assheton Committee (Cmd. 6525), which appeared in 1944, does not deal with the Foreign and Colonial Services or the various manipulative grades, or dwell in detail upon the professional and technical classes, each of which has its own training needs and problems. Its proposals are primarily concerned with the clerical-administrative sphere, which was, after all, the sphere in which training had been most neglected.

After touching briefly upon the defects for which the Civil Service is criticized the Committee go on to state, 'But whatever shortcomings there may have been in the past, our aim has been to consider in what ways, at their different levels, the servants of the State can be assisted to attain and maintain the wider outlook, greater adaptability and the technical knowledge which the State service will call for in the years that lie ahead.'[1] The objects of training, they suggest, are twofold. 'In any large-scale organization, efficiency depends on two elements: the technical efficiency of the individual to do the particular work allotted to him, and the less tangible efficiency of the organization as a corporate body derived from the collective spirit and outlook of the individuals of which the body is composed. Training must have regard to both elements.'[2]

The Committee laid down five main aims of training, which may be summarized as follows:[3]

(i) Attainment of precision and clarity in the transaction of business.

(ii) Continuing adjustment of the official's outlook and methods to the new needs of new times.

(iii) Inculcation of broad views to counteract the tendency towards robot-like efficiency and mechanization by the machine.

(iv) Vocational training, not merely to fit the individual to his present work, but also to develop his capacity for higher work and greater responsibilities.

(v) The payment of special regard to staff morale, in order to offset the adverse effects of routine work.

For the achievement of these aims a new organization was proposed. H.M. Treasury were to exercise general control of training in the Civil Service and for this purpose a Director of Training and Education was

[1] Report, para. 14.
[2] op. cit., para. 15.
[3] op. cit., para. 16.

to be appointed. The importance of each department having a systematized training scheme was emphasized and this was to be controlled by a Departmental Training Officer directly responsible to the Principal Establishment Officer. Special care was to be taken in selecting the instruction staff, and the use of up-to-date equipment and accommodation was considered vital. The close participation of the Staff Sides of the Whitley Councils was also recommended.[1]

In their classification of the types of training to be provided the Committee were perhaps a little confused. They defined the four main types of training as (i) vocational training, (ii) background training, (iii) further education and (iv) centralized training.[2] But four further divisions were also used in the Report, specifically to indicate the ends in view, namely, (*a*) initial training, (*b*) training for mobility, (*c*) training for supervision, and (*d*) training for higher administration. The latter headings speak for themselves and it is to be assumed that any or all of the preceding types of training may be employed as is appropriate to achieve these specific objectives. The Report suggests how the different types of training may be adopted for each of the main classes, i.e. Clerical, Typing, Executive and Administrative, with some reference also to the Professional and Technical Classes.

A summary of the Committee's proposals for each of the four main types of training will be of interest:

(i) *Vocational training*. Each department was to organize a scheme of training for its own recruits, who were not to be put on their actual duties straight away. At this stage they should be given a booklet, containing a brief history and outline of the functions of the department and a guide to office procedure. The technique of the model public office should be adopted wherever suitable. This initial stage would then be followed by a period on the actual work under the supervision of an experienced officer. During his early years the young officer would be moved from branch to branch at reasonable intervals in order to broaden his experience. Later on the problem of acquiring the faculties for supervision would be tackled. The interchange of staff in the higher ranges with the business world was not recommended, but it was thought that the secondment of officers to local government might sometimes prove useful.

(ii) *Background training*. The departments should aim at giving their staffs, by such methods as conferences and the circulation of an office bulletin, as much information as possible about their work. Each large department should have a house journal and a good library available to the staff. The exploration of the use of films was recommended.

[1] Report, paras. 19–23, pp. 11–12.
[2] op. cit., para 10, pp. 6–7, and later.

Visits to other branches were advocated as a useful means of broadening horizons.

(iii) *Further education.* Departments should encourage their staffs to acquire outside vocational qualifications by the provision, in approved cases, of time off and the payment of fees. Non-vocational further education should also be encouraged in co-operation with the authorities in every way short of paying the fees. All civil servants should be expected to pursue their education up to the age of 18 on a part-time basis.

(iv) *Centralized training.* Institutional training was not recommended for the Clerical grades and only to a limited extent for the Executive and the Professional grades, but for Administrative cadets the Civil Service should have its own central organization for training. It was not considered desirable that the Government should associate itself with the establishment of the proposed National Administrative Staff College, although if such were established some civil servants might attend experimentally.[1]

The Committee also gave special attention to the problems of training in higher administration. For example, they were favourable to the idea of granting sabbatical leave, say, to promising officers in their early thirties to pursue an approved course or undertake a specific task of research. Short-term transfers might be arranged to Services outside the United Kingdom. These proposals were clearly intended mainly for the Administrative Class, but the Committee disowned the notion that they should be confined to that class and stated 'On the contrary we attach considerable importance to the application of some of them to selected members of other grades, especially the Executive and Professional or Technical.'[2]

As a summing up of the Assheton Committee's aims a quotation from the closing paragraphs of their Report will not be out of place. They state:

> 'While our scheme is experimental in the sense of being the first attempt to devise a system of training for all civil servants, aiming both to increase the competence of the individual and to give the whole profession a higher conception of the contribution it can make to the welfare, happiness and good government of the community, some of the features are already in successful operation in the Service or elsewhere, and we do not doubt that the rest will also be productive of good and early results. But alone they will not suffice to attain our objective of a Civil Service keyed up to meet the demands of its generation not only successfully but acceptably to the community. For this the Service must be pervaded with a sense of its obligations

[1] The Administrative Staff College, which is now in being, receives such students.
[2] Report, para. 117, p. 32.

to the citizen as well as to the Crown. The faults we have recited earlier can be pointed out and to some extent prevented in the lecture-room, but if there is to be an ever-present consciousness of the importance of clarity of thought, directness of action, simplicity of expression, speed, initiative, considerateness and the other virtues in which civil servants are said to be deficient, these must be the key-notes of daily practice in all ranks from the highest downwards. It is our hope that if training – the idea that, besides being told what their jobs are, people need to be guided into the right way to do them – is given due prominence as a cardinal feature of good staff management, and if our scheme is worked with enthusiasm and vision, the whole Service will in due course be brought to an appreciation of the higher standards attainable and will be inspired by the force of example to attain them.'[1]

THE POST-ASSHETON ERA

The Report was well received though, as usual, the extremists wanting the moon failed to realize just how much the Assheton proposals did contain. These proposals were certainly not revolutionary, but the great thing was to ensure that they were carried out as quickly as possible. Then would come the time to look further in the light of experience.

Staff training was now placed positively upon the Civil Service map. With little delay a special Training and Education Division was set up at the Treasury, under a Director appointed from the university field,[2] and steps were taken to implement the main proposals. In 1945 a central school was established to provide training in special cases: for example, initial training of new entrants to the Administrative Class and certain technical training where the whole Service was a suitable field for selection, such as the instruction of training officers in the techniques of their new job. In the main, however, training was delegated to the departments who appointed their own training officers and usually equipped their own training centres. The larger ministries in their turn devolved training to their regions, retaining at headquarters only such training as could be most efficiently and economically provided centrally; for example, introductory courses for new entrants, courses for officers returning from the Forces and technical courses for which there would be insufficient demand in any one region.

Thus, it will be seen that staff training in the Civil Service is now conducted generally at three levels – Treasury, Department headquarters, and Region – and, while there is a constant flow of information and advice between these levels, the general practice is to allow in each

[1] Report, para. 119, p. 33.

[2] Strictly speaking the first Director, namely Mr (now Sir) A. P. Sinker, was already serving as a wartime temporary member of the Administrative Class.

sphere a reasonable latitude and scope for experiment. This training is being conducted on modern lines. Instructional methods appropriate to the adult are adopted and in particular the normal class-room atmosphere is avoided as much as possible. Discussion methods are favoured and practical demonstrations, by means of case study, role playing and the like, are widely used. Instructional visits to other offices and to outside organizations are included in the training scheme wherever suitable. Visual aids in the form of charts, films and film strips, are much in favour. Staff training handbooks have been prepared on such subjects as interviewing, letter-writing and statistics. H.M. Treasury issues to all new recruits a brightly written brochure, with the title *A Handbook for the New Civil Servant*, which briefly surveys the Civil Service as a career and the civil servant's rights and duties. In order to improve the conduct of official correspondence, the standard of which had fallen to a deplorably low level (partly owing no doubt to the influx of poorly educated types into the Service), Sir Ernest Gowers was commissioned to write *Plain Words* (1948) and *An A.B.C. of Plain Words* (1951). Issued through the Stationery Office, these books achieved unexpected success and became best sellers. *The Post Office Magazine* resuscitated from wartime suspension was joined by the other journals of a similar type.

For a few years the new training policy was pressed forward with enthusiasm and efficiency. Although it was extremely difficult to assess the immediate results of such training there can be little doubt that the post-war Civil Service has greatly benefited from this wave of instructional activity. For the time the doubters, of whom there are always many among the practical men, were forced to lie low.

By the autumn of 1951, however, this wave of enthusiasm had passed its peak, although the full objectives of the Assheton proposals were still far from achievement. The rod of economy entered the official classrooms where its normal scholastic counterpart had no place. In response to a Government demand that less money should be devoted to staff training – an obvious but expensive 'economy' if ever there was one – H.M. Treasury issued an edict that in future, except where technical training was in question, Civil Service staff training should become the task of the first line supervisor, as it had of course always been in the pre-Assheton era. For the advancement of this end more emphasis was to be placed upon the training of supervisors. A definite gain from this change has been the giving of more attention to training in supervision and management, subjects that had always been neglected but were becoming the most urgent concern of staff trainers everywhere.

But the loss following this change of policy has been far-reaching. The status of training officers was often reduced, particularly at Treasury level; the training staffs were cut and activities at the centres reduced or even abolished entirely. In many departments training quickly became a matter of minor importance. The enthusiasm with which this retrogressive movement was undertaken will surprise only those who do not understand the traditional outlook upon training of many civil servants. There is a large body of opinion in all grades that holds formal training to be so much waste of time: jobs can best be learned by doing them, as was ever the case in the happy past. Staff trainers are starry-eyed theorists not entirely unconcerned with the creation of cushy specialist jobs. Staff training in fact is considered an example, if a minor one, of empire building! These two schools of thought – the enthusiasts and the denigrators – are struggling all the time for supremacy. During the Assheton period the starry-eyed enthusiasts carried all before them: now the pendulum has swung in favour of the practical men. In the Civil Service as in the nation at large we suffer incalculably from the specious common sense of the rule of thumb. For, alas, the simple truth, in a world growing every day more complex, is that the empiric way will no longer do. The scientific approach is necessary in public administration as elsewhere and a return to nature – unfortunately, many will feel – is out of the question. A half-trained Civil Service is a luxury the nation cannot afford.

FURTHER EDUCATION FOR THE OFFICIAL

Official training activities at best cover only part of the problem of fitting the official to his work and keeping his mind alive to the world that public administration is devised to serve. There are also further education in the general sense and professional education in its theoretical and philosophical aspects. For some time civil servants have run an active further education movement to organize on their behalf a wide range of spare-time educational activities. Since the war the Civil Service Council for Further Education has been reconstituted on a tripartite basis, consisting of representatives of staff and official interests as well as co-opted members from the world of education. This is a body of the Whitley type associated with H.M. Treasury, which provides it with a Civil Service staff. There are also committees for Scotland, Wales and the English Regions,[1] appointed by the Treasury from local representatives of the Official and Staff Sides. The function of the Council and the committees is to encourage spare-time activities of an artistic, intellectual or skilled nature. The Council organizes arts and crafts exhibitions, publishes a quarterly journal but does not itself provide courses of study. Its main task is to encourage civil servants to use their spare time creatively, to bring to their notice existing facilities

[1] As well as a committee for Northern Ireland, which represents both the United Kingdom and the Northern Ireland Civil Services.

and to persuade the educational authorities to meet the needs of civil servants where such facilities do not already exist. The Council does not set out to encourage vocational studies in preference to other types of study. However, it has executive responsibility for the organization of continuation schooling for juveniles in the Civil Service, which is compulsory, on the basis of one day a week, up to the age of 16 and voluntary thereafter until the age of 18. All such officers are officially encouraged to continue their studies in subjects of their own choosing,[1] and executives, who may sometimes be inclined to place the day-to-day needs of their work above the long-term needs of the individual officer, are expected to release them.

The civil servant is not active in the furtherance of his strictly professional education. Indeed, study of public administration in the broad sense is not very advanced in this country. There are various reasons for this, apart from the general apathy of the majority of civil servants: for example, (i) the traditional academic supremacy of the Administrative Class (now being somewhat tempered by the inflow into the Service of large numbers of qualified members of the professions); (ii) the departmentalization of the Civil Service, which leads each department to consider the acquirement of its own techniques as of overriding importance and more general administrative studies as largely a waste of time; (iii) the predominantly empirical outlook of most civil servants, whose intensive concern for the trees often leave them little time to worry about the wood, and (iv) the essentially academic outlook of the universities, who seem as little concerned as the Civil Service to construct a bridge between the bread and butter activities of official staff training and the rarefied intellectualism of the high seats of learning.

There is, of course, the Royal Institute of Public Administration, established in 1922 by a band of enthusiasts to promote the study and improve the practice of public administration in all its branches. Membership is open to all officials, as well as teachers in the subject, and obviously the Institute is concerned only partially with the interests of the Civil Service. It arranges lectures by well-known administrators, organizes weekend and holiday conferences, provides library facilities, undertakes research, and publishes *Public Administration*, a journal with a world-wide reputation in this field. It also provides special services for its corporate members. The Institute is not an examining body and does not provide qualifications of any sort. Since the war the Institute, in line with so many other bodies of this type, has changed from a voluntary and somewhat amateurish organization to a partially professionalized and subsidized institution. The Institute's new responsibilities towards its corporate members (public authorities and departments of all types) tend to endow it with a near-official outlook and this

[1] Not specifically for examination purposes.

further restricts its capacity to meet the needs of individual officials or to do much to rescue them from the deadening influences of the large-scale organizations by which most of them are employed. As is the way of institutions its new air of impersonal efficiency is no substitute for the inspiration and enthusiasm of individuals.

The introduction of corporate membership has most certainly strengthened its finances, but probably at the expense of its individual membership, which is very small for an organization of its scope. However, the lack of support from the Civil Service is due as much to the apathy of the latter as to the failings of the Institute, which after all must find its support where it can. It is doing essential and invaluable work. If it had more enthusiastic Civil Service support it could certainly do much more than it does for civil servants as a body.

The activities of the Royal Institute of Public Administration and the provision of certain funds have recently encouraged the development of research in public administration. In accordance with the policy laid down in the Assheton Report a few higher civil servants have been given sabbatical leave both for research purposes and on an exchange basis for service in Commonwealth and foreign administrations. There are diplomas in Public Administration at a number of universities and even degrees in Administration at Manchester, but these are for internal students and are not readily available to serving civil servants. It is to be regretted that the Diploma in Public Administration, awarded by the University of London, which originally was freely open to external students, has now been made into a post-graduate qualification, available only to a restricted section of the Civil Service. The only other suitable examinations, namely those provided by the Royal Society of Arts in single subjects such as 'Outlines of Central and Local Government' (Stage II) and 'Public Administration' (Stage III), are somewhat restricted in scope but could be broadened by a system of grouping, were there sufficient demand. In fact the root difficulty of the provision of facilities for research and study lies in the sphere of demand. This is a matter for the Civil Service itself to grapple with, and we shall return to it in Chapter XII.

CHAPTER VI

SENIORITY, MERIT OR CHANCE?

Promotion is an important process in the Civil Service, as indeed it is in all graded services. It covers both advancement between grades within the same class and between different classes, although the latter process sometimes has something of the characteristics of recruitment. A civil servant has career prospects within the class to which he is recruited, but transfer to other classes is usually considered exceptional. This situation is certainly modified within the scheme of Treasury classes: for example, since the war the Clerical Officer's normal promotion outlet has led direct to the Executive Officer grade. While this present chapter is mainly concerned with the promotion process it should not be overlooked that this process is part of the greater problem of placement within the Service, the problem of so allocating the available personnel that the most efficient result is obtained through the maximum use of existing abilities. Such a result would also have the inestimable advantage of affording the highest satisfaction to the individual officials involved and thus would considerably enhance the general morale.

FITTING THE SQUARE PEG INTO THE SQUARE HOLE

Establishment branches are constantly concerned with filling vacancies arising here, there and everywhere from various causes. Officers have to be transferred within the department. Where no geographical change is involved this may not be difficult, although persons with the requisite experience may not always be available, or if available be releasable from other positions. In theory all the members of the same grade are available for any jobs allocated to that grade: in practice the range of work covered by one of the Treasury grades is so varied as to render some degree of specialization highly desirable. This is particularly so in the Executive Class. For example, an Executive Officer supervising a block of work in a Post Office department would require a completely different corpus of knowledge to supervise a block of work in a local office of the Ministry of Pensions and National Insurance, and vice versa. Within each department there is also a wide variety of work and it is generally considered desirable for officers to obtain experience in a number of branches. As was pointed out in a previous chapter this is also an ingredient of the training process. In small offices where staff absences might otherwise bring current operations to a standstill a high degree of interchangeability has to be aimed at by the manager. It is therefore a characteristic of the Civil Service that members of the general Treasury classes are expected to be versatile. They may eventually become specialists, but they are not recruited on that assumption.

Where the nature of the work varies – for example, as between case work and supervision, desk work and public relations, considerative work and inspection – it is clear that establishment branches must take into account an officer's particular flair, if the best results are to be achieved. Moreover, an officer allotted to a type of work for which he is not particularly fitted will be discontented and liable to spread his discontent to others. It is no easy task to match official with job and the blind application of the theory that all the members of a grade are interchangeable may lead to a good deal of unease and inefficiency. In practice this situation is bound sometimes to occur in a large-scale organization.

Inefficient personnel management may not be the only reason for unsatisfactory results in this sphere. It cannot be assumed that the staff is completely mobile. Where a department is decentralized the effective allocation of some members of the staff may involve a geographical movement which is unduly expensive or actually prevented by social and economic circumstances. Civil servants are expected under their terms of service to be mobile, but it is not usually expedient to transfer persons against their will, particularly in the present housing situation. Expenses of removal and subsistence allowances are paid in cases where transfer is made for the benefit of the Service, but such upheavals are often so unattractive that officers may even refuse a promotion that involves uprooting their homes. Wives, of course, have a considerable influence upon such decisions. All this means a high degree of immobility unless the department is concentrated geographically. Particularly for those serving in areas they do not like there is usually a Whitley agreement on the order of precedence to be followed when transfers are made; marital status, personal disabilities and hardship grounds being taken into account.

Although there are similarities between the work of the same grade in different government departments there are also vital differences that substantially alter the relative attractiveness of the work to different individuals. Transfers between departments can be arranged, but this is not easy unless a department, usually because of some exceptional expansion, offers transfers to fill up gaps for which it is unable to find experienced officers. Transfers on a personal exchange basis are possible between officials in different departments, but these are not easily arranged, and such voluntary transfers usually involve loss of seniority, since such transferees have to go to the bottom of the seniority list in their new department. The British Civil Service has no machinery for rationalizing transfers between departments. Despite certain arrangements to the contrary, which will be mentioned later, the broad assumption is that an officer is the servant of the department to which he is assigned and has no rights elsewhere in virtue of his membership of an all-Service class. Constitutionally, departmental loyalties still override general Service loyalties. To some extent an inherent parochialism in the system defeats the desirable policy of fitting the square pegs into square holes.

These are only a few of the difficulties that confront the establishment sections, and indeed all senior officers and managers with responsibility for staff allocations, in their endeavours to make the most of the human resources at their disposal. Moreover, this is not only a problem of making use of the positive capacities of the efficient, but also of getting the best out of the inefficient despite their negative qualities. With these preliminary observations in mind it is time to examine the more dynamic problem of selection for promotion.

PRINCIPLES OF PROMOTION

Historically, in all graded services the practice of arbitrary selection is at an early stage tempered by the emergence of an order of precedence – based upon privilege, heredity, prestige of office, and possibly relative power – in accordance with which certain rights, including consideration for other official positions, are decided. Seniority has always been considered an important attribute, as indeed it is if merely as a measure of the experience of the individual official, and promotion in accordance with the seniority list of a grade has for long been a common practice in the Civil Service as elsewhere. Where selection by this method was rigid it led inevitably to the placing of incompetents in high positions and at a time when officials could retain their posts indefinitely this was a serious drag upon the Civil Service's general efficiency. It was not to be wondered at, therefore, that under such conditions patronage had a certain virtue in allowing the alternative of direct appointment from outside in place of routine advancement within. The Trevelyan-Northcote Report, 1853, condemned this system and in its place advocated selection by merit. Each subsequent enquiry supported this view and a dictum of the Playfair Commission, 1875, is well worth quoting. They wrote: 'A man should be promoted, not because those above him are unfit, but because he is the best man for the place. If this course be pursued no man is branded as unfit, and it would not at all follow that the senior man, passed over for one promotion, might not be the fittest man for the next.'[1] To some extent the principle was tempered for the

[1] Quoted in Report of Royal Commission on the Civil Service, 1929–31 (Tomlin), p. 79, para. 293(1).

more junior grades; in which case it was widely agreed that seniority should be given more weight. The general practice was to follow the seniority list, but not slavishly, so that an officer adjudged not suitable for the higher post could be 'passed over'. In the main the seniority principle was supported by the staff who felt that it was the one method not open to favouritism and other underhand influences.

The trouble is that the words 'seniority' and 'merit' have merely to be uttered in conjunction to prejudge the issue. Seniority seems to conjure up automatically the idea of bureaucracy, of working to rule, of selecting the elderly merely because of their age and, therefore, lack of enterprise: merit on the other hand suggests both justice to the chosen and vigour to the system. Thus, to defend seniority is to mark oneself down as a stick in the mud.

The truth is that we are not called upon to make this particular choice. Seniority and merit are complementary factors: a system that denies either is almost inevitably bad, for if the first on its own means stagnation and lack of enterprise, the second is almost as likely to be challenged because the standards adopted are not generally acceptable by those to whom they are being applied. The real difficulty indeed is to define merit in this particular context and to evolve a method whereby the merit choice can be made in a way acceptable to the majority. Ultimately, in many merit systems the choice is made by individuals who are rightly making a personal judgment in the light of standards that are not easy to lay down. In fact, merit selection has been advocated by practical investigators, and applauded by publicists and scholars, but the problems involved in applying it are left, not merely unsolved, but often unrecognized. An effective promotion system has to achieve at least three important goals, namely (i) to select the best man for the higher position, (ii) to satisfy those to whom it is applied that it is fair and just, and (iii) to have a creative influence on the whole staff structure. Merit selection is aimed primarily at (i); seniority selection is effective generally in achieving (ii); an ineffective merit system or an excessive seniority system are likely to fail under (iii) by their adverse effect upon individual initiative and the general morale of the Service.

THE PROMOTION MACHINERY

Promotion in the Civil Service is primarily a departmental and not a service matter. Responsibility for the selection of his staff rests with the Head of the Department, traditionally the Minister of the Crown, by administrative delegation in practice the Permanent Secretary. At the highest levels this principle is modified by the constitutional practice of consultation between the Permanent Secretary of the Treasury, acting in his capacity as Head of the Civil Service, and the Prime Minister in filling the departmental posts of Permanent Secretary, Deputy Secretary, senior Finance officer and senior Establishment officer. The principle is also tempered by the fact that the Administrative Class is, as an all-Service class, transferable between departments, and by the fairly recent growth of promotion pools.

In the earlier period of the modern Civil Service, when the majority of departments were still sufficiently compact for the senior officers to know personally all the staff of the department, it was not difficult for the head to exercise this prerogative. With the general guidance of the seniority list, as the key to experience, and the personal reports of senior officers under whom members of a specific grade were working, it was not difficult for such a head to reach an honest and effective decision. It was a grave responsibility, but one not beyond his capacity to fulfil. With the growth of the central departments the task passed beyond the range of practical fulfilment and unavoidable mistakes of judgment caused a widespread dissatisfaction among the staff who were not easy to convince that *bona fide* mistakes, however regrettable, were not due to favouritism or worse.

It was for this reason that the newly appointed Civil Service National Whitley Council decided at an early stage to tackle the problem of promotion. The present promotion machinery stems back to their first report, issued in 1921. The new system provided for (i) the constitution in each department of a properly organized promotion board, and (ii) the introduction of a standardized report for officers within the range of promotion.

Departmental promotion boards are now appointed by the head of the department, to whom they act in an advisory capacity. The final decision still rests with him, although in a large ministry he will usually find it expedient to accept the recommendations of the board as they stand. He can, where he considers it necessary – e.g. for filling a post requiring special experience or qualifications – waive the normal procedures but, as such a decision is bound to create difficulties with the staff representatives, it is usually resorted to only where circumstances are exceptional. The promotion board will include the principal Establishment officer and other senior officers. It may reach its decision informally after consideration of all the available evidence, or it may first interview recommended candidates. For the latter purpose interviewing panels may be set up, consisting of officers senior in grade to those being interviewed. It is desirable also to include on such panels officers who have a reasonably intimate knowledge of the work of the branches in which the candidates are serving.

Staff representation on these promotion boards is not usually considered expedient. In the first place it would be difficult to find staff representatives who were not themselves involved in the specific promotional process, unless the staff themselves selected fairly senior people who are almost as likely as the official element to be out of touch with the outlook of the rank and file: in the second place the staff interests might find that participating in the responsiblity for choosing would create invidious difficulties with their own constituents unless they religiously selected the most senior aspirant. In any case they would find their important function of criticizing the official decisions largely abrogated by their direct participation. However, they may be given an opportunity to make recommendations and such a system is at present being tried out in the Post Office.[1]

One of a promotion board's biggest problems is to ensure that they have all the facts needed to make a proper comparison between all the officers eligible to fill the particular vacancies, which are almost invariably restricted to the members of the grade next below the one in which the vacancy exists, a field which may be further restricted by the imposition of a minimum period of service in the lower grade. These boards have before them the normal personal records of the officers concerned as well as any special reports that have been made during that officer's career; they have also specific recommendations of senior officers and some of them will have personal knowledge of at least some of the officers involved. The real problem is to reduce so much information to a common denominator and to fill the gaps where scrappy personal knowledge is in question. To assist in this a system of standardized periodical reports was introduced.

ASSESSMENT OF THE INDIVIDUAL

A scheme of systematized reports has three main aims, all closely interwoven, namely:

(i) the achievement of an objective assessment of the capacities of the individual officer in the performance of his duties;

(ii) a just forecast of his capacity for different and more responsible work; and

(iii) the gearing of such assessments to a common standard throughout the promotional area, which may be a large central department with branches throughout the country.

The third and culminating objective is very difficult to attain, since the basic assessments must necessarily be made by different supervisory officers in a number of different branches, possibly dealing with different types of work and probably distributed over a wide geographical area. This is one of the main reasons for the introduction of interviewing boards to assist, or act for, the promotion board.

[1] See E. N. Gladden, *Civil Service Staff Relationships*, p. 134, for details of an interesting promotion scheme in the Admiralty in which the staff co-operated.

The main object of the annual report form introduced for the Civil Service as a result of the proposals of 1921 was to rationalize the process of making such assessments and to provide the materials upon which sound conclusions on the reportee's achievement and capacities could be drawn. The Model Report Form proposed by the National Whitley Council and later amended in the light of experience[1] is reproduced on pages 104–5.

Such a report is made periodically, usually each year, on officers within the range of promotion in all grades below a certain salary level.[2] It will be seen that the Model Report prescribes two distinct operations, namely (i) assessment of the officer's performance on his present work, under the twelve quality headings shown, by means of a marking on the following scale:[3] A – Outstanding, B – Very Good, C – Satisfactory, D – Indifferent, and E – Poor; and (ii) assessment of his suitability for promotion under one of four headings, namely, 'Exceptionally well qualified', 'Highly qualified', 'Qualified', and 'Not yet qualified'. The report is normally made by an officer at least two grades above the reportee and countersigned by a more senior officer. The former should insert, under 'general remarks', a note on any special qualifications or weaknesses not covered in the schedule, and the latter may add his remarks on the report in general. The report is treated as confidential and not communicated to the reportee except in the case of an E marking, details of which have to be given him unless broadly it is due to inexperience or, owing to health reasons, its communication is likely to have an adverse effect upon the officer. In fact this information is merely passed on to the officer to give him an opportunity to put right his failings, a matter that should have already received attention in the ordinary course of business.

Each department is left to adopt its own type of report. There is no standardization throughout the Civil Service. Some departments have adopted the Model Form, some have adapted it to their specific needs, others – notably the Inland Revenue Department – have devised report forms of their own.[4]

The Model Form has been criticized, mainly on the grounds that it does not give a complete picture, and amendments to the schedule of character factors have been suggested. It has been pointed out that these character factors are in some cases ambiguous: e.g. 'initiative' may refer either to intellectual initiative or to the initiative of the energetic and adventurous temperament. In some departments, therefore, the reporting officers have been supplied with a set of definitions, or 'pointers', as

[1] Revised in 1938.
[2] At present £1,250.
[3] But A or B markings are not appropriate under heading No. 11—Official conduct.
[4] Attempts since the war to introduce a standardized form have so far failed.

they are called. The introduction of further headings, such as 'mental powers', 'speed of working', 'adaptability' – three notable omissions – has been suggested. There is also the difficulty of integrating the various character factors into a comprehensive judgment on the individual, complicated by the fact that different levels in the hierarchy call for different types of general capacity. The main difficulty, however, is to obtain equivalent standards of marking, particularly in a widely distributed staff organization. It is almost necessary to devise a 'coefficient of marking ability' for each reporting officer in order to bring each report to a common denominator, a fantastic idea perhaps, but one that at least suggests the almost insurmountable difficulty of devising a just scheme of comparison for a promotion system in a large-scale organization.

Various alternative solutions have been sought, particularly in America where much thought and experiment have been devoted to the problem. Ultimately all reporting systems depend upon an act of judgment, or more usually a series of such acts. Broadly two kinds of process have been applied in an effort to improve upon the report under character factors in a restricted range of markings as in the Civil Service Model Report. In the first an attempt has been made to add a numerical element to the process by which the different character factors are individually scaled and mutually weighted. The most popular is the rating scale method under which each element is assessed on a scale rising to 100, a total numerical assessment being reached by adding up the individual assessments, suitably weighted, in accordance with the relative importance of each quality required for the efficient performance of the work under review. The numerical result by which the candidates are eventually graded has an appearance of precision which is misleading, to say the least, and masks the fact that the whole scheme is based upon a series of personal judgments. Scientific precision in this sphere is unattainable and it is dangerous not to recognize the fact.

The rating scale appears to be much less popular in America than it was. It has never found favour in this country. An alternative method has been sought in the direction of simplifying the marking process by breaking it down into a number of simple stages. The Probst system, which is based upon a number of short answers, is perhaps the best known.[1] Under this method the reporting officer is asked to mark a series of short statements about the reportee: on the following lines: Lazy; Slow moving; Quick and Active; Too old for the work; Minor physical defects; Indifferent and not interested; Talks too much; Good team worker; etc. Only those headings that definitely apply to the

[1] This was experimented within the Inland Revenue Department in 1931. See E. N. Gladden's *Civil Service Staff Relationships*, p. 140.

MODEL REPORT FORM

CONFIDENTIAL E 53. ESTAPORT (Code 5.53.0)

ANNUAL REPORT ON MEMBERS OF THE STAFF

1st January 19........

Name.. *Rank*.......................... *Branch*....................

Date of Birth.................................... *Date of entry into (a) Public Service*..............................

b) Department (if different from (a)).................................... *(c) Present Grade*....................

(For notes on compiling the report, see overleaf)

SECTION I. PERFORMANCE OF DUTIES IN PRESENT GRADE

	Marking (see note (1))	*Remarks*
1. Knowledge (*a*) of Branch	....	....
(*b*) of Department	....	....
2. Personality and force of character	....	....
3. Judgment	....	....
4. Power of taking responsibility ...	....	....
5. Initiative	....	....
6. Accuracy	....	....
7. Address and tact	....	....
8. Power of supervising staff ...	....	....
9. Zeal	....	....
10. Ability to express himself herself clearly (*a*) in writing...	....	....
(*b*) orally	....	....
11. Official conduct (see note (2)) ...	....	....

General Remarks (including note of any special qualifications not included above):—

SECTION II. DEGREE OF FITNESS FOR PROMOTION

Indicate by placing a cross against the appropriate degree of fitness:—

Exceptionally well qualified	....	Qualified	....
Highly qualified	....	Not yet qualified	....

Remarks

(May be continued overleaf)

I HEREBY CERTIFY that in my opinion the conduct, standard of efficiency, and degree of fitness for promotion of the officer named hereon are as stated.

Signature.. Rank..
(Certifying Officer)

Remarks by Countersigning Officer.

Signature..
(Head of Sub-Department)

(For professional and technical qualifications as supplied by the officer see form annexed)

NOTES

SECTION I

NOTE (1). Insert in this column A, B, C, D, or E, against each item according to the following appraisement:—

A. Outstanding. B. Very Good. C. Satisfactory.

D. Indifferent. E. Poor.

NOTE (2). An A or B marking is inappropriate for this item.

NOTE (3). This report is to be regarded as confidential: but an E marking against any item must be communicated in duplicate by the head of the sub-department to the officer concerned except in the following circumstances:—

(i) Where in the opinion of the head of the sub-department communication is considered likely to affect adversely the officer's health.

(ii) Where the marking is due to inexperience owing to less than one year's service on the grade (except in cases of unsatisfactory conduct, laziness, etc.);

(iii) Where the weakness has already been notified and it is clear that no useful purpose can be served by repeated notifications. In such cases the officer should be advised of the proposal to discontinue further notifications to the same effect as those he has previously received. Any change, for better or worse, should be notified to the officer.

The officer should be required to sign and return to the Establishment Officer one copy of intimations of E markings as evidence that he has been notified: he may, if he so desires, add observations.

SECTION II

NOTE (4). The estimate of fitness for promotion should be related to the officer's capacity for the performance of the duties of the grade above. If he is marked "Exceptionally well qualified" or "Not yet qualified" the reasons for the markings should be stated; and in general reporting officers should make the fullest use of the "Remarks" space.

GENERAL

NOTE (5). Every effort should be made to arrive at a just estimate of the qualities of the officer at the time the report is made. Reporting Officers should rely on their own judgment and experience and should in no circumstances have access to previous reports on the same officer by other reporting officers.

Remarks (continued from overleaf):—

individual concerned are marked and the resulting assessment is worked out by means of a special scoring device. A different set of virtues and failings is selected for each type of appointment. Whatever can be said in favour of such a pseudo-automatic system it appears to be inevitably restricted to the assessment of work of a routine nature.

In Britain the line of development most thoroughly explored has led in the direction of rendering the individual character factors more precise by attempting to define more carefully the meanings of the different headings, either by means of definitions or by inserting pointers to indicate the particular aspects of the main quality to which the judgment should be orientated. This is done by means of questions, e.g. 'Energy'. (Is he thorough in his application to work? Does he put his heart into it?)[1] It seems that this type of report is the most suitable for Civil Service use and that improvement of the present system should be sought in this direction.

This is, in fact, the way in which events appear to be moving. Despite the failure of the Staff Side to agree on a revised form, a new Model Form has recently been made available, in which more specific assessments are provided for. Section B of this new form, covering 'Qualities and Performance of Duties', is reproduced as an Appendix to the

[1] Quoted from the Inland Revenue Form (E1).

present chapter (see pages 110–11). Other sections of the form have been brought into line, but they follow generally the pattern of the Model Form which we have been discussing.

Yet when all is said and done, and assuming that the real difficulties of obtaining a series of comparable reports have been overcome, the resultant report can present little more than an emasculated version of the real personality of the reportee and fails to do more than suggest how effectively he may be expected to grapple with a real job of work. The real problem of the selectors is so to equate these reports and all the other information available to them as to choose the best man for the job, and there are so many imponderables in any system which is too large for the selectors to have intimate personal knowledge of all the candidates that it is not surprising that they sometimes fail in this. It seems possible that in any organization beyond a certain size, the job of selection is too big to place entirely upon the shoulders of a group of senior officers, and that some active element of individual competitive participation needs to be introduced.

WORKING THE SYSTEM

Application of the general principles of promotion through the machinery of the promotion boards and periodical reports varies throughout the Civil Service. This is due partly to the varying size of the central departments and the degree of geographical dispersion of their staffs and partly to the different attitudes adopted by the departments' Whitley councils in applying the general scheme. The system is most adequate to the needs of the smaller departments where the personal knowledge of the heads is sufficient to bring an element of reality into the selecting process. In the larger departments the defects of the system are more manifest, although here special factors may create unusual difficulties: for example, frequent changes in the selection policy adopted at the top, inconvenient age groupings in the staff that render periods of stagnancy inevitable, and factors affecting the expansion or contraction of the department's activities at different periods.

It is important that the promotion system should be accepted as just by the staff themselves and, of course, Whitley co-operation in devising the system has gone a good way to ensure this. In some instances an even closer participation of the staff in the process of selection has been attempted. One important aspect is the question of appeal. How far should an official within the range of promotion who has not been selected be given the right to appeal and to what authority? The practice varies. Again the smaller departments have an advantage, for there it is not too burdensome a task for the head himself to see any aggrieved officer if he so desires. It is important to the health of the system for an officer who feels that he has a grievance to be able to get it off his chest, as it were. In the larger departments there may be an avenue of appeal, but unless an oral hearing is possible – and frequently such appeals can only be made on paper, usually within very restricted terms of reference – this is not very satisfying to the aggrieved individual, who unless he succeeds will feel that no real review has taken place. In any case the appeal is to the official who is ultimately responsible for the promotion; namely, the permanent head of the department. There is no provision for appeal to a higher authority and thus no true appeals system exists.

The experience of other countries, notably Australia, where a system of central appeals has been in operation for some time, suggests that the solution of this problem is not easy. For in removing grounds for one sense of injustice the appeals system can easily introduce others and in effect merely shift the problem from one point to another. But the difficulty of finding such a solution must not be allowed to blind us to the fact that there is a problem. Securing that justice is done both to the individual civil servant and to the Service as a whole, is of extreme importance and a matter to which much more consideration needs to be given.

One way of introducing an objective element into the promotion process would be to use competitive examinations. This is of course practicable through the entrance examinations during the officer's early years of service, when he is given facilities to enter the ordinary competitions for posts in a higher class or may even be afforded an opportunity to sit a limited competition reserved for his grade alone. Since the war, as we have already seen, such competitions have been widely introduced into the Civil Service, so that an entrant to a class lower than his capacities justify, now has good opportunities to obtain advancement in this way during his early years of service. There is even a so-called promotion examination for Clerical Officers between the ages of 21 and 28, during which period no officer of this grade can obtain advancement to the Executive Officer grade by normal promotion. But this is really a special type of entrance examination, particularly as the successful candidate is available for posts in any departments, and indeed is more likely than not to move out of his present promotional field.

The difficulty with the promotional examination is that it cannot easily take into account the qualities of mind and character that are so important as soon as the official begins to rise in the hierarchy. On the other hand it cannot be said that the application of the examination process to promotion has been widely tested in this country, for the idea receives little support inside the Service. Nor does much consideration appear to have been given to the application to promotion selection of methods adopted in the country house system of recruitment. Yet one would have thought that to test candidates for more senior positions by giving them case studies or special tasks to carry out might have at least been more revealing than subjecting those on the final short list to a desultory general conversation of no more than twenty to thirty minutes duration, which is the method at present often adopted by promotion interview panels.

There is in fact one notable example of a promotion examination in the British Civil Service, namely in the Customs and Excise Department, where the important post of Surveyor is filled by examination from among officers of the next lower grade who have eighteen years service to their credit. This examination appears to have been introduced because of the difficulty of filling posts widely distributed over the country, from officers of experience who were loath to uproot themselves and often moved unwillingly, with consequent loss of efficiency.[1] The examination, a written one, is based entirely upon the technical work of the particular department. This one instance of a promotion examination shows how in its great variety the British Civil Service can break away from general practice and thus render difficult the making of dogmatic pronouncements on its methods.

From what has been written it will be clearly seen that the promotion system in the Civil Service is based firmly in the departments. It is not to any great extent a Service system and in this respect at least the Service is not one but many. Opportunities vary not only as between the grades but also as between members of the same grade in different departments. Some steps, however, have now been taken to mitigate this situation.

At one time it was difficult, below the top levels, to make promotions between the departments and any suggestion that vacancies should be pooled was anathema to officers in departments where the number of prospective vacancies was above the average. Limited pooling schemes had been introduced before the Second World War to ameliorate the differences in opportunity for promotion from the Clerical to the Executive Class which had arisen inside the Post Office[2] at that time. After the war, however, when the separateness of the departments had been somewhat broken down under the exigencies of the great emergency, the principle of pooling a margin of vacancies was generally accepted and, with the approval of the Staff Sides, pooling schemes were introduced by the Treasury. The general method is for departments where the proportion of prospective vacancies is below average to be

[1] Since this examination was first introduced this problem has become much more general by the spreading out of the departments, but the particular solution has not been copied.

[2] This large department is, exceptionally, divided into a number of promotion fields.

assigned a certain number of appointments from the pool, which is made up of posts contributed by departments with a high proportion of such vacancies. Officers recommended by the below-average departments as fully suitable for promotion are seen by a specially constituted Treasury Pool Board, who compare the candidates and choose the most suitable to fill vacancies in the pool. The selected officer may have to move out of his department: departments have to accept officers brought up elsewhere, but, although they no doubt prefer members of their own staffs to be promoted, in practice they do not lose by an inflow of 'new blood', or should one rather say 'different blood', since the newcomers are likely to be rather older than their own potential promotees. This scheme has been applied to promotions from the next grade below to the Executive Officer, Higher Executive Officer and Senior Executive Officer grades respectively. It has been of great value in preventing the great discrepancies between promotion opportunities that were prevalent in the Civil Service between the wars. It is a simple and logical procedure, but its earlier introduction was obstructed by the prejudices and vested interests that exist in the Civil Service as in all professions.

It is clear that in large Service classes like the Treasury classes with which this book is mainly concerned, the operation of a general scheme of promotion is fraught with almost insuperable difficulties. The same problems do not arise in the departmental classes whose field of opportunities is strictly defined and many of these classes have specialized duties that would in any case confine their members to their own departments. For example, there are in the Post Office large Manipulative groups for which there would be little employment elsewhere. On the other hand since the war the professional groups, many of which worked in small departmentally recruited pockets before the war, have been reorganized on a Service basis and it is possible, the numbers not being too large, for promotion to be made between the departments. It is probably easier fairly to compare the capacities of officers in different departments who are masters of a specialist technique than to compare those with varying experience in the vastly miscellaneous field of general administration.

In this chapter we have briefly summarized the principles and methods of promotion applied inside the Civil Service. It would be foolish to deny that much thought and goodwill have been devoted to the solution of the many difficult problems arising, but optimistic to suggest that satisfactory solutions have invariably been achieved. During the course of this and previous discussion numerous references have been made to the co-operation between the staff and official elements, upon which the success of the system so much depends, and it is now time to consider this very important problem as a whole.

APPENDIX TO CHAPTER VI

Extract from Revised Report Form (1955)

B Report on Qualities and Performance of Duties

CHARACTER AND PERSONALITY *Tick appropriate boxes* REMARKS

1. Responsibility
Seeks and accepts responsibility at all times . . . . 1 ☐
Very willing to accept responsibility . . . . 2 . ☐
Accepts responsibility as it comes . . . . 3 . . ☐
Inclined to refer up matters he could himself decide. 4 . . . ☐
Avoids taking responsibility . . . . 5 . . . . ☐

2. Relations with Colleagues
Wins and retains the highest regard of all . . . 1 ☐
Is generally liked and respected . . . . . . 2 . ☐
Gets on well with everyone . . . . 3 . . ☐
Not very easy in his relationships . . . . . . 4 . . . ☐
A difficult colleague . . . . 5 . . . . ☐

***3. Contacts with Public**
Outstandingly effective in dealing with them . . . . 1 ☐
Considerate and firm as required . . . . 2 . ☐
Handles them quite well . . . . 3 . . ☐
His manner tends to be unfortunate . . . . . . 4 . . . ☐
Poor at dealing with them . . . . 5 . . . . ☐

CAPACITY

4. Penetration
Gets at once to the root of any problem . . . . 1 ☐
Shows a ready appreciation of any problem . . . 2 . ☐
Usually grasps a point correctly . . . . . . 3 . . ☐
Not very quick in the uptake . . . . 4 . . . ☐
Often misses the point . . . . 5 . . . . ☐

5. Constructive Power
Always produces a comprehensive solution . . . 1 ☐
Generally makes a valuable contribution . . . . 2 . ☐
His solutions are normally adequate . . . . . 3 . . ☐
Seldom takes any constructive action . . . . . 4 . . . ☐
Fails to respond to a new situation . . . . . 5 . . . . ☐

6. Judgment
Judgments consistently sound and well thought out . 1 ☐
His view of a matter is nearly always a sensible one. 2 . ☐
Takes a reasonable view on most matters . . . . 3 . . ☐
His judgment tends to be erratic . . . . . . 4 . . . ☐
His judgment cannot be relied on . . . . . . 5 . . . . ☐

PERFORMANCE OF DUTIES

7. Output
Outstanding in the amount of work he does . . . . 1 ☐
Gets through a great deal of work. . . . . . . 2 . ☐
Output satisfactory . . . . 3 . . ☐
Does rather less than expected . . . . 4 . . . ☐
Output regularly insufficient . . . . 5 . . . . ☐

* To be completed only for officers with relevant experience.

B Report on Qualities and Performance of Duties—*continued*

PERFORMANCE OF DUTIES—*continued* *Tick appropriate boxes* **REMARKS**

8. Quality

Distinguished for accurate and thorough work . . 1 ☐
Maintains a high standard . . . . 2 . ☐
His work is generally of good quality . . . . . . 3 . . ☐
His performance is uneven . . . . 4 . . . ☐
Inaccurate and slovenly in his work . . . . . . 5 . . . . ☐

9. Expression on Paper

Brilliant on paper . . . . 1 ☐
Written work always clear, cogent and well set out . 2 . ☐
Generally expresses himself clearly and concisely . 3 . . ☐
Written work just good enough to get by. . . . 4 . . . ☐
Cannot express himself clearly on paper . . . . 5 . . . . ☐

10. Oral Expression

Extremely effective . . . . 1 ☐
Puts his points across convincingly . . . . . . 2 . ☐
Expresses himself adequately . . . . 3 . . ☐
Barely competent . . . . 4 . . . ☐
Ineffective. . . . . 5 . . . . ☐

***11. Figurework**

Exceptionally good at all kinds of figurework . . 1 ☐
Handles and interprets figures very well . . . . . 2 . ☐
Competent at figurework . . . . 3 . . ☐
Handling of figures leaves something to be desired . 4 . . . ☐
Poor at figures . . . . 5 . . . . ☐

***12. Management of Subordinates**

Always inspires them to give of their best . . . 1 ☐
Manages them distinctly well . . . . 2 . ☐
They work quite well for him . . . . 3 . . ☐
Does not control them very skilfully . . . . . . 4 . . . ☐
Handles them badly . . . . 5 . . . . ☐

***13. Organization of Work**

An exceptionally effective organizer . . . . . . 1 ☐
Shows considerable organizing skill . . . . . . 2 . ☐
Plans and controls work satisfactorily. . . . . . 3 . . ☐
An indifferent organizer. . . . . 4 . . . ☐
Cannot organize . . . . 5 . . . . ☐

14.

. . . . 1 ☐
. . . . 2 . ☐
. . . . 3 . . ☐
. . . . 4 . . . ☐
. . . . 5 . . . . ☐

* To be completed only for officers with relevant experience.

CHAPTER VII

TRADE UNIONISM AND JOINT CONSULTATION

Inside the Civil Service trade unionism, where it exists, is bound to be modified considerably by the special nature of State employment and the peculiar loyalties of the public official. Although the history of mutual combination by civil servants to protect and further their own interests can be traced back to earlier, less conventional days, there has always been an air of respectability about this movement and a disinclination to accept the assumptions of a full-blooded trade unionism. Combinations of officials are referred to as 'staff associations' and the label 'trade union' is usually avoided.[1] An important factor is that in the British Civil Service, where the political administrator remains aloof from establishment activities, the normal master-servant relationship does not exist. The employer or 'Official' element is supplied by the senior civil servants in charge and thus both sides are really members of one and the same interest group. The mythologies of the class war are not there to confuse the issue, although one has to admit that confusion may arise in other ways.

BRIEF HISTORY

Leadership in the Victorian Civil Service was essentially authoritarian, tempered with a good measure of paternal benevolence. The upper stratum expected their intellectual inferiors to know their place and, providing they did, were usually willing to give sympathetic consideration to their modest aspirations: as far, that is to say, as regulations might permit. It could safely be left to the fiscal strictness of Her Majesty's Treasury, as guardians of the Nation's financial resources, to refuse anything that transcended the barest justice. There is therefore no reason to be surprised that the legal recognition of trade unionism by the Trade Union Act of 1871 was not accepted, even by any large number of subordinate officials, as granting a similar privilege to the servant of the State. Certainly the administrative-clerical classes as a whole, typifying the blackcoated worker, continued right up to the First World War to consider mutual aid in seeking better conditions of service as a sign of ill-breeding, not calculated to enhance their status as civil servants.

Nor is it surprising that recognition when it did come in 1906 was

[1] This is not the case with the Industrial Civil Service or with such an organization as the Union of Post Office Workers which has always advocated a more activist approach.

granted by the Postmaster General[1] to the rather more menial sections of the Civil Service. For a quarter of a century at least the chronically underpaid manipulative workers of the Post Office had been struggling for better conditions and one of the strongest weapons in the official armoury was the refusal to listen to representations by staff unions except in accordance with procedures that made it difficult for representatives to act without prejudicing their own official prospects.

There were indeed earlier examples of incipient trade unionism in the Civil Service, even before 1879 when the letter carriers of the Post Office began to consider united action in their own defence. In reply to Tom Paine's statement on behalf of his former colleagues in the Excise Service,[2] Pitt stated in the House of Commons in 1788 that the only proper mode of applying to Parliament was through the Commissioners of Excise and that he would never countenance an application to the Legislature by petition from the Excise Officers themselves. This statement, which could have been made as authoritatively a century later without appearing the least old-fashioned, indicates that even in the eighteenth century the house union might be tolerated provided it made its representation through 'normal official channels'. Associations were formed for special purposes, as in 1846 when one was established to pursue reform of the pensions system. This was dissolved as soon as a select committee had been set up to investigate the problem.[3] In the 'sixties of the nineteenth century, and probably earlier, revenue officers were again in the picture. Through a Central Committee representing certain grades statements were made both to the Commissioners of Inland Revenue and to Parliament not only suing for pay increases but also proposing an extensive re-classification of the Excise Branch.[4] The Royal Commission, as a method of investigation into Civil Service conditions, also had its influence on the shaping of such associational activities. Both the Playfair (1874–5) and the Ridley (1886–90) Commissions received information from civil servants and from groups of civil servants on behalf of their colleagues.[5]

Already in these early manifestations of staff collaboration in the Civil Service, manifestations that were no doubt much more widespread than the surviving records disclose, there clearly appears – in addition to the natural objective of such activities to advance and protect the interests of the membership – their supplemental but hardly less important function as collectors and disseminators of information.

[1] On February 13th, 1906, by Mr Sydney Buxton.
[2] In *The Case of the Excise Officers* (1772).
[3] Select Committee on Superannuation Allowances, reported 1857.
[4] See E. N. Gladden *Civil Service Staff Relationships* (1943), pp. 13–16.
[5] See *Introductory Memoranda relating to the Civil Service*, H.M. Treasury (1930), p. 71, which also mentions in this connection the Tweedmouth Committee on Post Office Establishments, 1895–7.

The success of Post Office unionism in 1906 was followed by a steady advance in staff co-operation throughout the Civil Service, so that by 1914 even the blackcoated civil servants were building up their own associations. Collective bargaining as a principle was by that date more or less generally accepted, though progress was very slow in many departments, where the old method of solicitation for the removal of grievances by memorial was still favoured. Traditionally couched in language that mixed pomposity with servility, the memorial had the dual advantage to the administrators of allowing their staffs the psychological relief of bringing their grievances out into the open and at the same time permitting those grievances to be quickly incarcerated in the official pigeonhole from which they would only emerge, if ever, after a good deal of procrastination. The Treasury suggested[1] that any reluctance to recognize associations arose not from any fundamental antagonism but because of the difficulty of reconciling the doctrine of ministerial responsibility with direct recognition by the Treasury of an association representing a grade common to the whole Service. That is as may be, but there can be little doubt that in 1914 the *élite* of the Civil Service still regarded staff activities as generally obnoxious and their instigators as vulgar and distinctly disloyal, while the rank and file themselves, rightly or wrongly, entertained a strong suspicion that those who were intrepid enough to stand up for the rights of their colleagues were foolishly, if nobly, jeopardizing such opportunities for advancement as might in the future arise.

ENTER WHITLEYISM

The First World War offset to some extent its tragic destruction of many promising civil servants, among those who rushed into the armed forces before the system of voluntary recruitment was superseded, by ensuring that those who returned from the battlefields of Flanders and the Somme to the humdrum offices of Whitehall should no longer feel the same subservience as in the past. The juniors of the post-war Civil Service were not prepared to go cap-in-hand to their superiors or to be content with fair words that masked specious excuses. If in other spheres the Civil Service was destined, for some years at least, to follow the even tenor of its ways, in the sphere of staff relations a revolution was certainly at hand.

While the international struggle was still at its height a significant movement had been taking shape inside the nation's factories. The workers were demanding a greater share in the management of the industries in which they worked. A Committee, under the chairmanship of the Deputy-Speaker of the House of Commons, the Rt. Hon.

[1] *Introductory Memoranda*, p. 74.

J. H. Whitley, which had been appointed by the Minister of Reconstruction, reported[1] during 1917 and 1918 in favour of the introduction into industry of a system of joint councils on which representatives of the workers should share with the management the decision of questions particularly concerning the workers' interests. After substantial initial successes this system of Whitley Councils, as they came to be called, was not destined to make universal headway. The times were not yet ripe. In the Civil Service the new system was accepted for the industrial establishments, where the Government felt they had to set an example, but originally there was no intention that it should be adopted for the administrative sectors. Indeed the Reconstruction Committee had not had any such application of their scheme in mind.

The new plan, however, commended itself very favourably to the rank and file of the Civil Service. The staff associations, growing in strength by the inflow of new members, put pressure upon the Government to apply the Whitley scheme throughout the central departments and persisted in their representations with such good effect that the understandable reluctance of the Government was overcome. The departments and associations discussed jointly the application of the scheme to the Civil Service and produced, in May 1919, an agreed report.[2] This was a consummation that in itself demonstrated at the very outset the potentialities of the Service as a field for operating the Whitley method of joint consultation. The report recommended the establishment at an early date of a National Whitley Council and appropriate departmental Whitley councils for the non-industrial classes of the Civil Service.

It is laid down in the constitution adopted for the new system that 'the objects of the National Council shall be to secure the greatest measure of co-operation between the State in its capacity as employer and the general body of civil servants in matters affecting the Civil Service, with a view to increasing efficiency in the public service combined with the well being of those employed; to provide machinery for dealing with grievances, and generally to bring together the experience and different points of view of representatives of the administrative, clerical and manipulative Civil Service.'[3]

The main functions of the National Council, modified to meet the needs of the Civil Service from the more detailed definitions suggested in the

[1] Interim report on Joint Standing Industrial Councils (Cmd. 8606); Supplementary Report on Works Committees (Cmd. 9001); Second Report on Joint Standing Industrial Councils (Cmd. 9002); Report on Conciliation and Arbitration (Cmd. 9099); Committee on Relations between Employers and Employed, Final Report (Cmd. 9153).

[2] Cmd. 198.

[3] The terms of the constitution of the National Whitley Council are reproduced as an appendix to *Staff Relations in the Civil Service*, H.M. Treasury (H.M.S.O. 1955).

Whitley Reports for industrial joint councils, are covered by the following six headings:

(i) 'Provision of the best means for utilizing the ideas and experience of the staff.'

(ii) 'Means for securing to the staff a greater share in and responsibility for the determination and observance of the conditions under which their duties are carried out.'

(iii) 'Determination of the general principles governing the conditions of service, e.g. recruitment, hours, promotion, discipline, tenure, remuneration and superannuation.'

(iv) 'The encouragement of the further education of Civil Servants and their training in higher administration and organization.'

(v) 'Improvement of office machinery and organization and the provision of opportunities for the full consideration of suggestions by the staff on this subject.'

(vi) 'Proposed legislation so far as it has a bearing upon the position of civil servants in relation to their employment.'

The scope of these functions is very wide, covering not only many of the normal objectives of trade unionism, but also those of a professional body. There was no intention, however, that the councils should displace the staff associations, and to avoid any possibility of this happening staff representatives on these councils were to be selected by the associations. There is no provision for individual membership. Employee organization in the Civil Service is therefore divided into three distinct but closely inter-related sectors; namely, the National Whitley Council, the departmental Whitley councils, and the staff associations. Broadly their respective fields of responsibility may be defined as follows: the National Council deals with matters of interest to grades in more than one department, the departmental council deals with the affairs common to the various grades within its own department, while the association pursue the interests of the grade or grades, which it has been formed to represent, whether its members serve in one or a number of departments.

The National Whitley Council has a membership of fifty-four; one-half of whom, appointed by the Government, is known as the 'Official Side', the other half, appointed by groups of associations, being known as the 'Staff Side'. Membership is not confined to civil servants. Normally the Official Side, which is appointed by the Chancellor of the Exchequer, consists of higher civil servants, while those selected to represent the staff are usually important association officials, who may or may not be civil servants.

At first sight this joint council on which civil servants or their representatives sit on both sides of the table would seem to have a somewhat artificial character, differing fundamentally from the typical industrial council on which the 'we' and the 'they' are more clearly differentiated. In fact the highly responsible attitudes of the senior administrative officers who make up the Official Side, coupled with their inherent outlook as members of a select band, are quite decisive in removing any such artificiality. While the Official Side have welcomed and encouraged the co-operation of the staffs in the spirit of the new system they have never been free in granting concessions that would impose an undue burden on the State. Indeed, as representatives of the Government it is certain that the Official Side will never come to a decision that is likely to be contrary to the wishes of the Government of the day. As decisions on the National Council are operative, subject always to the constitutional overriding powers of the Cabinet and Parliament, as soon as they have been reached, it is common sense to assume that the Official Side will always make the position absolutely clear to their political chiefs before an agreement is concluded.

The jurisdiction of the National Whitley Council does not extend to matters of purely departmental interest. Consequently there are in most government departments a departmental Whitley Council independently appointed, with Official and Staff sides very much on the plan of the National Council. There is also provision for district or regional committees to deal with the Whitley problems of staffs distributed in offices throughout the country. It must be emphasized that this departmental system constitutes a distinct layer without hierarchic connection with the National Council, which does not constitute a court of appeal from the departmental councils. Membership of the two systems is independently determined but, as far as the staffs are concerned, coherence between the activities of the two layers is achieved by virtue of the fact that membership rests upon the associations. Had a more precise inter-relationship been devised it would have been necessary to modify the principle of ministerial responsibility.

THE STAFF ASSOCIATIONS

After the First World War the range and membership of the staff associations in the Civil Service greatly extended. Usually they are bodies set up to deal with the interests of a specific class, or of a series of allied classes. It is a law of their inner being that they should wish to continue to expand, even to the extent of covering interests that are not essentially assimilable, and in the minds of many an association leader is the dream-picture of the all-comprehensive Civil Service association that will offer a united front to the authorities. Usually the association begins as a small voluntary group with elected representatives who carry out all the necessary work in their spare time. Eventually the job passes beyond the scope of the voluntary official and full-time officials are appointed: sometimes from outside the Service. The larger Civil Service associations today have professional officers and some of them constitute very powerful organizations in the trade union movement.[1] They differ mainly from the ordinary trade union in not having the strike weapon at their disposal, although in fact it is vetoed by custom and not by law. In cases of ultimate disagreement, the absence of this final sanction, however undesirable its use may be in a public service, must affect considerably both the spirit and the effectiveness of the Civil Service staff association. Another restriction is the essential aim of the Civil Service to keep clear of political activities. While the policy of the associations varies in this respect, it would in the main be true to say that association workers are persons of strong political views who sometimes find it difficult not to confuse their own personal aims with the interests of their constituents. The tendency is certainly for the larger and more influential associations to take a more active interest in political affairs. Some associations have affiiliated to the Trade Union Congress, as they are again entitled to do since the repeal in 1946 of the Trade Disputes and Trade Unions Act of 1927.[2]

There is no closed shop in the Civil Service, but it is administratively desirable that associations should achieve as near to one hundred per cent membership as possible. It is the official attitude, therefore, to encourage the civil servant to belong to his appropriate association and new entrants particularly are made aware of the advantages of staff co-operation. The point is made in the introductory booklet for new entrants to the Civil Service issued by H.M. Treasury. As will be stressed later modern large-scale administration depends very much for its efficiency upon being able to gauge the views of its personnel. This will ensure an encouraging attitude to trade unionism on the part of the official interest but the fact that Whitleyism depends upon complete staff co-operation in itself presupposes such an attitude.

In the main the associations have made good use of the Whitley system. Had such a scheme not been devised with official sanction it is clear that some sort of Civil Service staff council would have had to be formed to deal with matters of common interest to associations. Thus the National Staff Side as the voice of all civil servants serves a very special purpose in its own right. There have of course been disagreements and for periods some associations have not co-operated. This has usually happened at the departmental level where on a few occasions an association has left the Staff Side rather than continue to agree to

[1] See Table on p. 119.

[2] This Act, passed as a consequence of the General Strike of 1926 to which certain Civil Service organizations gave support, made it illegal for a civil servant to be a member of an association catering for outside members or having political interests.

differ with its co-members. On the National Staff Side associations representing the higher staffs withdrew as a consequence of the policy of the Staff Side during the General Strike in 1926. This was in many ways a pity, but hardly a wounding blow in light of the small size of the associations concerned. However, since the Second World War the common front has been restored and the Staff Side is more representative today than ever before.

TABLE V

Civil Service Staff Associations, represented on the Staff Side of the Civil Service National Whitley Council

Association of First Division Civil Servants (2,955)
Association of H.M. Inspectors of Taxes (2,251)
Association of Officers of Ministry of Labour (2,999)
Association of Post Office Controlling Officers (10,863)
Civil Service Clerical Association (146,847)
Civil Service Union (24,007)
County Court Officers' Association (1,700)
Customs and Excise Group of Departmental Associations (7,202)
Federation of Civil Service Professional and Technical Staffs (15,530)
Inland Revenue Staff Federation (36,048)
Institution of Professional Civil Servants (49,458)
Ministry of Labour Staff Association (11,607)
Postmasters' Association (560)
Post Office Engineering Union (65,832)
Society of Civil Servants (39,544)
Society of Telecommunication Engineers (5,233)
Telecommunications Traffic Association (1,552)
Telephone Contract Officers' Association (760)
Union of Post Office Workers (159,816)

Associated with the National Staff Side is also the Federation of Sub-Postmasters, whose members are not civil servants. Among those associations that are not represented on the National Staff Side are the National Association of Women Civil Servants, the National Guild of Civil Servants and organizations representing certain small specialist groups, such as the Civil Service Legal Society.

N.B. The figures in brackets indicate the representative capacity of the individual organizations as at the end of 1955. (See *Whitley Bulletin*, Vol. XXXVI, p. 54.)

ARBITRATION MACHINERY

Remuneration is a constant subject of staff agitation. It is the first task of the associations to press on behalf of their membership claims for improved salaries. Disagreement with the department or the Treasury is not an unusual outcome of such negotiations. It was thought at the introduction of the Whitley system that such difficulties would be solved by the new machinery, but success in this sphere depends largely upon compromise and where, in the public interest, the Official Side feels itself compelled to refuse concessions which involve expenditure there is bound to be deadlock between the two sides. To solve such deadlocks arbitration under the Industrial Courts Act of 1919 was applied to the Civil Service in 1925. There had already existed, largely as the outcome of wartime conditions, a Conciliation and Arbitration Board for Government employees, which had sat between 1917 and 1923. This Board had done effective work and its discontinuance by the Government on the score that it was no longer necessary was received critically by the staffs, whose agitation was instrumental, after strong Parliamentary pressure, in inducing a change of policy on the part of the Government.

Under the new arrangement a division of the Industrial Court, appointed to cover Civil Service cases, was made competent to deal with claims affecting the emoluments, weekly hours of work, and leave of 'any well-defined category of civil servants who, for the purpose of a particular claim, occupy the same position, or have a common interest in the claim', but the cases of individual officers are excluded. The need for this arbitration machinery is demonstrated by the fact that between 1926 and 1936 the number of Civil Service cases considered by the Industrial Court was approximately 44 per cent of all cases brought before it. In October 1936, when it was decided to separate the Civil Service side from the Industrial Court, the present Civil Service Arbitration Tribunal came into being. The Tribunal consists of a chairman appointed by the Crown, together with one member representative of the official interests and one member representative of the Staff Side of the National Whitley Council, drawn respectively from panels specially set up for the purpose by the Minister of Labour and National Service. The Tribunal does not adjudicate upon claims from grades whose salary range rises above £1,450 a year. Proceedings are conducted with a minimum of formality in accordance with flexible rules laid down by the court itself. Cases for the staff are usually presented by leading officials of the associations concerned, while the official viewpoint is put forward by a representative of the department or the Treasury. Although hearings are open to the public there is no attempt at rhetoric. The Tribunal considers its findings in private and issues its award within a few days of the sitting.

There can be no doubt that the Civil Service Arbitration Tribunal serves an essential purpose. It has afforded aggrieved sections of the staff the opportunity to air their grievances and, on sustaining their case, to obtain redress. It is true that the findings of the court cannot, over a period in which so many changes have taken place in the national situation, be interpreted in relation to some unswerving standard of equity, for in fact the influences of the current economic situation and the overriding considerations of national economy can be clearly detected in decisions reached over the years. But after all no servant of the State can ask for more than that his just aspirations shall be weighed in relation to the needs and resources of the community that he has chosen to serve. During 1949–50 when the Tribunal, while showing sympathy with the staffs, refused in accordance with the Government's policy of a national wage freeze, to adjudicate for the time being on the claims laid before them, it was considered both within the Civil Service and in wider circles that the whole principle of arbitration had been negated.

One effect the existence of the Tribunal has certainly had. It has enabled H.M. Treasury to divest itself of some of the characteristics of the stern and heavy father and at the same time freed it to press with all its resources the case for public economy. On the other hand the shifting of the immediate responsibility to the Tribunal, even if ultimately the responsibility of implementing the Tribunal's findings must rest upon the Government, had undoubtedly enabled a more friendly attitude to develop between the Treasury and the rest. This is of course to a great extent due to the success of Whitleyism, but it is difficult to feel confident that that success would have been so evident had the last word on salary matters devolved upon the National Whitley Council.

ACHIEVEMENTS IN STAFF CO-OPERATION

Opinions on this or that aspect of staff co-operation vary and for long the success of Whitleyism was held to be in the balance. In the departments its efficiency has varied both in place and time. At the time of the Tomlin investigation, for example, some heads of departments advocated the abolition of the system, and Staff Side enthusiasts have not infrequently raised their voices in disappointment at the meagre results achieved.

There can be little doubt, however, that on balance there have been considerable gains both to the staffs and to the Administration in the development of staff co-operation in the Civil Service since the First World War. The whole atmosphere has changed from a situation in which the master-servant relationship predominated to one in which the official elements are first and foremost in encouraging co-operation and condemning those who stand aloof. It is understandable that there was an interim period during which this was not universally so and that for some time there were areas of the Service – possibly a few still linger – in which administrators of the old school placed a black mark against the names of those who devoted themselves to their colleagues' interests. As late as 1939 the decision on this point may well have been still in the balance, but events since then have surely turned the scale in favour of the new system.

From the very outset the National Whitley Council was responsible for some excellent reforms in the general administrative field. Not only did it sponsor the new Reorganization of 1920, to which ample reference has already been made, but it continued steadily through joint co-operation to improve personnel methods in many directions, such as promotional procedure, consideration of suggestions by the staff, organization of training schemes, and in keeping many bread and butter matters in close adjustment to changing facts. The staffs were keenly concerned in protecting the interests of their temporary colleagues, in obtaining due adjustments in the war bonus system that caused so much heart-burning after the First World War and, when the Tomlin Commission had reported, in co-operating closely in the implementation of its report which, if it made no spectacular proposals, threw out a number of suggestions that led to improvements in detail, e.g. with regard to superannuation.

Possibly the most serious criticism is that the associations and Whitley councils have been too much concerned with bread-and-butter matters. They have paid too little attention to improving the efficiency of their constituents, to furthering the more purely professional interests of civil servants. It has already been made plain that even in staff raining, in which field the Staff Side was for long undoubtedly ahead of the Official Side, interest was very moderate until the Select Committee on National Expenditure came upon this particular scene in 1942. Civil servants have never been eager to equip themselves professionally nor has any Civil Service association vied in this with such an organization as the National and Local Government Officers Association, whose activities in a parallel public administrative field are so worthy of emulation.

During the Second World War the National Whitley Council gained greatly in reputation and prestige. The Whitley councils and the associations had co-operated closely with the Administration in the war preparations that had been going forward steadily since the *démarche* at Munich in 1938. In particular, their participation in the planning of the evacuation schemes for the departments in the event of intensive bombing of the centres of administration, especially Whitehall, or of invasion was to be of great importance in the months ahead; for it soon became apparent that the average official viewed with concern the radical dislocation of his home life that evacuation made inevitable, and in the absence of an immediate and obvious threat – upon which the smooth operation of such a scheme of administrative dispersal could not wait – the individual member of the staff could not easily be convinced that his enforced evacuation was really necessary. This and many other wartime problems were co-operatively faced by the National Whitley Council, working through special standing committees. The Civil Service was called upon to set an example in relinquishing peacetime privileges – especially with regard to leave and hours of work – in face of the dire national emergency. The staff representatives, naturally eager to voice the views of the majority in patriotic response to the Government's calls, did not always find it easy to convince some of their constituents that these sacrifices by example would not eventually constitute a heaven-sent excuse to take away from the Civil Service advantages that some official elements had always grudged.

The contribution of the Whitley and staff organizations to the running of the wartime administration was of great importance and deserves a study of its own. Not only did the normal problems continue, frequently with aggravated acuteness, but new ones were created by the need to organize and to serve the crowds of temporary officers who entered the Service, often from a very different occupational environment, and also by the creation of a number of brand-new ministries containing but a nucleus of permanent civil servants. Later on there were the problems of post-war resettlement to be faced and, as we have already seen, plans were put in hand well in advance to deal with such matters as recruitment and training. The staff associations greatly expanded their membership. They were therefore called upon to strengthen their own organizations, often by additions to their professional appointments. The National Whitley Council, which from the early days maintained a small office staff under a Staff Side Secretary (a civil servant seconded from his department for a term of years), strengthened its own central organization and the status of the Staff Side was raised by making the chairmanship into a full-time appointment. A more recent reorganization has resulted in the appointment of a Secretary General to take over the executive duties of the Chairman of the Staff Side, who in future will be elected for a term of two years. Today the Civil Service staff movement is well organized, well supported and appears to be more firmly based than ever before.

CO-OPERATION IN ADMINISTRATION

Had the Civil Service staff movement not arisen in its present form on a surge of spontaneous enthusiasm in the years following the First World War and become consolidated into the effective system of joint consultation that now exists, it is no exaggeration to suggest that the Administration itself would have had to introduce some such system. The fact is that when an administrative organization develops large-scale characteristics, so that it is no longer possible for contacts between the administrators at the top and the rank and file to be conducted on a paternalistic basis, some effective form of consultation becomes an absolute necessity to administrative efficiency. Administration is a human activity depending upon a high standard of co-operation between all who are engaged in it. Except where large blocks of purely routine work exist it is not amenable to mechanization and even there regimentation is an expensive substitute for free participation. The highest success of administrative processes can only be achieved where the minds of administrative workers are receptive and friendly to the processes they are called upon to operate. There is something intangible about administration that renders the least obstruction, which may often be unconscious, not only difficult to discover but disproportionately destructive of the efficiency standards that the leader has in view.

In a large-scale administrative organization staff or personnel management is an art that assumes an ever-increasing importance and the administrative leader cannot achieve the best results in this field unless he has an easy means of discovering the views of his subordinates and of preparing their minds on numerous occasions to the acceptance of new methods whose introduction they may often be disposed at first to resent. In a small organization such matters can be talked over in a friendly informal atmosphere; in a large one the administrator has need of properly constituted channels of communication. This, however, is merely one side of the problem. The administrative leader who does not recognize that his most promising ideas spring as bright particles in the minds of a hundred colleagues is already doomed to sterility. It is only by making full use of the ideas and experience of all who are in direct contact with the day-to-day activities of the organization that the most efficient administration can be achieved, and this depends upon the existence of a communications system on the lines of Whitleyism in the British Civil Service.

CHAPTER VIII

CONTROL OF THE CIVIL SERVICE

On the extent and effectiveness of the control of a public service will largely depend the degree to which either the civil service or the bureaucratic spirit flourishes within it. Constitutionally the British Civil Service is subject to the political group in the central government, and the real test of the reforms effected since the middle of the nineteenth century lies in their success in building up a politically neutral but administratively efficient professional corps. In practice control is multifarious, operating both upon the Civil Service from outside and within the central departments in their daily working. The actual situation is extremely complex and has not yet been comprehensively explored by scholars.[1] Consequently the present brief account can hardly do more than sketch out the more important channels along which such control operates. In this particular context it will be necessary to consider not only the Civil Service as a body of officials, but also the wider environment, both political and social, in which it works, as well as the departmental work for which it is responsible.

CIVIL SERVICE LAW

As is well known there is no separate branch of administrative law in Britain. The civil servant in carrying out his daily work is subject to the ordinary law of the land, as is any other citizen, and his official activities are not conditioned by a special system of law, such as the 'droit administratif' of France, with its distinctive code and specialized system of administrative courts.

Furthermore, there is no comprehensive Civil Service statute, as exists in many modern countries, under which the structure and conditions of employment of the Civil Service are legally defined and made subject to the interpretation of the courts of law. The only branch of public personnel management that has been comprehensively covered by the statute law is the important, if somewhat limited, subject of superannuation, embodied in a series of Statutes going back to 1834.[2]

The reason for this special interest is obvious in the light of the House

[1] See, however, N. E. Mustoe *The Law and Organization of the Civil Service* (1932).

[2] An earlier Act of 1822 providing for a contributory scheme was repealed in 1824. See comprehensive survey in H.M. Treasury's *Digest of Pension Law and Regulations of the Civil Service* (H.M.S.O., 1952).

of Commons's concern with finance and the importance of ensuring that a prospective burden of this type should have its prior sanction.

In earlier days the public official as a servant of the Crown was appointed by Royal Warrant or Patent,[1] in accordance with which he operated, or he might be the personal servant to a holder of such an appointment which included the right to delegate part or all of his duties to deputies and assistants. It is significant that Trevelyan and Northcote in their Report of 1853 visualized a switch of authority for personnel control to Parliament when they recommended that their proposals should be embodied in an Act. In face of opposition the Government of the day, after foreshadowing such legislation in the Queen's Speech early in 1854, decided to legislate for the Civil Service by Order in Council under the Royal Prerogative. Following the two important Orders in Council of 1855 and 1870 establishing the Civil Service Commission and introducing open competition, a series of such Orders were issued laying down rules applicable to the Civil Service and its conditions of service. These were consolidated in an important Order in Council in 1910, but after the First World War two Orders in Council of 1920 gave H.M. Treasury the power to make regulations to modify these arrangements, and this has since been the main authority for such changes. Thus we see that even the Royal Prerogative has been subjected to the process of delegation; albeit necessarily in face of the growing complexity of the task of administrative regulation.

There are in fact a number of statutes that affect the civil servant and few modern Acts of Parliament fail at least to define tasks for which the Civil Service is to be responsible. Thus the Trade Disputes and Trade Unions Act of 1927 (subsequently repealed) affected the civil servant's right to belong to a trade union with outside affiliations or political objectives. The Official Secrets Acts place him under special obligations with regard to the communication of official information (a limited application of 'droit administratif'). Numerous statutes define the powers of specific officials, such as inspectors who may, for example, be given special powers of entry and the right to demand the disclosure of specific information. Most modern departments operate under a statute which creates a Ministerial office and gives its occupant power to appoint such officials and servants as he may need, subject to the consent of the Treasury. The staff numbers of the several departments and offices of the central government are set out in the annual estimates, which are eventually covered by the Appropriation Act, although only the vote figures actually appear therein.

[1] In fact the practice still survives for appointment by the Crown of certain officials holding high posts, members of administrative boards in control of departments and some inspectors, who hold office under Letters Patent, Orders in Council or Royal Warrant. There is also the case of the Special Commissioners of Income Tax who are appointed under Treasury Warrant.

MINISTERIAL DIRECTION

Civil servants hold primary allegiance to the ministerial head of their department, but through him, as the Crown's appointee, they remain truly the Queen's servants. Thus a civil servant's primary loyalty is to his department and not to the Civil Service as a whole, which exists in convention rather than fact. The doctrine of ministerial responsibility which gives the Minister complete administrative autonomy within his own sphere of authority inevitably divides up the Civil Service vertically into a number of separate provinces. Thus the civil servant, although he has but one master, the Crown, suffers under the disadvantage of being the subject of only a ministerial fraction of that master's authority. The minister on the other hand must take full responsibility for the official actions of his servants and it is no defence that day-to-day administration has grown so vast and complex that he cannot today know even a fraction of what is going on in his name. The rules, that were perfectly logical in the not so far off days when a minister could have personal knowledge of all his secretariat and their doings, still continue to operate in an administrative situation whose intricacies would have amazed the minister's predecessors but a hundred years or so ago.

But much of the difficulty is solved by delegating responsibility for staff control to the permanent secretary, who is the professional head of the ministry. After all, the modern department, despite its thousands of officials, is legally but the minister's secretariat writ large. The task performed by Samuel Pepys in the seventeenth century with the aid of a few personal assistants is today performed by the complex organization of the Admiralty with its many branches and thousands of staff. It is an interesting side-light upon this situation that the senior grades of the Administrative Class all have the term 'secretary' as part of their official title.[1]

RECRUITMENT CONTROL

The largest modification of ministerial control of the Civil Service took place when patronage was taken out of the minister's hands and an impartial commission was set up to examine the credentials of candidates for the public offices. The control of the Civil Service Commissioners may be highly specialized and confined to one short stage in a civil servant's career, but nevertheless it is the most vital and pervasive control, for not only does it prevent the serious failings and malefactions that inevitably accompany any patronage system of public appointment, but it also makes possible the imposition of a general

[1] Namely, in descending order of importance, 'Secretary', 'Deputy Secretary', 'Under Secretary' and 'Assistant Secretary'.

staffing pattern upon officials recruited to many departments with differing functional requirements. The selection of temporary staffs still remains with heads of departments, but a temporary officer cannot receive permanent status without the approval of the Civil Service Commissioners, whose certificate is necessary to entitle the individual officer to profit from the Superannuation Acts. In this sense these Acts are themselves an important factor in Civil Service control, a rather roundabout means which is certainly not untypical of British constitutional practice.

TREASURY CONTROL

The importance of H.M. Treasury as a controlling agency among the central departments is inherent in its overriding finance functions, but it has mounted with the centralization and consolidation of the State's financial machinery. Significantly the premiership has been closely associated with the First Lordship of the Treasury, although today the formal leadership of the department falls to another member of the Treasury Board, the Chancellor of the Exchequer. Staff, or establishments, control has inevitably become associated with finance and although in our present context the establishment aspects of Treasury Control is of primary interest it should not be overlooked that finance is the overriding master.

Even in the days of comparative ministerial autonomy the Treasury had acquired a special leadership in such general staffing matters as then existed; for example, the initiative in the abolishing of both sinecure offices and the employment of deputies, as well as in other matters calling for general advice and regulation. The sphere of the Treasury's patronage was so wide, since it included the important revenue collecting departments, that the Department's parliamentary secretary was formerly known as the Patronage Secretary, his task being to dispose of the patronage of the Treasury, the Revenue Departments and certain other offices among nominees proposed by members of the Government.

The influence of Sir Charles Trevelyan at the time of the nineteenth century reforms has already been recorded. Apart from his outstanding personal contribution, there is little doubt that his occupancy of the senior permanent post at the Treasury was vital in ensuring that his influence should percolate through the strong walls of patronage and custom that hedged round the central offices of the State at that time.

As the importance of establishment work grew, the participation of the Treasury in this branch of administration extended and was quickly recognized. The Order in Council of 1870 gave the Treasury powers to make rules in certain matters of staff organization not directly associated with finance, and these functions were gradually extended in the field of establishments as the modern Civil Service structure emerged. After the First World War establishment matters were separated from questions of departmental finance with which they had previously been associated inside the Treasury and reorganized within a new Establishment Department of that ministry. As we have already seen shortly after this the Treasury's rule-making powers in personnel matters were extended and consolidated under Order in Council of 1920. This growth of the Treasury as an all-powerful establishment agency has been an important factor in British Civil Service history, for it meant that in virtue of the great size and variety of the tasks of the new Civil Service, the Treasury became the depository of a vast experience in personnel matters at a time when the art of personnel management was hardly yet recognized outside the governmental field. The importance of the Treasury and the British Civil Service generally as forerunners in this specialist sphere of management should not be overlooked.

As a result of this development the autonomy of the central departments has been considerably modified. On establishment matters they have to conform to general Treasury rules and advice, although the departmental heads retain a certain discretion in some directions and have power to issue their own instructions in this connexion. As an example of this may be cited regulations restricting the rights of members of a department to carry on spare-time activities that may impinge upon the department's sphere of responsibilities.

The introduction of the Whitley machinery certainly modified the controlling powers of the senior administrators by bringing in the staff interest to participate in the decision of matters affecting conditions of service and other personnel matters. This subject has already been treated at length in Chapter VII and it is not likely that its great importance in the web of control will be overlooked. It is interesting to recollect that the two main layers of the Whitley system, namely the National and the several Departmental Whitley Councils, are separately organized in conformity with the principle of ministerial responsibility. Here constitutional principle overrides the requirements of maximum administrative efficiency, rightly under our particular system of government.

WORK CONTROL

Another aspect of Treasury Control that affects the Civil Service rests in its responsibility to further the efficiency of the departments in their work processes. This functional aspect deserves separate if somewhat summary attention, for it is to be remembered that work problems transcend the boundaries of this present study. We are concerned with the Civil Service as a body of professional workers. A book on the work of the Civil Service would necessarily be encyclopaedic in scope and not within the competence of any one author. Nevertheless, it would be unrealistic to ignore the problem of techniques, which indeed must come into the picture from the very beginning when the qualities and qualifications of the recruit are under consideration.

In the sphere of control the work processes are of primary importance, since it is through both their detailed regulation and critical review that some of the most effective lines in the web of control operate. It is by this means certainly that the departments exercise a close control over their staffs. Instructions are issued, laying down the methods and procedures to be adopted in carrying out the day-to-day work of the branches and outlying offices. These instructions often build up a comprehensive code which, inside the offices, may have the effect of law. By means of internal inspection and audit the conduct of business is largely judged in relation to the way in which these instructions have been implemented. This process can indeed be carried too far by restricting too much the discretion of the supervisory staff and leading to hide-bound working. For this reason the operation of the instructional system is probably one of the most illuminating tests of the effectiveness of a department's working. Like the law of the land it will make an indelible impression on those who are constantly subject to its pervasive influence.

At the general Service level direct work controls are inevitably of less importance. They are essentially a ministerial responsibility, although there is plenty of scope for the exchange of information and advice. Through their Organization and Methods and Staff Training Divisions the Treasury exercise an important control, but it is in essence advisory and not control in the imperative sense. At this level the existence of certain common service agencies, on which the departments depend for services in carrying out their day-to-day administration, is of vital importance. The Civil Service must use the stationery and office appliances supplied by H.M. Stationery Office, the accommodation and furniture obtained by the Ministry of Works, the general information made available by the Central Office of Information.

Organization and methods, although it is closely involved with the human element and crosses the establishment boundaries at many points, is very much concerned with the work processes, consideration of which is outside the scope of the present work. Yet this activity is so much in the public eye and so much the responsibility of the Civil Service that it would be inexpedient to dismiss it so summarily.

The main aim of O & M, as it is now usually termed, is by objective investigation to devise the most effective means of shaping and improving the organization and conduct of business. In a general sense the idea is not new and has been present in the various types of efficiency audit which have been widely adopted in different spheres.

The present enthusiasm for the idea goes back to the 1942 Report of the Select Committee on National Expenditure, already mentioned in connexion with staff training, but the need for it is implicit in the increasing complexities of the State's administrative machinery. The Committee blamed the Treasury, perhaps a little unfairly but understandably in face of the grave urgencies of wartime, for its previous lukewarm interest in the improvement of the machinery of central administration. Under the guidance for the time being of an outside expert,[1] an expanded and reorganized Treasury division was immediately instructed to implement the Committee's proposals.

The larger departments were encouraged to set up their own O & M branches, H.M. Treasury's resources being made generally available, but mainly concentrated upon the smaller departments. The Treasury's position is really one of mentor and guide. Its services are advisory and provided at the invitation of heads of departments. Training is provided at the Treasury for O & M officers throughout the Civil Service. Even within the departments O & M is advisory, the decision whether its findings and advice should be followed being left to the executive heads. Of course, pressure can always be exerted from higher levels, especially where obstructionist attitudes are apparent, but it is the firm policy of O & M investigatory teams to get over their ideas by taking the executive staffs into their confidence as they go along. O & M is not to be confused with inspection.

There are few specific rules in the practice of O & M. It represents more an attitude of mind than an array of accepted techniques.[2] Its important objective is to inculcate in officials a habit of objective examination, a capacity to stand outside and look impartially into the organization and processes in which they are involved. O & M men are not experts: they are selected officials who, after serving a term on the work, are expected to return to normal duties, taking with them their new knowledge and experience and disseminating the new attitude as widely as possible. O & M is really the application of common sense to the examination of day-to-day experience. It is none the less difficult to implement because its need is so obvious. It has all the inertias of routine and the prejudices of the lazy mind to break down.

PARLIAMENTARY CONTROL

It is through criticism of the civil servant's activities and not of the civil servant as a person that Parliament is able to maintain some control over the central administration. This arises not from some restriction on

[1] Mr I. J. Pitman.
[2] See particularly H.M. Treasury's *The Practice of O and M* (1954, H.M.S.O.).

the legislature's competence, but from the fortunate fact that the conduct of officials is not usually the point at issue. If professional integrity and morale were low no doubt the position would be very different. As it is, the Cabinet system ensures that Parliamentary criticism of the Civil Service shall operate indirectly through the criticism of policy and interrogation of the responsible minister. Question time is undoubtedly the most effective of the Parliamentary means of administrative control. Ministers are called upon to answer questions on the day-to-day detail of their administration. Such questions may be *bona fide* searchings after illumination, or artfully designed probings into weak spots; frequently they are based upon complaints put forward by an M.P.'s constituents. In any case the Minister, who has due notice of the question, cannot plead ignorance. He must find out what has happened. For this purpose an urgent inquiry is directed from his Private Office[1] down the line to the spot where the alleged incident occurred: written explanations are forwarded and official interpretations are provided, together with such additional information as may in the experience of the officials be considered likely to anticipate the supplementary question which the Minister may be asked. This procedure is well calculated to elicit the truth, for the senior officials will not accept excuses from their subordinates or risk their reputations by misleading the Minister. If he, by manipulating the evidence, tries cleverly to evade the issue and fails, the blood will then be on his own head. There can be little doubt that this system works and has a salutary effect inside the departments, where every official is constantly aware that a mistake on his part affecting the rights of a member of the public may have political repercussions. It is sometimes argued that this type of interrogation tends to excessive red tape methods, but the time actually involved in propounding answers to Parliamentary questions is not relatively so great and the value of the method is not easily overestimated. The main element of red tape, which is an inevitable expense of any system that involves public accountability, rests in the need for the Civil Service to document its activities to a degree that a businessman would consider excessive. This would still be necessary without the particular institution of Question time.

Parliament's other method of controlling administration in the central departments is through its Select Committees, which have power to interrogate responsible officials and to examine work processes. However, the three Select Committees in question, namely on Public Accounts, Estimates and Statutory Instruments respectively, are each concerned with a specialized sphere and there are wide administrative territories in the departments that are not under their purview. It is significant that these committees are not concerned with policy but

[1] Situated in the Headquarters of a Department, the Minister's Private Office is staffed entirely by civil servants.

with the way the departments have carried out Parliament's wishes within the respective spheres. The Public Accounts and Estimates Committees are concerned with matters of finance, forming part of the structure of financial control, the Treasury's participation in which has already been touched upon. From this influence the civil servant is never released. It is in fact important to the success of any system of financial control that public officials at all levels should be daily conscious of guarding the public purse and treating all costs as though they were to come out of their own pockets. In the operation of this particular control the position of the Comptroller and Auditor General is important. Although himself a public official, subject very much to the general conditions of the Civil Service from which he is usually selected, he stands in an independent category as a servant of Parliament, appointed by the Crown and removable only on an address from both Houses of Parliament. It is in his capacity of Auditor that he exercises his closest control of the Civil Service. His Department, the Exchequer and Audit, is directly responsible for auditing the accounts of the other central departments, while he acts as expert adviser to the Public Accounts Committee to whom the audited accounts are passed for review. At this stage we encounter what is probably the most interesting contact between Parliament and the administration, namely the Accounting Officer, a civil servant, who is made personally responsible for the correctness of the Department's Appropriation Accounts. By general practice the Accounting Officer is the Permanent Secretary himself, who will be assisted by an officer in charge of the financial side of his department's work, usually under some such title as 'Accountant General'. The Accouting Officer is expected to make personal submission on his financial stewardship direct to the Public Accounts Committee. This is no light burden to add to his general responsibility to the Minister for the Department's administration. Naturally he sees that his subordinates do not let him down in this important sphere.

There is one other significant method of control which if not strictly Parliamentary is usually operated at Parliament's behest. It would be impossible to consider Civil Service history for a moment without coming across it and we have certainly on numerous occasions had reason to be aware of its great importance. We refer to the practice of calling for a periodical inquiry into the Civil Service and its working through the appointment of either a Royal Commission or a select committee. The inquest has been important in the process of British government from the earliest times: in the sphere of the Civil Service it has been particularly valuable, for there the situation is a difficult one to examine and interpret. Parliament and public are concerned to inquire into a responsibility of the Executive, which is in itself very much a specialist closed shop. An impartial public inquiry at fairly distant intervals seems to be as good a means as any. The historic authority of the various official reports, to which reference was made in Chapter II, is a standing proof of the value of this means of control.

PROFESSIONAL CONTROL

The Civil Service is in a sense a profession and indeed a noble profession, for it has a high tradition of service and self-effacement, which distinguishes it from a mere occupation, a means of earning a living. It is in this special civil service spirit, which has no taint of bureaucracy, that Sir Edward Bridges, in a notable pronouncement[1], discovered the professional attitudes of the British Civil Service. Otherwise the Civil Service lacks certain characteristics that are essential to a profession, namely, autonomy and powers of self-regulation, often in other fields legalized by statute. The Civil Service in its subordination to the political organs of the State can never achieve the autonomy of a profession without becoming bureaucratic. Its standards of competence have been so closely determined by the system of competitive recruitment that so far no strong urge has been felt to take steps consciously to improve these standards. The multifarious nature of the Civil Service tends also to act against a single professional unity. Indeed the content of his lecture suggests that Sir Edward Bridges had the Administrative Class mainly in mind and it is common practice to consider the other reaches of the Civil Service as being of small professional importance, an attitude that is usually strenuously resisted only by those civil servants who are also members of other professions.

The question of professional morale will be considered in the next chapter: here we are concerned with control, a matter of power rather than influence. There is no autonomous body solely concerned with the strictly professional interest of the Civil Service. The Staff Side of the National Whitley Council and the individual staff associations, usually to a much lesser degree, are the only bodies with aspirations in this field and they are much more actively concerned in the trade union than the wider professional interests of their clientele. It is not that professional matters are outside their scope, but that bread and butter problems must take priority under a sort of Gresham's Law in staff relationships that relegates professional problems to a subsidiary position.

In default of an independent professional body, leadership of the Civil Service has been exercised, through precept and example, by the Administrative Class. Its close working relationship with the political leaders, as secretaries and advisers, has given this class a controlling responsibility, quite apart from the great influence of its intellectual quality and high standards of integrity. Only the exercise of patronage

[1] See *Portrait of a Profession* (Rede Lecture, 1950).

has been taken from it. Otherwise members of the Administrative Class virtually control everything that goes on inside the Service. It is they who have the final word in all major administrative policy. It is their edict that goes forth in all matters of organization, personnel management, and administrative procedure.

They form a homogeneous group that effectively assimilates such recruits as do not already think with minds moulded in the older universities. They belong to the same London clubs and pass the same type of highly respectable lives. There is little reason to believe that the picture of middle class conformity, so excellently word-painted by Mr H. E. Dale,[1] although related to the pre-war Administrative Class, has been substantially challenged by post-war expansion. In times of emergency they go first to their own contemporaries at Oxford and Cambridge for reinforcement, preferring the contemplative academic experience of the university to the practical administrative experience of other, less favoured, members of the Civil Service.

It is little mitigation of this situation to suggest that today half the present Administrative Class have been recruited from below. Few of those who thus came up from the middle grades occupy the leading positions, which are still largely the monopoly of the higher university element. These others belong to two broad types. Those who have come up at an early competition stage and those who have been selected at later stages in their careers. The former are a special feature of the post-war Civil Service and there is no reason to suppose that they will not be as effectively assimilated to the Administrative Class as were their forerunners. Even here the departmental authorities retain a controlling power, since their approval is required before a candidate can present himself for the limited competition.[2] Such approval is likely to be withheld where the department is of opinion that the applicant is not of the right calibre. With regard to those selected at later stages in their career the element of chance has no doubt entered into the process to a high degree. Before the war there were very few, but the war created a need that the authorities were unable fully to meet from other sources. With regard to the individual much depended upon his having the right opportunity in the right place at the right time, and even in such instances the decision having been made by a member or members of the Administrative Class it is likely that the generally held conception of the sort of person fitted to be a member of that select corps will have had an important influence on the final decision. Among the competent, even brilliant, type of civil servant in the other ranks there are those who are always on the side of authority and quite exceptionally adept at formulating the answer that will be most acceptable to those at the top. It is

[1] *The Higher Civil Service of Great Britain* (1941).

[2] As an experiment this requirement is being suspended in 1956 and 1957.

no secret that they get on better than those who are outspoken and speak their minds on matters on which their opinions are sought. It is less that the administrator will consciously eliminate such types than that their own chiefs will see that they do not even appear in the running. Thus, in the final reckoning all who are selected from within the Civil Service to enter the Administrative Class will have had to conform to tests laid down by members of that class. They must be *personae gratae*, and it is rarely that a mistake is made.

The present organization of the Civil Service, coupled with the intellectual predominance and the social homogeneity of the Administrative Class, thus places an almost overwhelming controlling power in the hands of that Class. The Administrative Class is in fact one of the most powerful oligarchies in existence. It has ruled over its own particular sphere for the best part of a hundred years almost without challenge. Its quiet, impersonal and highly responsible exercise of its great power, springing from a great sense of duty, has so obscured the realities of its position as to disarm criticism. Yet despite its efficiency, devotion to duty and sense of mission this power is no less pervasive. The rest of the Civil Service exercises initiative only by its good graces. In this sense the only will in the Civil Service is the will of the Administrative Class. On its record of public service it stands unchallenged, setting an example that the lesser breeds of official strive, almost hopelessly, to emulate.

THE GENERAL PROBLEM

The vast web of control in which the Civil Service is enmeshed is an essential element of our historically moulded system of democratic government. It grew up, conforming with and meeting changing needs: it continues to grow in the same empirical spirit. It is highly effective in its extensive complexity, although the system does tend to generate problems here and there that are not amenable to simple logical solutions. However, providing the underlying principles are right, we need only be concerned whether the system works. The system of control in which the British Civil Service is involved certainly works, and of this the high reputation of that Service throughout the world is some corroboration.

Certain proposals have from time to time been made for its improvement. It has, for example, been authoritatively argued that there is little logic in associating the two types of Treasury function and control, namely finance and personnel management, under the same departmental roof. In many national systems Civil Service management is attached to the office of the President or Executive Head of the Government as a separate responsibility. However, there seems to be little point in making changes merely on the grounds of logic, especially in a system such as ours in which the political side is so illogical. In practice the financial and personnel functions of the Treasury are in the hands of separate specialist divisions. The chief political executive and the chief finance minister are associated at the head of the Department. A formal separation on the administrative side could be more apparent than real. The truth is that the Treasury has long ceased to be what its name implies. It is the chief co-ordinating department, looking both outwards across the nation and inwards throughout the central departments. It is the centre of communications through which the political executive exercises its main directive functions. The shift since the end of the war of the centre of gravity of economic planning to the Treasury from the Cabinet Office points to the underlying logic of the Treasury's situation at the centre of both political and administrative power, the nodal point at which these two worlds meet.

As this book goes through the press a significant change at the Treasury is announced. With the retirement later in 1956 of the present Permanent Secretary, Sir Edward Bridges, and of his Deputy, Sir Bernard Gilbert, it is proposed to appoint joint Permanent Secretaries. One will be responsible to the Chancellor of the Exchequer for the financial and economic work of the Treasury; the other, combining the duties of Head of the Civil Service and of Secretary of the Cabinet, will be responsible to the Prime Minister for the present work of the Treasury in connexion with the Civil Service and the Machinery of Government and also for the work of the Cabinet Office.

Certain proposals to set up a special administrative court or to appoint committees of Parliament to supervise the work of the departments have received authoritative support. If adopted such schemes would certainly modify the system of Civil Service control, although such new bodies would be concerned with the work processes rather than the Civil Service as a body of staff. One proposal for the improvement of Civil Service control, however, does call for special mention. This was made in 1942 by the Select Committee on National Expenditure in a notable Report[1] already referred to in connection with the development of organization and methods and staff training. The proposal was that a Select Committee should be appointed sessionally to conduct on behalf of the House of Commons 'a continuing review of the Machinery of Government with special reference to the economic use of personnel'. The new committee, which was to have no executive power, was to be interested in the active functioning of the administrative organization and to operate by inquiry, observation, criticism and submission of reports and recommendations to the House. The committee was to be assisted by an Assessor comparable in status with the Comptroller and Auditor General and to be invested with power to make inquiries on behalf of the committee. The proposal did not com-

[1] Sixteenth Report of the Session 1941–2; see particularly para. 125, p. 38.

mend itself to the government-of-the-day. But the fact that governments and senior civil servants are at one in disliking a proposal for the introduction of closer oversight by a parliamentary committee should not blind us to the need for some means of throwing light upon Civil Service activity without increasing bureaucratic controls.

The real gap in the present system of Civil Service control is in the sphere of information. The general democracy is woefully ignorant of the daily practices of its chief servant and occasional master. This may be partly due to Press misinformation, public apathy and sheer ill-will – matters to be discussed in the next chapter – but it is also an inevitable outcome of the complexity of modern administrative organization and practice. It is to some extent fortuitous that the British Civil Service is so well intentioned and efficiently led. Its direction by the politicians ensures that it does not misuse its power, but ministers have too many responsibilities to be able to exercise any close administrative control over their little kingdoms. They are very much in the hands of their professional advisers when it comes to administration and are bound in practice if not in theory to accept their advice on matters affecting the personnel of the department. There are times when they do go their own way, notably when matters of national policy are involved, and the Civil Service has to toe the line against its better judgment, e.g. on the occasion of the removal of the marriage bar in 1946 when it was desired to encourage married women to remain in industry where their services continued to be needed. Sometimes the administrative inexpediency of the politicians' judgment can be assessed, as when the Labour Government proposed the recruitment of ex-regular officers to fill Higher and Senior Executive posts. Such direct recruitment from outside to fill posts normally filled by promotion from inside the Executive Class not only affronted the professional sense of justice of that class, but also foreshadowed the introduction of a form of group patronage that would have undermined seriously the whole Civil Service system. In the face of criticism from inside the Service the proposal was dropped.

An advantage likely to follow the acceptance of the National Expenditure Committee's proposals would be the gradual instruction of an authoritative body of opinion inside Parliament on the working of the departments and the Civil Service. This expanded capacity to bring informed criticism to bear upon the Administration would be a great gain to the Parliamentary system and an important safeguard against the misuse of administrative power. There is no reason why the enlightened understanding of such a body of Members of Parliament should have any restrictive effect upon the professional neutrality of the Civil Service or restrict unduly the responsibility of ministers, who indeed might very well gain from having their colleagues' assistance in overseeing their administrative vineyards.

CHAPTER IX

CIVIL SERVICE MORALE AND OBLIGATIONS

In Chapter I emphasis was placed upon civil service as the manifestation of a special type, an *esprit de corps* and a sense of self-dedication of the official to the service of the common weal. Civil service in this sense has been an essential balancing factor in a developing democracy, which as a form of government has throughout history demonstrated an ingrained tendency to become distorted and corrupt. The need in the circumstances for such a balancing factor in the shape of the professional administrative corps of the modern state is universally accepted if not so widely achieved. This accounts to some extent for the world-wide interest that has been taken in the British Civil Service and its methods.

As a matter of fact, although democracy needs the impartial conduct of a civil service in the management of its administrative business, its inherent principles do not necessarily lead in this direction. The outstanding modern example of a civil service born and bred in the atmosphere of democracy, that of the United States of America, demonstrates clearly the dangers of pressing democratic principles in spheres for which they are not designed. The practice of rotation in office, which assumed that every citizen was capable of conducting every citizen's business, and the spoils system which gained such an impetus from this practice were logically based on Jefferson's democratic principles and have persisted to the present day despite the successful attritions of many reformers who have recognized that however good democracy may be in the political sphere it is less appropriate where the techniques of administration reign. Other modern civil services have grown out of aristocratic institutions with much more efficient results. In France, for example, the traditions of the Civil Service go back to the *ancien régime*, as remodelled by the Napoleonic drive for administrative efficiency: in Germany the Civil Service, even under the degenerative regime of a Hitler, was still inspired by the ideals of the state services of seventeenth and eighteenth century Prussia.

Even in Britain it was the example of the aristocracy, which had so long been habituated to conducting the administration of the country through the unpaid appointments of Justices of the Peace, that triumphed, first by substituting a non-patronage service for the exploitative bureaucracy of the East India Company, last by transmuting the patronage system of the central government in Britain into an intellectual *élite* inspired by the classical philosophies of Plato and Aristotle. As Gladstone had foreseen when controverting the foolish prognostications of the anti-reformers in 1854[1], under the new open competition system the rag-tag and bobtail of the patronage-mongers were to be replaced by the highly educated sons of the upper classes.

In the early days of open competition, when entry to the Civil Service was for the first time freely open to all, it was in fact only the sons of those who could afford to pay for an education at Oxford or Cambridge who could hope to enter the top class of the Civil Service. It was this leadership group, who came to occupy most of the leading posts in the departments, that set the high standards of conduct and determined the particular morale of the Victorian Civil Service. They were of the same breed as the temporary politicians whom they served. They thought in the terms of the public schools where most of them had studied: they lived the same sort of lives and knew the same people. Their standards of conduct were determined by the Royal Court and the aristocracy, whose very obedient servants they were.

These new officials did not enter the Civil Service for gain. Even the poorer sons of the aristocracy who chose the Civil Service as a career, chose it with their eyes open. Scales of pay were better then than they are now, but they were never lavish and under the new system there were to be no perquisites. These civil servants were, and indeed their successors continue to be, dedicated men who preferred to serve their Sovereign and country to the struggle for money and power that went on mightily around them in the hey-day of Victorian capitalism.

This new leadership group, based upon an intellectual superiority proved both in the halls of the ancient universities and in the examination room at Burlington Gardens, set the example of high devotion, impartial achievement and great integrity for which the British Civil Service is still esteemed. The other classes, the Second Division and the rest, accepted their pre-eminence and followed their example. The educational gulfs between the classes were wide enough to prevent any challenge of the Administrative Class's superiority coming from below. But the conditions of service offered by the State, if not lavish were sufficient to distinguish the Civil Service career at most stages and to place it in a category of its own. Public esteem did the rest.

Of course the situation was not static. The great drive towards universal education that characterized the half century following the Civil Service reform of 1870, changed the relative position of the classes. Natural brain-power allowed youths of the lower middle and working classes gradually to climb the educational ladder, but these elements were well assimilated by the time they sat their examination – otherwise

[1] Letter to Lord John Russell, January 20th, 1854. Quoted in John Morley's *Life of Gladstone* (1903), Vol. I, p. 649.

they were not likely to have chosen this particular career. The politicians too changed even more rapidly under the impact of an expanding democracy to which the aristocratic British Constitution adapted itself with remarkable success. Different types began to sit in the ministerial chairs in Whitehall. The men changed, the system changed; but the spirit of service continued and was even strengthened. This has been the real miracle of British government during the hundred years following the Trevelyan-Northcote reforms, which we may without exaggeration term the Civil Service Century.

It is not the object of this present chapter to examine this theme further or to forecast what changes may well be on the way. That is a problem for the second part of this book. What we are concerned with here are the various factors that affect the morale and special obligations of the Civil Service in Britain.

RULES OF CONDUCT

The special nature of official employment imposes certain duties on the civil servant, whose conditions of service therefore include important obligations, apart from the advantages and disadvantages discussed in Chapter III. It is a matter of grave concern to the community that its public servants should maintain high personal standards of conduct and carry out their official duties with high integrity. This is not the situation in some countries, where holders of public office are not prevented from taking advantage of their official positions to offset inadequate remuneration from public funds: nor was it always the case in this country before the patronage system was brought to an end. The morale of a public service, it need hardly be emphasized, depends upon other things besides monetary rewards and the perquisites of office. A minor official on a comparatively low salary, such as a postal or Customs official, may often be exposed to considerable temptation when carrying out his ordinary duties and it is necessary that the discouragement to submission to such a temptation should be sterner in his case than in that of the ordinary citizen who succumbs to a similar fault.[1]

In fact official morale depends to no small extent upon the general standards of the community in which the particular service operates, for it is clear that even if we have a right to expect the official to set an example, it would be unrealistic to insist that the gap between the two spheres should be a wide one.

Much depends no doubt on the degree of enthusiasm with which the civil servant approaches his work. A person who devotes himself to the

[1] This is the reason why legal penalties imposed for minor defalcations in which petty officials are concerned often appear to be out of all proportion to the misdemeanour committed, particularly as they involve also the loss of all earned pension rights.

service of the State knows that he is inevitably sacrificing certain marginal opportunities. He will not grow rich and, even if the risk of utter poverty is absent, to sacrifice such a chance of wealth has a discouraging effect upon the spirit of the energetic person. To be really efficient the public official must, therefore, believe in his life's work with almost religious devotion. But if this high endeavour necessarily springs within the soul it can be maintained and matured, except in the heart of the exceptional individual, only by a system that proffers justice to its servants. Hence the need for the good conditions of service that have already been discussed in this study.

Public criticism has its contribution to make in the building of this high morale in the Civil Service. For even the official who is inspired by the ideal of service will soon lose his enthusiasm if he feels that his contribution is consistently depreciated by those whom he serves. Reasonable criticism will help to keep the ordinary official up to the mark. Constant vigilance on the part of the public is the only safeguard against the growth of bureaucracy. On the other hand a tendency to make the Service a scapegoat for everything that goes amiss and to hold up the official as an inferior sort of human being will gradually undermine the highest morale, rendering the average official despondent and apathetic in the performance of his daily tasks.

It is by no means certain that unwise and ill-informed criticism in the Press in Britain has not had some influence in this direction. In a democracy some of this criticism is understandable, even when it includes an element of scurrility. There may be political reasons for attributing to a civil servant's incompetence the failure of some particular policy, and in every community there are individuals who through enviousness or other undesirable motives will join in the hunt for an official scapegoat, but there can be little doubt that the main cause is ignorance. The public are woefully ignorant of the working of public offices and of the many intricate problems of public administration. To remove some of this ignorance is not the least of the useful functions that the public relations officers of the central departments are called upon to perform. But a much more energetic offensive against this particular form of ignorance needs to be undertaken and on a much wider front.

The British Civil Service recognizes the need to maintain specially high standards of personal conduct. There are few specific vetos – and these will be discussed in the following sections – but the civil servant is expected to conduct his private affairs in such a way as to avoid bringing discredit upon the Service. Normally there is no official inquisition into a civil servant's private life, which is not the concern of his department. His personal activities – for example, with regard to matrimonial difficulties – will be considered only so far as they may affect the efficient performance of his official duties and this will to a large extent depend upon the type and responsibility of the work that he performs.

In one direction, however, official rules are stringent. Any personal applications made by a civil servant on matters affecting his salary and conditions of service must be made to the head of his department.[1] Any attempt to manipulate outside influences – for example, through Parliament – to obtain preferment within the Service, and this applies particularly to advancement by promotion, will be met by official disfavour and thus defeat the object in view.

USE OF OFFICIAL INFORMATION

The public official often has access to secret information: even subordinate officials become aware of information whose communication outside official circles might prove detrimental to public policy, and there are occasions when an official by using information obtained in the course of his normal duties could gain advantages that might well be substantial. It is obvious, therefore, that the civil servant, in so far as he is aware of facts that, if published, might affect public policy, is under a special obligation to use official information with the utmost discretion. He is subject in this matter to the Official Secrets Acts, to special departmental pronouncements and to a code of conduct that is generally recognized as correct Civil Service practice.

The Official Secrets Acts impose special penalties for the disclosure of official information. Their operation is not, of course, confined to members of the Civil Service. A section of the Official Secrets Act of 1889 that is of particular significance reads as follows:

'2. (1) Where a person, by means of his holding or having held an office under Her Majesty the Queen, has lawfully or unlawfully either obtained possession of or control over any document, sketch, plan, or model, or acquired any information, and at any time corruptly or contrary to his official duty communicates or attempts to communicate that document, sketch, plan, model or information to any person to whom the same ought not, in the interest of the State, or otherwise in the public interest, to be communicated at that time, he shall be guilty of a breach of official trust.

(2) A person guilty of a breach of official trust shall:

(*a*) If the communication was made or attempted to be made to a foreign State, be guilty of felony, and on conviction be liable at the

[1] The normal procedure is, of course, to make such applications collectively through the appropriate staff association, but the individual civil servant's right to make application by memorial though rarely used nowadays has not been rescinded.

discretion of the court to penal servitude for life or for any term not less than five years, or to imprisonment for any term not exceeding two years, with or without hard labour; and

(*b*) In any other case be guilty of a misdemeanour and on conviction be liable to imprisonment, with or without hard labour, for a term not exceeding one year, or to a fine, or to both imprisonment and a fine.

'(3) This section shall apply to a person holding a contract with any department of the Government of the United Kingdom, or with the holder of any office under Her Majesty the Queen as such holder, where such contract involves an obligation of secrecy, and to any person employed by any person or body of persons holding such a contract, who is under a like obligation of secrecy, as if the person holding the contract and the person so employed were respectively holders of an office under Her Majesty the Queen.'

These statutes are wide in scope, covering at once activities that are highly treasonable and disclosures that might be considered little more than indiscreet, but they are not a complete guide to a civil servant's conduct in such matters. Communication of information to the Press, for example, may be covered by departmental rules under which an official is forbidden to make an official communication to the newspapers except under proper authority, and prohibited from corresponding with them in his personal capacity on any official subject.

The publication by civil servants of articles and books that have a bearing upon official matters is not, however, forbidden providing the Official Secrets Acts are not contravened. It is not the object of the rules to prevent the reasonable dissemination of information or to discourage the scientific approach of officials to matters of professional interest. Permission to publish must be sought from the departments concerned or from H.M. Treasury. If the information contained in the work comes primarily from official sources and it is considered that copies would be of value to the Administration the right is reserved of placing publication in the hands of the Stationery Office or alternatively, where the author is allowed to retain responsibility for publication, to ensure that copies are available for official use at an agreed price. There is no evidence that these rules are ungenerously administered. If, therefore, the Civil Service as a profession is disinclined to discuss in print the problems of its operation the cause must be sought elsewhere than in rules by which matters of official secrecy are rightly hedged.

Civil servants are under special obligations with regard to the patenting of inventions made by them in the course of their official work. It is left to their departments to decide whether the inventor should be allowed controlling rights or required to assign all rights in the invention to the Crown, possibly reserving to himself a share in any commercial proceeds. He may apply to a Departmental Awards Committee for an award, with the right of appeal to the Central Committee of Awards, which consists of nominees of those government departments that are most concerned with inventions, under the presidency of a high legal authority. Much will depend upon the nature of the invention and the circumstances in which it has emerged. It may be a by-product of the official's activities or of little official value, in either of which cases few difficulties will arise in the assignment of the patent to the official. On the other hand many inventions are the result of team work. Specific assignment is difficult and if the work is carried out by officials specially devoted to experiment and research – an expanding category – there will normally be no claim to patent rights, although the latter may be considered in cases of exceptional brilliance and utility.

There are, no doubt, many circumstances in which a civil servant could use official information to his own advantage, for example, by anticipating the results of official action that may be contemplated, such as the imposition or raising of controls and changes in the tax schedule proposed in the Budget or estimating the effect of official policy on foreign exchange rates. A case of the latter type, which had received a good deal of publicity in the Press and the courts, was investigated by a Board of Enquiry set up by the Prime Minister, Mr Stanley Baldwin, on February 1st, 1928. The closing paragraphs of the Report[1] are so important that they are printed as an Appendix to the present chapter. It had been alleged in the course of the case of *Ironmonger and Company v. Dyne*, heard in the Kings Bench Division of the High Court, that three officials of the Foreign Office had been using their official knowledge in speculative transactions in foreign currency for the purpose of private profit. While concluding, after examining all the available evidence, that neither of the officers concerned had used, or endeavoured to use, any official information for the purpose of their transactions, the Board of Enquiry were justly critical of the activities of the officers concerned, which were of a gambling nature and inconsistent with their obligations as civil servants. This case clearly illustrates how necessary it is that civil servants should not merely avoid breaking the law or contravening the rules of their department, but should also refrain from conduct that merely raises suspicions incompatible with their official positions. This is indeed a high standard in an erring world!

During the period shortly following the Second World War, when the central administration was expanding rapidly and it had become even more difficult than usual for members of the public to understand the workings of the departments, there was a good deal of public discussion of the emergence of a new type of agent or 'contact' man, who was

[1] Cmd. 3037, February 1928. See Appendix, p. 155.

specially skilled in bringing interested members of the public into touch with the official most likely to be in a position to deal expeditiously with applications for licences and suchlike matters. Bribery and corruption were rather more than hinted at. A tribunal under the chairmanship of Sir George Justin Lynskey, a judge of the High Court of Justice, was therefore appointed by the Home Secretary to enquire whether there was any justification for allegations that payments, rewards or other considerations had been 'sought, offered, promised, made or received by, or to Ministers of the Crown or other public servants in connection with licences or permissions required under any enactment, regulation or order or in connection with the withdrawal of any prosecution and, if so, in what circumstances the transaction took place, and what persons were involved therein'.

In its Report[1] the Tribunal, although critical of the attitude of certain political officials, completely exonerated the civil servants into whose activities they had been called upon to investigate. Once again the high reputation of the Civil Service had been completely upheld. The Lynskey Report, however, deserves study, since it shows how easily powerful temptations may assail the public official who comes late into the official sphere, after experiencing an easier code outside, and how thinly drawn in modern society may be the dividing line between the path of official rectitude and the incline to venality.

PARTICIPATION IN NON-OFFICIAL BUSINESS

Restriction of the civil servant's participation in outside activities is not completely determined by rules guiding his use of official knowledge. Speculation in foreign currency, as in the case just mentioned, may be unwise in any circumstance, yet only culpable if the official is working in a department in which he has access to useful official information. Nevertheless, the civil servant's outside business activities are subject to certain definite rules. Generally he can engage in lawful business providing his personal attendance is not required by it during official hours. This is laid down as a minimum for universal application which departments may supplement to meet any special circumstances attaching to their own activities. The rule[2] reads:

(i) No officer may at any time engage in any activity which would in any way tend to impair his usefulness as a public servant.

(ii) No officer may engage in any occupation or undertaking which might in any way conflict with the interest of his Department or be inconsistent with his position as a public servant.

[1] Cmd. 7616 (1949).
[2] Quoted from Order in Council of January 10th, 1910, Clause 17.

(iii) It is the duty of any officer, who may have any doubt as to the propriety of undertaking any particular work, to consult the head of his department, or the Establishment Officer.

Outside business activities may give a civil servant an interest in contracts with government departments. Such participation is stringently regulated and an official is bound to disclose fully any interest of this type to the Head of his department, who has discretion to permit the transaction. In this case steps will be taken to ensure that the officer concerned does not participate in the transaction on the department's behalf. Failing such authority no government contract may be let to an officer of the contracting department or to a partnership or company of which an officer of such a department is a partner or director.

One of the circumstances considered likely to impair the efficiency of a public servant is serious pecuniary embarrassment. There are long-standing rules dealing with the bankruptcy and insolvency of civil servants. A civil servant becoming bankrupt or insolvent must report the fact immediately, on pain of dismissal, to the Permanent Head of his department, to whom he is called upon to submit with the least possible delay a full statement of the position. The Head has discretion to decide whether disciplinary action is called for, dismissal being the penalty in cases of dishonesty or discreditable transactions. In the meantime, unless there is evidence of the latter, the officer concerned is allowed to continue in his post providing that his duties do not involve the handling of public moneys.

There are numerous rules in the departments with regard to borrowing, gambling or resort to a moneylender. All are designed to maintain the integrity of the public service and are important, since financial difficulties can lead to other unsatisfactory situations. For example, a senior officer borrowing from a subordinate could place himself in the position of being pressed to grant favours in other ways in order to liquidate his obligation.

There can be no doubt that the general standards of the Civil Service in this connection are very high. The rules are strict, as indeed they should be, and strictly administered in the public interest, but there is humanity in their application, every case being treated on its merits. In at least one large department, which handles considerable sums of public money, the departmental Whitley Council has operated a scheme to aid, with tact and in confidence, officers who find themselves, not dishonestly, in financial difficulties. Under the scheme a staff committee administers the official's salary while the debt is being liquidated. Nor are the departmental regulations dealing with this subject always devoid of humour as the following quotation shows:

'Finally, I would like to advise members of the staff on the actual experience of the cases that have come before me that resort to a moneylender is fatal. However bad an officer's financial position be it cannot but be made worse by resort to a moneylender. There are bad moneylenders and very bad ones. *There are no good ones*, and those who write the nicest letters and have the kindest faces are the worst.'

There is one problem that has a close bearing on this and the previous section, namely, the acceptance by the civil servant of outside appointments. The services of a public official may, by virtue of his inside knowledge and official contacts, be of special value to a business concern, which may make it worth his while to transfer his services to the new field of activities and, in view of the gap between the salaries of highly placed individuals in the official and non-official spheres, it is not difficult for the business concern to make a very favourable offer to the official whose services they want. There is, of course, nothing to prevent a civil servant resigning his post and taking up an outside appointment, although usually he will think twice of relinquishing his pension rights unless adequate compensation is offered. Many, however, do so every year. It is, nevertheless, a grave fault for a high official to seek to use his official position to obtain preferment outside the Civil Service and any such action may lead to dismissal.[1] The question of imposing some restrictions on the civil servant who wishes to transfer his activities to another sphere has often been raised.[2] It is difficult to solve this problem without doing injustice to the individual and possibly the only effective way is to ensure that the counter-attractiveness of outside service is not too pronounced. For officers holding high rank in the Civil Service and the Armed Services the Government has imposed a two-year embargo following retirement upon the taking up of appointments in firms concerned with government loans, subsidies or contracts, or in which the Government is closely interested in any way financially.

Since the war the position has been considerably eased by permitting civil servants to transfer to posts in the public corporations, academic institutions and international agencies, without sacrificing their pension rights.

RESTRICTIONS UPON CITIZENSHIP

The civil servant, who is in many ways by the very nature of his duties made more than usually conscious of his citizenship, is bound by his official obligations to be something less than a citizen. As an individual he has a right to his own political views, and in his private capacity he

[1] See *Report of Board of Enquiry* (1936), Cmd. 5254 and *Minute of the Prime Minister* (1936), Cmd. 5255.

[2] See, for example, *Statement relating to Report of the Royal Commission on the Private Manufacture of and Trading in Arms*, 1935–6, Cmd. 5451, para. 15.

can support his own party and vote for the candidate of his choice. Publicly there are restrictions upon the degree of his participation in political affairs.

In this country policy is determined by the political parties and imposed by the Ministers of the Crown, both corporately and individually. The civil servant acts in a professional capacity and the less he airs his personal views the better. There has been some falling away from this ideal of recent years especially among the lower grades of the Service, whose political activities as trade unionists cannot with confidence be said always to have advanced their own professional interests. It has to be admitted, however, that political participation is much less important in the lower reaches; although, with the expanding participation of the State in social fields, even the most junior officers may become involved in matters that have important political implications. It is impossible, for example, for a junior clerk in an employment exchange to handle the registration of an unemployed person without being brought into contact with situations in which the political aspects of public policy may be criticized or appraised. He must always be on his guard against incurring the charge of partisanship and even when his sympathies are involved he must not forget that there are other aspects to the question which the next Parliament may call upon him officially to implement.

Nevertheless, with the rapid growth in the size of the Civil Service it has come to be recognized that there are grave disadvantages in excluding such a large body of citizens from the full rights of citizenship and that the rules appropriate to a compact leadership group may no longer be suitable to a much larger group. Since August 1925 the industrial staffs under the Defence Departments had been exempted from the general embargo upon Parliamentary candidature. In response to pressure from the staffs after the war to extend the area of exception the Chancellor of the Exchequer, Sir Stafford Cripps, set up in April 1948 a special committee under the chairmanship of Mr J. C. Masterman to inquire into the wider problem of political participation. The Masterman Report of June 1949[1] was received with great disappointment by the Civil Service. It proposed the extension of the area of exemption to all industrial and minor and manipulative grades, but refused to include any of the clerical grades. In some directions it even recommended a tightening up of existing practices. Under the new arrangements, in order to comply with the provisions of the Succession to the Crown Act, 1707, all civil servants would have to resign before nomination day, but members of the exempted grades who were not elected would be reinstated on application within a week of declaration day. Reinstatement

[1] *Report of the Committee on the Political Activities of Civil Servants*, Cmd. 7718 (1949).

after ceasing to be a Member of Parliament would be granted subject to certain conditions.

The Government accepted the principles set out in the Masterman Report but, after protracted discussions with the staff representatives, the proposal that the Civil Service should be divided horizontally into two groups, a politically free and an excluded group, was modified by the introduction of an intermediate group with restricted rights.[1] Political activities in the national sphere are defined as (i) adoption as a Parliamentary candidate, (ii) holding in party political organizations offices impinging wholly or mainly on party politics in the national field, (iii) speaking in public on matters of national political controversy, (iv) expressing views on such matters in letters to the Press, books, articles and leaflets, and (v) canvassing on behalf of Parliamentary candidates. A similar list covers local political activities. The politically free group comprises broadly all industrial civil servants and the non-industrial staffs in the minor and manipulative grades as proposed by the Masterman Committee. These may participate in any of the activities listed. The intermediate group covers broadly the typing and clerical grades and those of equivalent status, manipulative supervisory grades and other senior grades of equivalent status who are not actually members of the Executive class. Subject to receiving the Department's permission, which will depend largely upon the extent to which their personal duties are compatible with such activities, these officers may be allowed to participate in any of the activities listed except adoption as Parliamentary candidate. The politically restricted group, which can participate in none of these activities at the national level, includes the Administrative, Executive, professional and all other senior classes not definitely included in one of the other groups. Permission may still be granted by Departments to members of this group to participate in local political activities. Their position has not therefore been modified by the new rules. The totals in the three groups in April 1954 were as follows: (i) Free Group: Industrial 427,223, non-Industrial 270,560, (ii) Intermediate Group 278,439, (iii) Excluded Group 119,918.

CONCLUSIONS

It is a matter of great importance as well as of considerable interest that the high standards of morale and public service, for which the Civil Service in Britain is universally recognized, were built up during a period following the introduction of open competition in 1870. At a time when the general philosophy of the nation endorsed with enthusiasm the principles of the open market and the doctrine that the devil was welcome to the hindmost, a special enclave was being created in the

[1] Cmd. 8783.

employment field, within which the public official was exhorted to place the public weal before his own personal advantage. The Civil Service existed as a neutral non-competitive group within the capitalist system and as such undoubtedly had a steadying influence upon the rest of the national economy.

There were, of course, a number of factors conspiring to produce this situation and the nation had reason to be pleased that this was so. Revulsion from the inefficiencies of patronage was the impetus, but there can be no doubt that the *noblesse oblige* of an aristrocratic ruling class had an imponderable influence upon the new official corps. As the educational system expanded, widening year by year the basis of the leadership group, the time-honoured principles of public service were inculcated in the souls of those who chose public administration as their life's work. If they held other views they were unlikely to seek within the government departments life's unrestricted excitements. It speaks volumes that the prestige of State service should have continued to attract in abundant measure sufficient talents to cope with the increasing complexities of the work. The general rule that the civil servant should be politically neutral in approaching his work served to reinforce the solidarity of the Civil Service.

We have already mentioned in Chapter III the effect of the recent economic and social changes on the position of the Civil Service in the community: the changing attitude of the official to politics is likely to have equally radical repercussions. In a democratic world the State should have no concern with its servant's political views. The public official who, on entering his profession, signs away his personal right to disagree with the political views of the regime has already become a slave. An expanding bureaucracy is then synonymous with a slave state. Yet with the advent of totalitarianism in politics the strain on the allegiance of some officials becomes too great and the temptation of the State as employer to examine the political credentials of its servants becomes stronger and stronger. A stage may be reached when it feels that it can no longer afford to regard with impartiality the views of those who do not accept the principles upon which its whole existence rests. In the last resort the Democratic State is no more bound to accept the service of those who publicly proclaim that they will not on the 'appointed day' honour their bond, than to accept the allegiance of the criminal who rejects the moral law of the community.

It is, nevertheless, a matter for regret if the State is called upon to face the problem of the servant who does not accept the assumptions upon which it works. Witch hunting is never a happy pastime for the democrat and in an atmosphere of suspicion intolerance is liable to expand until justice becomes a farce. Victimization thrives wherever totalitarian philosophies have currency.

Even before the Second World War, when totalitarianisms of the Right were in the ascendant, the political integrity of the Civil Service was considered by some to be threatened and accusations of victimization were made. There were cases where sympathisers of Fascism were alleged to be under observation and although the Government denied that it had any concern with the political views of its servants, it is difficult in such a situation for it so to control its subordinate authorities that undue precautions are not taken. The spirit of the times, fear-ridden with incalculable consequences, favours the suppression of the unorthodox.[1]

Since the war the Government has discarded its attitude of non-concern. Events in the wider world have had no little influence in bringing this about. Thus in his statement to the House of Commons on March 15th, 1948, the Prime Minister, Mr Clement (now Earl) Attlee, stated categorically:

> 'Experience, both in this country and elsewhere, has shown that membership of, and other forms of continuing association with, the Communist Party, may involve the acceptance by the individual of a loyalty which in certain circumstances can be inimical to the State. It is not suggested that in matters affecting the security of the State all those who adhere to the Communist Party would allow themselves thus to forget their primary loyalty to the State. But there is no way of distinguishing such people from those who, if opportunity offered, would be prepared to endanger the security of the State in the interests of another power. The Government has, therefore, reached the conclusion that the only prudent course to adopt is to ensure that no one who is known to be a member of the Communist Party, or to be associated with it in such a way as to raise legitimate doubts about his or her reliability, is employed in connection with work, the nature of which is vital to the security of the State.
>
> 'The same rule will govern the employment of those who are known to be actively associated with Fascist organizations.
>
> 'I should emphasize that this action is being taken solely on security grounds. The State is not concerned with the political views, as such, of its servants, and as far as possible alternative employment on the wide range of non-secret Government work will be found for those who are deemed for the reason indicated to be unsuitable for secret work. It may, however, happen that it is impossible to find suitable employment elsewhere in the Civil Service for individuals with specialist qualifications and in such cases there may be no alternative to refusal of employment or dismissal.'

It was made clear that the decision in such cases would not rest with the security services, whose function was only to provide information.

[1] Notably in the case of a Major Vernon in the Air Ministry; see *The Strange Case of Major Vernon* (National Council of Civil Liberties).

In accordance with constitutional practice the final decision was left with the Minister, but an Advisory Body of three eminent retired civil servants was appointed to examine the evidence in all cases where the Minister decided that a *prima facie* case had been made. In the meantime the officer concerned was to be suspended and placed on leave with pay while the case was under consideration.

It is not completely clear, in view of the constitutional position of the civil servant within the Service, why this new procedure and machinery were really necessary. The Minister is finally responsible for the officials within his own department. Except in the case of specialists for whom there were no alternative posts available, normal staff control should have prevented unsuitable persons from holding specific posts or made it possible to change them, without challenge, as soon as it was discovered that they were not suitable. Such changes, whatever the position of the officer, would in normal course be little more than of a routine nature. The explanation presumably is that an unhealthy situation had already developed in certain reaches of the Service and that the integrity of the Civil Service was being threatened by the attitudes of certain individuals whose hearts were less concerned with the practice of public administration than with the building of some New Jerusalem that they conceived it to be their business to impose upon their less enlightened brethren. It may be concluded that authoritative action by the Government was necessitated by the fact that the political heads were not all equally enthusiastic to preserve the political neutrality of the Civil Service and also that some such publicity was needed to make the Service as well as the community aware of this serious development. Otherwise there appears to be little in the situation that could not have been dealt with in the course of ordinary Civil Service management. One consequence of all this is that the Civil Service Commission now request candidates at their examinations to disclose whether they are members of Communist or Fascist organizations.

It is hardly surprising that the staff associations have viewed these innovations with concern and have done everything possible to safeguard the interests of their members. A number of individual cases have been referred to in the Press and some comparatively obscure civil servants have obtained a notoriety that they would not otherwise have earned, but there is no evidence that any real injustice has been done.[1]

[1] On March 16th, 1954 the following figures (quoted in "Whitley Bulletin" Vol. XXXIV, p.70) were given in reply to a Question in the House of Commons. Total number of officials affected by the imposition of security procedures up to that date:

	Dismissed	Transferred
Non-industrial	7	54
Industrial	17	18
	24	72

Politically the Civil Service is no longer so unconcerned as it used to be. It is in the nature of the modern world that this should be so. Influential new ideas tend to erode the civil servant's loyalty, while he himself, rightly or wrongly, tends more and more to associate his relationship to the State as employee with his relationship to the Nation as citizen. A new spirit of public service is needed to maintain and rejuvenate the high traditions of the past. How this new spirit may be encouraged is clearly a problem for the second, and more speculative, part of this work.

POSTSCRIPT: MACLEAN AND BURGESS

In consequence of the Maclean-Burgess affair of 1951,[1] when two Foreign Office officials disappeared behind the Iron Curtain in suspicious circumstances, later to become self-declared traitors, the Government, on November 23rd, 1955, set up a Conference of seven Privy Councillors[2] 'to examine the security procedures now applied in the public services and to consider whether any further precautions are called for and should be taken'.

While concluding that there is nothing organically wrong with the Government's security arrangements, the Conference, in a Report to the Government early in 1956[3], state that 'the chief risks are presented by Communists and by other persons who for one reason or another are subject to Communist influence', and that one of the main problems today is 'to identify the members of the British Communist Party, to be informed of its activities and to identify that wider body of those who are both sympathetic to Communism, or susceptible to Communist pressure and present a danger to security'. They go on to state that while the problem is a general one it is recognized as of special importance in certain areas of the public service, such as the Foreign Service, the Defence field and the Atomic Energy Organization.

'Character defects as factors tending to make a man unreliable or expose him to blackmail or influence by foreign agents' are of great importance and it is the duty of 'Departments to inform themselves of serious failings such as drunkenness, addiction to drugs, homosexuality or any loose living that may seriously affect a man's reliability'. Consequently the Conference state that it is not only the responsibility of Heads of Departments, but of supervisory officers generally 'to know their staff' and not fail 'to report anything which affects security'.

[1] *Report concerning the disappearance of two former Foreign Office Officials* (Cmd. 9477), 1955.

[2] These were the Lord President of the Council; the Lord Chancellor; the Secretary of State for the Home Department; Lord Jowitt; Members of Parliament for Lewisham, South, and Vauxhall; and the Permanent Secretary to H.M. Treasury.

[3] *Statement on the Findings of the Conference of Privy Counsellors on Security* (Cmd. 9715), 1956.

'A serious character defect may appropriately be the determining factor in a decision to dismiss a particular individual or to transfer him to other work.' 'The fact that a public servant is a Communist not only bars his employment on secret duties, but may also in some departments have an unfavourable effect on his prospects of promotion.' The Conference go on to recommend that no individual should be employed on secret work who is living with a wife or husband who is a Communist or Communist sympathizer.

A significant pronouncement in the white paper runs: 'The Conference is of opinion that in deciding these difficult and often borderline cases, it is right to continue the practice of tilting the balance in favour of offering greater protection to the security of the State rather than in the direction of safeguarding the rights of the individual.' Further, it may sometimes be necessary to decide against so employing a person 'because after the fullest investigation doubts about his reliability remain, even although nothing may have been proved against him on standards which would be accepted in a Court of Law'.

It can be assumed that such serious deviation from normal constitutional practice would not have been recommended without good cause. The proposals, nevertheless, have serious implications for the future of the Civil Service. It must be clear to all but the wilfully blind or the sentimentally doped that support for the policy and methods of the Communist Party is incompatible with membership of the British Civil Service. Yet it is equally certain that the change in attitudes implicit in the measures proposed to counter this threat is incompatible with the inherent spirit of civil service. This is of course a dilemma of our modern society which is not peculiar to the public service and glib answers on the basis of political theory or mere sentiment will not provide the certain solution for those who have to take responsibility for results.

The Conference recommend that the Tribunal of Three Advisers previously appointed should continue to hear appeals under the more stringent measures now proposed and that the whole matter should first be discussed with the representatives of the staffs concerned.

APPENDIX TO CHAPTER IX

Extracts from Report of the Board of Enquiry[1] *appointed by the Prime Minister to investigate certain Statements affecting Civil Servants.* (*Cmd.* 3037, 1928.)

54. We think in conclusion that we shall not be travelling outside our terms of reference if, as three Civil Servants of some experience and

[1] Consisting of Sir Warren Fisher, G.C.B., G.C.V.O., Sir Malcolm Ramsay, K.C.B. and Mr M. L. Gwyer, C.B.

jealous for the honour and traditions of the Service, we indicate what we conceive to be the principles which should regulate the conduct of Civil Servants – whether engaged in Home Departments or on diplomatic missions – in their relation to the public.

55. His Majesty's Civil Service, unlike other great professions, is not and cannot in the nature of things be an autonomous profession. In common with the Royal Navy, the Army and the Royal Air Force, it must always be subject to the rules and regulations laid down for its guidance by His Majesty's Government. This written code is, in the case of the Civil Service, to be found not only in the Statutes but also in Orders in Council, Treasury Circulars and other directions which may from time to time be promulgated; but over and above these the Civil Service, like every other profession, has its unwritten code of ethics and conduct for which the most effective sanction lies in the public opinion of the Service itself, and it is upon the maintenance of a sound and healthy public opinion within the Service that its value and efficiency chiefly depend.

56. The first duty of a Civil Servant is to give his undivided allegiance to the State at all times and on all occasions when the State has a claim upon his services. With his private activities the State is in general not concerned, so long as his conduct therein is not such as to bring discredit upon the Service of which he is a member. But to say that he is not to subordinate his duty to his private interests, nor to make use of his official position to further those interests, is to say no more than that he must behave with common honesty. The Service exacts from itself a higher standard, because it recognizes that the State is entitled to demand that its servants shall not only be honest in fact, but beyond the reach of suspicion of dishonesty. It was laid down by one of His Majesty's Judges in a case some few years ago that it was not merely of some importance but of fundamental importance that in a Court of Law justice should not only be done, but should manifestly and undoubtedly be seen to be done; which we take to mean that public confidence in the administration of justice would be shaken if the least suspicion, however ill-founded, were allowed to arise that the course of legal proceedings could in any way be influenced by improper motives. We apply without hesitation an analogous rule to other branches of the public service. A Civil Servant is not to subordinate his duty to his private interests; but neither is he to put himself in a position where his duty and his interests conflict. He is not to make use of his official position to further those interests; but neither is he so to order his private affairs as to allow the suspicion to arise that a trust has been abused or a confidence betrayed. These obligations are, we do not doubt, universally recognized throughout the whole of the Service; if it were otherwise, its public credit would be diminished and its usefulness to the State impaired.

57. It follows that there are spheres of activity legitimately open to the ordinary citizen in which the Civil Servant can play no part, or only a limited part. He is not to indulge in political or party controversy, lest by so doing he should appear no longer the disinterested adviser of Ministers or able impartially to execute their policy. He is bound to maintain a proper reticence in discussing public affairs and more particularly those with which his own Department is concerned. And lastly, his position clearly imposes upon him restrictions in matters of commerce and business from which the ordinary citizen is free.

58. Between the regular investment or management of a private fortune on the one hand, and speculative transactions in stocks, exchange or commodities on the other, there are obviously numerous gradations, and it may often be difficult to draw the precise line of demarcation between what is lawful and what is prohibited; it may even be inadvisable to make the attempt, because many things, though lawful, may yet be inexpedient. But some transactions fall indubitably on one side of the line rather than upon the other. It might well be desirable for a Civil Servant in all circumstances to avoid transactions wholly speculative in character; but where he is employed in any Department to which, whether rightly or wrongly, the public attribute the power of obtaining special information, such as the future course of political or financial events likely to affect the rise and fall of markets, then we assert unhesitatingly that participation in such transactions is not only undesirable or inexpedient, but wrong. The knowledge that Civil Servants so employed are engaged in them could not fail to shock public confidence at home, and, especially if matters of foreign exchange are involved, to produce a deplorable effect upon opinion abroad.

59. We content ourselves with laying down these general principles, which we do not seek to elaborate into any detailed code, if only for the reason that their application must necessarily vary according to the position, the Department and the work of the Civil Servant concerned. Practical rules for the guidance of social conduct depend also as much upon the instinct and perception of the individual as upon cast-iron formulas: and the surest guide will, we hope, always be found in the nice and jealous honour of Civil Servants themselves. The public expects from them a standard of integrity and conduct not only inflexible but fastidious, and has not been disappointed in the past. We are confident that we are expressing the view of the Service when we say that the public have a right to expect that standard, and that it is the duty of the Service to see that the expectation is fulfilled.

PART II

DISCUSSION

CHAPTER X

THE BENEVOLENT OLIGARCHY

The outstanding position of the leadership group in the British Civil Service has already been discussed in this book. Indeed, it is too widely recognized for its truth to be challenged. The idea of Plato's guardians has probably never come closer to practical realization than in the Administrative Class. Nor is this a matter for surprise when one remembers the great influence of the classical learning of Greece and Rome in moulding the minds of occupiers of the top posts during the Civil Service's formative phase. The objectivity of open competition had the virtue of eliminating patronage while at the same time increasing the homogeneity of the *élite*. Such a large proportion passed through the classical faculties of the two older universities that they were able spontaneously to impose their outlook and principles upon the whole of their group. They were chief ministerial advisers as well as administrative leaders and it followed as a matter of course that the rest of the Civil Service should accept their outlook and seek to emulate their standards. This would have happened even if it had not been a part of their job to regulate the conduct of business inside the departments.

Before the Second World War few had been recruited to the Administrative Class from below and the assimilation of these few had presented little difficulty. In assessing the fitness of outstanding subordinate officials to become members of their class the standards applied were obviously cast in the *élite's* own image. The adoption of any other would hardly have done credit to their self-confidence. The pattern thus imposed upon the Civil Service may have been admirable but it had the vice of creating a vested interest inside the Central Administration, whose great power was effectively masked, but hardly diminished by the constitutional supremacy of the political executive. In relinquishing control of matters of technical administration to their professional advisers the ministerial heads of departments left a sphere of growing importance to the leaders of the Civil Service, who thus at the price of political neutrality wisely discovered a whole new important world for themselves. Non-interference by the politicians, whose competence to participate in purely administrative matters was in any case not likely to be high, coupled with sheer ignorance of Civil Service practices and of the requirements for administrative efficiency on the part of almost everyone else, have assisted greatly in reinforcing the power of the Civil Service *élite*. It is with no intention of detracting one iota from the greatness of the service to the community rendered by that group that we discern at a vital spot in the British system of government an institution that has some of the characteristics of an oligarchy.

On the face of things there is no mystery: the community selects its Civil Service leaders by an impartial system of open competition, but after that it is the leadership group itself that determines what should happen to itself. By adopting a self-denying ordinance and ensuring the achievement of a high standard of administrative effectiveness it has earned the right to live on its own terms, albeit sheltered from the winds of creative criticism.

ACCEPTANCE OF THE POSITION

The lack of effective outside criticism is a serious matter and the position is merely aggravated by the considerable volume of unbalanced criticism in the Press that does neither the Civil Service nor the nation one bit of good. In the past the impasse has been broken from time to time by the putting in hand of a grand inquest upon the Civil Service on the nation's behalf. Such an inquiry was projected in 1953 when a Royal Commission was set up under the chairmanship of Sir Raymond Priestley. But despite important pronouncements in Parliament comparing this new Commission with the periodical inquiries of the past, there can be no doubt that the parallel was not a good one. The terms of reference of the Royal Commission were restricted to an investigation of the Civil Service's conditions of service which had too obviously got out of step in the press of post-war social and economic development. The Service's general organization, invariably the concern of previous major investigations, was accepted as satisfactory and not requiring radical change.

Thus the Royal Commission's terms of reference precluded evidence that might have thrown doubt on the present structure of the Civil Service and the Commissioners were left in little doubt as to the general acceptance, both by the Official interests and by many of the staff groups, of the continuing validity of the present system, including the paramountcy of the Administrative Class within that system. Only the scientists and professional groups have put up an effective fight against this attitude, mainly through a comparison of pay scales; and this is a fight which they have been waging for equality with the Administrative Class for some time. They are contestants for power and not protagonists of a new order. The other grades have been too concerned with their own very real bread and butter problems to show any radical dissatisfaction with the present regime. In any case they have become so used to accepting the inevitable that it is doubtful whether they would have had a very vigorous case to put even if the Royal Commission had been in a position to listen to it. This fatalistic attitude on the part of such a large body of workers is not the least of the shortcomings of the present system.

THE NON-COMPETITIVE RETREAT

A paradoxical outcome of the institution of open competition was the conversion of the central administration of the State into a non-competitive retreat in the midst of a national economy of growing competitiveness, a retreat in which the normal laws of competition did not operate. When Trevelyan and Northcote advocated the reorganization of the Civil Service on the basis of a division of labour that separated the intellectual and the routine work of the departments into self-contained compartments they were effectively ensuring the supremacy of the group that had access to the right type of education. What that right type should be was itself determined by the moulding of the new higher examinations on the model of liberal studies already adopted, on Lord Macaulay's advocacy, for the Indian Civil Service.

Administering in those days was still rightly reckoned an art not calling for special technical skill. The very effectiveness of the new system in producing competent administrators was calculated to perpetuate the idea that administration could best be learned by doing and that there was no science to be studied. For long the tasks of the higher administration were fairly simple, personal secretarial service to the minister forming an important part of the work of the higher staffs. The somewhat menial nature of much of this work and the degree to which success depended upon the civil servant's personal relationships with his political chiefs – on being *persona grata* in a social sense – is demonstrated by the writings of Algernon West[1], a well-connected patronage man who began as a temporary clerk in the Inland Revenue at six shillings a day and rose, via Gladstone's personal secretaryship, to be Chairman of the Board of Inland Revenue. It was only gradually, as the central departments expanded beyond the personal orbit of an individual minister, that matters of policy and organization became the primary task of a small band of senior administrators. It has been explained how the simple scheme of 1853 had by the early years of the twentieth century begun to change into a more complicated tripartite system, in which a new intermediate or middle class of executives had emerged to deal with matters of audit and accounting that were considered to be below the interest of the higher administrative recruits and not calculated to make full use of their talents. Although this so-called executive work is still considered an activity inferior to pure administration, whatever that may be, it is doubtful whether similar reasons could today stand a moment's chance of acceptance.

[1] See *Recollections, 1832 to 1886* (1899).

There were at the time factors other than mere differences in the intrinsic difficulty of the work to account for the caste-like levels of the three main classes. In the first place, with administration was associated power arising from the occupancy of the directing posts of the Civil Service. Administration has always been associated with power, which accounts for the keenness with which such posts have always been sought. In the second place, the competitive system, by the interaction of the requirements of the examinations with the development of the educational system, had built up vested interests inside the educational world who were powerful advocates of the maintenance of the system in order to afford outlets for a regular annual band of school-leavers at the appropriate levels. Their great influence is indicated by the strength of the evidence submitted on their behalf to the MacDonnell and Tomlin Commissions. Lastly, the work itself at the different levels gained a special prestige from the educational calibre of the actual holders of the official posts. In this way the examinations tended to determine the importance of the work processes instead of vice versa. Few of the cleverer members of the several classes were ever likely to be given work commensurate with their abilities, but the incumbents of posts at the several levels accepted the position and acknowledged the supremacy of those above them without question. For the competitive entrants to a lower class to challenge the position of their seniors in the class above was tantamount to challenging their own right to office. This scheme of watertight classes in the clerical-administrative sphere reached its apogee with the Reorganization Scheme of 1920, which undoubtedly measured up to the situation existing at that time.

Nevertheless, the writing was already on the wall and the world that had shaped the great Victorian Civil Service was rapidly passing away, although it was to be some time before anyone would recognize this truth. One has only to examine the public pronouncements made in honour of the centenary of the Trevelyan and Northcote Report during 1954 and the evidence to the Royal Commission (Priestley), especially by the Treasury and the representatives of the Administrative Class, to realize that the presuppositions of the past are still being assumed, so far as the leadership group is concerned. This is not surprising when one realizes that the one great innovation of the Reorganization period, the introduction into the Civil Service of Whitleyism in place of the decided paternalism of the past, has been so effectively accommodated within the system without greatly altering its main assumptions. The foundations were being eroded in a much more drastic manner by other forces. The danger came from without rather than from within and it is a great tribute indeed to the original builders that even today the edifice has an appearance of timelessness in a world of change.

THE EMERGING SITUATION

Today the Civil Service is no longer a comparatively compact non-competitive islet in a sea of capitalist competitiveness guided by different principles and with standards fit to set an example to a less select world. It has grown considerably and its differences from the rest of the community have narrowed with the great expansion of public administration into the territories of private enterprise. The changed situation has been officially recognized by the Treasury's insistence on the need to relate Civil Service conditions with those of the outside world. The Civil Service can no longer take pride in setting a high example to those who have not been subjected to such effective selection processes. The flow of social and economic events, speeded up by the Second World War and assisted by the official philosophy that the Civil Service could at least set an example in the making of sacrifices, has in any case altered radically the relative position of the civil servant in the general field of employment.

Quite apart from these general changes in the reality between the Civil Service and the wider community there are those changes, still in full flow, that are affecting the internal realm of public administration. The work of the Civil Service has extended into fields that hardly existed a hundred years ago. Even the regulatory and advisory tasks of government departments have become much more complex and they have been widely supplemented by service-providing activities that have actually been invented to meet the needs of a more socially conscious community. These have themselves been instrumental in shaping the new type of state that that community requires. Obvious examples are the systems of employment exchanges, public health and national insurance. Public administration, which was an art largely acquired by sitting at the foot of the Throne and by observing during a menial apprenticeship how the skilled controllers of power manipulated the simple pieces in accordance with time-honoured ways, has now grown into a science that needs to be learned the hard way and calls upon the services not only of the administrator-writer and the paper keeper, but of a band of experts – messengers, technicians, supervisors – commanding a wide range of skills and calling for varied talents. Apart from this manysidedness which has expanded the work of the Civil Service beyond the realms of administration into vast fields of research, service provision and even production, the sphere of the central departments has expanded beyond the confines of Whitehall into every parish in the land. This extension is not of course unique or without precedent. It is its new comprehensiveness that is startling. Central government has for long extended beyond the purely regulatory sphere into such executive fields as posts, tax collection and defence, all with far-flung branches, but even within these almost immemorial activities of government the scene has become complicated almost beyond recognition.

The picture needs only to be contemplated for a few moments to suggest the inadequacy in such a context of the Trevelyan-Northcote solution of a simply organized Civil Service selected on the basis of general literary skills. This assumed a simple administrative world in which (i) the leaders could be chosen young and left to acquire their skill by affording office assistance to their betters and other ranks could graduate in the same way on basic clerical work: (ii) the work of the various central departments was so similar that the clerks and administrators could be interchangeable[1] and that no one else mattered much; (iii) the staffs mostly worked in offices within or closely accessible to Whitehall; and (iv) the work was largely clerical, involving few contacts with the public. Such a solution visualized leadership as advising ministers on fairly simple policy matters on common sense lines and paid no attention to the element of management called into play by the spread of large-scale organization. It visualized the leadership as centred in London and making little calls upon managerial skills distributed throughout the country. It visualized the work of the branches as mainly office work involving simple clerical processes, such as copying and record keeping, and ignored not only the specialization of such services, e.g. in establishment and accounting branches, but also the emergence of the service-providing departments calling for specialist techniques even if they were based fundamentally on clerical routines. It is true that the development of the original pattern into the tripartite scheme of Reorganization in 1920 and the retention of certain departmental variations were for long successful in keeping the system in step with realities, but this can hardly be said to be true now and it is significant that the process of standardization was actually continued after the Second World War, leading to a further reduction in the number of departmental variations, although it is doubtful whether this rationalizing trend, however tidy it might appear from the Treasury's standpoint, was in line with realities. Significantly the new Ministry of National Insurance (now Pensions and National Insurance), although calling for the application of specialist techniques, was staffed on the standard Treasury class pattern.

It is hardly surprising, in face of this changed situation and the inadequacy of an outworn system of internal organization, that the Civil Service is now finding it difficult to recruit and to retain all the skills it needs. On the one hand it has become a much less attractive field of employment; on the other, it needs even more talents than it was able to use in the past. Over and beyond all else it seems clear that with the

[1] It is interesting to note that some of the most effective criticism of the 1853 proposals was directed by heads of departments against this very assumption!

increased demand upon the national labour pool for higher level talents and skills of all kinds the potential supply available for the Civil Service will have diminished in any case. The question of quality is therefore of paramount importance. The position is also adversely affected by the decline in Civil Service efficiency due to staff inflation since 1939.

THE PROBLEM OF THE *ÉLITE*

Before any satisfactory scheme of reform can be contemplated the problem of the *élite* will have to be faced. The Civil Service is one of the few institutions in the world in which the leadership rests in a segregated group which, if not self-perpetuating, is selected by rules largely within its own formulation. In this it has an analogy, if a distant one, with the single party of the communo-fascist state. It is no palliation to point to the methods adopted by outside management to recruit its own ranks by the selection of juniors for special grooming into the succession. The ruling groups in outside enterprise are not homogeneous in the sense that most of their members have come in through the same channel. There are plenty of other ways of entry and there is much more internal competition than in the Civil Service.

It is no longer satisfactory that the leaders of a central department should come predominantly from among those who have worked all their lives in the peculiar atmosphere of headquarter divisions in Whitehall and have demonstrated their prowess by their effectiveness as personal assistants to Ministers. Leadership implies wide knowledge and experience inside the administrative machine in dealing with staff and problems on the spot, including of course direct contacts with the people served. In reply to this it can be justly said that many of the present members of the Administrative Class have come up the line and that there is more provision for movement between the classes than in the past. This is true and all to the good, but the point is that the idea of a select ruling class is out of date and should be superseded.

Not the least criticism of the system is that it has a bad effect inside the Civil Service. There is a distinct sense everywhere of the *we* and the *they*. The specially brilliant top *we* are of a different clay from the lowlier *they*. The *we* are too sure of their superiority to be arrogant, but they can hardly help showing this superiority even when their condescension is masked with the charm that long established members of the Administrative Class almost invariably cultivate. Their very virtue creates more than a commensurate vice in the other reaches of the Service. Members of senior grades outside the Administrative Class, who have worked in headquarter offices will appreciate fully how this almost indefinable difference so clearly exists as to weigh upon their souls. They are made to feel in subtle ways that they do not belong to the inner circle. And if it is doubted that the *we* do not intend this, the comparison between the quality of the Administrative and Executive Classes as set out in Treasury evidence to the Royal Commission on the Civil Service need only be consulted.[1]

It works in wider fields, for there is a similar gap between headquarter offices and the regions, where the Administrative Class has no particular interest. Headquarter staffs tend to despise the regional workers as simple hewers of wood: regional workers, certain that the tempo and difficulties of their work in close contact with the public far transcends the stresses of the specialist work at headquarters, despise the headquarter staffs for their inflated assessment of their work while at the same time envying them their opportunities.

There is some truth in the view that outside the Administrative Class the Service tends to be apathetic and to lack enterprise. They find that bright ideas are dangerous, that they are expected to think in accordance with a well-established pattern of thinking. If they have surplus energies it is better to expend them in outside activities. They are content to become competent if unimaginative members of their grade. The mediocre who can achieve nothing more make just as good officials as those others who might do something if they had the opportunity. This is bad and although it is not the whole story it goes a good way towards explaining the excessively unimaginative nature of much Civil Service administration. In these days when good management and supervision at the extremities are just as important as good leadership in Whitehall (the major part of which should be supplied by the politician-administrators in any case) it is a fatal defect. The leadership idea needs to break out of Whitehall into the field where the real administrative battle goes on. This cannot happen under the present restrictive regime. The *élite* must be abolished in an institutional sense and the scope of leadership greatly widened in the Civil Service of the future.

THE WAY TO REFORM

It would be presumptuous for one man with the limited vision even of a life's experience inside one field to lay down the lines on which reform in that field should travel. This is a job for an authoritative committee of investigation and unfortunately, as we think, this major overdue task has been withheld from the present Royal Commission. It is true that the present writer did have the temerity to offer a detailed scheme in a previous work.[2] This was designed mainly to introduce a degree of flexibility into a situation that has since been superseded. The principles

[1] E.g. Evidence 21–2, Cmd. 3263.

[2] *The Civil Service: Its Problems and Future.* First published in 1945, but actually written before the Second World War.

of the proposed scheme are still valid, but to some extent they have been introduced – for example, by the extension of the system of pooling – or rendered unnecessary by the very breaking down under the stress of war of the hidebound departmental staffing patterns to which they were to apply. Certain other proposals[1] that were embodied in the scheme are appropriate to any scheme of reorganization. These will be mentioned in the course of later discussion. It was not at that time suggested that the Administrative Class should be abolished in its present form. It was felt that more urgent reforms were called for in much wider spheres and that it would be unwise to go further than propose recruitment of the Administrative Class from within the Service to the extent of fifty per cent. This was sufficiently radical at that time when such selections were few and far between and is an objective that will certainly not be improved upon by present recruitment and promotion methods.[2]

Obviously the abolition of a distinct Administrative Class would not mean the cessation of direct recruitment from the universities. There can be no suggestion of a one-class Civil Service recruited at the bottom. The university recruit should come in at a sufficiently high level to facilitate the use of his special qualities and qualifications, but not so high as to assure him of leadership posts without further effort and very little further experience.

At the moment an Assistant Principal is roughly equivalent to the Higher Executive Officer, but does not take the full responsibilities of that grade which is staffed by civil servants who have already had some years of valuable practical experience as Executive Officers. The Assistant Principal is really an apprentice, practically certain to become a Principal at the age of 30 or thereabouts. Now the rough equivalent of the Principal on the Executive side, inferior in status of course, is shared between the two grades of Senior and Chief Executive Officer. The real position of these grades in the hierarchy is indicated by the fact that the university recruited Principal with but a few years administrative experience is equated on the Executive side with officers of at least twenty and usually thirty to forty years' experience, who are already virtually at the apex of their career. The parallel is inequitable and from the practical viewpoint defective. The difference between administrative and executive activities (which comprise a large element of management and supervision) is no longer a difference in kind and the gap between the two scales of reward is completely unrealistic.

Of course the difference, in so far as it does not rest upon the maintenance of a vested interest, largely arises from the need to pay a relatively high price for university trained people. This phenomenon of

[1] *The Civil Service: Its Problems and Future.* (2nd Edn. 1948), p. 117.

[2] The present high percentage of promotees in the Administrative Class is largely due to the war-time expansion.

the market is perhaps as near as we come at the moment to Burnham's managerial revolution[1], the birth of an oligarchy of the educated. Yet there is less justification for giving the university product a privileged position today than there was in the past, for it becomes less and less true in this era of socially financed education and State scholarships that university education is paid for by the individual, who consequently has a right to expect an adequate return for his outlay. After all education is sufficiently its own reward and should only call for a special return in virtue of its capacity to give better results, a matter that can only be proved in practice. Clever people are not invariably practical or full of wisdom. Knowledge is a tool whose use has to be learned by experience. The most that any well-educated youth has a right to ask from life is the opportunity to use his knowledge in the service of his fellow men.

Entry to most professions is gained through knowledge and the initial reward is determined partly by convention and partly by the market: the Civil Service test is similar in some respects, but it has two special characteristics that put it in a category of its own: it does not presume to test professional competence, which has still to be acquired, and it has an oligarchic element which virtually gives exclusive right of entry at a particular time of life and protects the successful from competition from other quarters and at other times.

The solution seems to lie in the direction of absorbing the university element into the Service at the present Higher Executive level, or thereabouts, and resting further advancement on actual capacity, which in many cases would be amply demonstrated by virtue of the higher education. This would mean making that particular grade more attractive for the cadet, a change that would be justified in any case when the responsibilities of the Executive Class are fully considered. These university talents would no longer be concentrated in London at headquarter level and the effect upon the Executive Class, which would be extended upwards to absorb most of the present Administrative posts to Under Secretary level, could not be other than highly beneficial both to its efficiency and its morale. It might be asked how the special private secretary posts would be filled. The obvious answer is that any youthful member of the Executive grades would be eligible on secondment for a period of years. It would still form an excellent means of training as at present, but from a much wider field. On the other hand the practice, sometimes at present resorted to, of placing in posts requiring experience young men merely because they belonged to the Administrative Class would no longer be necessary, thus avoiding the loss of efficiency arising from the use of such posts in providing training for promising men. There are plenty of posts of sufficient executive responsibility throughout the Service which would become available for this purpose. Posts above

[1] James Burnham *The Managerial Revolution* (1941).

the new top Executive grade would be common to the Service as a whole, selection resting entirely upon capacity.

This amalgamation of the Executive and Administrative Classes into one Civil Service class concerned broadly with public service management, would produce an unwieldly corps and still leave a number of difficulties to be overcome. In view of the varying needs of the Service and the different techniques used by the various branches it is considered that a much higher degree of after-entry specialization will need to operate in future. It is no longer a sensible doctrine to hold that all clerks or executives are interchangeable. The broad liberal education may still provide the best basis for the administrative career, but the growing complexity of the Civil Service's functions undoubtedly calls for more after-entry specialization. Since the war the need for special experience has led to the separate organization and specialization of one branch of Executive work, namely, the Information Officer group, still generally interchangeable with the Executive class, but forming a separate career inside the Departments and between the Information branches of the several departments. Similar arrangements could be made for other specialist groups, establishment work offering a special example. There would be no question of going to the American extreme of regarding posts from an individual standpoint, each with its job specification and separate recruitment conditions. The Executive Class would be generally recruited as heretofore, specialization taking place afterwards when, through training and experience, the officer had shown in which direction his special aptitudes and inclinations lay. Normally these specialists would remain within their chosen 'career-within-a-career', but there would be reasonable opportunities for horizontal interchange in order to maintain cross-fertilization at different levels.

It would be for consideration whether the Civil Service today would not gain from being grouped according to function into a series of vertical sub-services. The all-Service idea is now being outmoded by technical advances and, of course, size. The Post Office already forms a large sphere on its own; the Social Service Ministries could be grouped, and so could perhaps the Defence Ministries, as well as those dealing with economic and industrial matters. Another possible development could be the emergence of separate Regional Civil Services based upon a new governmental pattern (which it is obviously beyond the scope of this book to discuss). The problems of staff mobility at the moment strongly support a solution on these lines though the variety of functions within the regions would make complete interchangeability very difficult. On the other hand a closer co-ordination of common services a regional levels and an increase in the authority and autonomy of the regional directorates could have valuable administrative advantages.

This is as far as we are warranted in pursuing these ideas in the present context. What we have in view is the breaking down of the artificial barriers of the present class system, the substitution of a system of equal opportunity and a reclassification of the administrative sectors of the Civil Service on the basis of function or service, or possibly a mixture of both. What is important is not the formulation of a precise solution, but that a serious problem should receive wide discussion. In superseding the Benevolent Oligarchy it is important that individual virtues of the present system should not be thrown out with its vices. The alternative, perhaps unfortunately, is certainly not to maintain things as they are, since the situation for which they were so admirably designed is rapidly passing away. It is surely better to decide what we need in its replacement than to be forced into solutions representing the line of least resistance, except in the minds of those who will move heaven and earth to maintain the *status quo*.

CHAPTER XI

THE EVILS OF ORGANIZATIONAL INFLATION

The new complex multi-functional administration of the Central Government, so like and yet so different from its counterpart of a hundred years ago, has shown a remarkable capacity to evolve adequate new organizational patterns to deal with its extended responsibilities. It is a universal characteristic of organization that in default of planning and foresight it matches itself to its new environment under the moulding activities of individual administrators who are often unconscious of what they are doing. So long as they can achieve the limited objectives for which they have been made responsible they are often quite prepared to let the structure look after itself. Of course when an entirely new branch has to be set up a coherent organizational plan will be devised (today with the close co-operation of the O and M man) and from time to time the whole structure will be better for a complete overhaul leading to reorganization; but for most of the time a sort of spontaneous growth is going on.

To some extent the application of a systematic personnel plan, as represented by the Civil Service grading system, has considerably facilitated this development and ensured that the resulting administrative pattern should retain a high degree of homogeneity. To deal with the growing personnel problem the procedures of staff management have been worked out with a high degree of acumen and latterly on a broad co-operative basis. The measures adopted have been described in earlier chapters dealing with recruitment, training, promotion and the rest. The net result, however, has been to reduce the participation of the individual, who is inevitably overwhelmed by the vastness of the machine in which he works. This is indeed the problem of the new world that is emerging around us. This world is being designed by man for his own edification, but he has to fight continuously against the danger of becoming its slave. Emancipation from its thraldom often calls for an understanding that the ordinary layman cannot hope to command. It is the object of this chapter to consider the place of the individual civil servant inside the administrative machine.

THE MAKING OF A BUREAUCRAT

The Civil Service, as the result of a hundred years of steady evolution, has become a highly organized and closely regulated system. This development was inevitable if an effective instrument to meet the multi-functional requirements of government was to be forged. Whether considered as a series of service classes or of separate departmental units – and in fact it has the characteristics of each – the Civil Service has become so large as to leave little scope for individuality in its ranks. Even the Administrative Class has today become too large for its uniqueness and ubiquity to be much more than a fiction.

The newcomer soon discovers that he is a generalized staff unit regarded as a human being only by those with whom he has daily contacts. As the chain of command above him lengthens away into the higher reaches, often into other geographical situations, it loses its humanness and becomes a part of the legal system to which he has become subjected. The system is quite impersonal. A new member soon learns that he is a cog in a large machine, and not a very important cog at that. He is of course told that if he perseveres in mastering his job, merit will receive its just reward in good time, but what he discerns around him in the results of previous history does not inspire confidence, and if his personal view is not very perceptive the grouses of his older colleagues will soon make him aware of the other side of the coin. He will discover that in the best of regulated services opportunity rests in the lap of chance as everywhere else, and when he has become experienced enough to judge he will see that the hierarchy around him is not arranged in accordance with any scale of competence that he can comprehend. He might even, were he a cunning fellow – and fortunately such are not usually attracted to Civil Service administration as a career – conclude that his best prospects could even rest in his cultivating opportunities that operated outside the normal channels. It is a good thing to cultivate one's own garden; it is even better to cultivate one's chief's. It is a mistake even to take up golf if one's chief's passion is for classical music, although as a long-term guess the cultivation of golf is more likely to be remunerative than music even in the comparatively intellectual Civil Service. He would soon learn, for example, that outspokenness though invited by those at the top and welcomed as a part of official policy is not usually received very warmly by his immediate superiors. Yesmanship is an immemorial characteristic of bureaucracy and the ability to determine which way the ultra-bureaucratic wind blows can be of incalculable advantage to the aspiring junior.

Few who are subjected to the outlook and 'mores' of a routinized service for a number of years will be strong enough to retain their independence of mind. The long-serving civil servant is notoriously inclined to accept the decisions of authority without question. It is indeed accounted by some a virtue of the system that it should have this effect upon its participants. The rebel is not easily borne in a bureaucracy which places its narrower loyalties above the wider loyalties of life. For this reason it is bad tactics on the part of a junior to show his chief that he is so ambitious that he would like to take his talents into a more expansive field. Such divine impatience is an implied criticism of the importance of the chief's own imperium. The efficient civil servant soon learns to dissemble: he is more likely to be judged by what he says than by what he does. His voice may travel far, the quality of his work will only be known to those around him. If his chief chooses to give him less than his due, or even if he gives him his due but is half-hearted in his advocacy, his official light will be dimmed amongst a galaxy of better advertized talents.

In the environment of officialdom only the strong-minded will retain any real freedom of spirit. The system may be designed to protect the weak against the strong, in fact it has the inevitable effect of encouraging the growth of a slave mentality and of placing a premium upon caution. To some extent this effect is a result of the very success of building up an efficient system of personnel management. It arises even from the initial recognition that officials are human and entitled to justice. The rejection of patronage and the search for ways of defeating favouritism, which has been greatly influenced by the emergence of an effective system of staff participation, have decreased in every direction the scope for arbitrary decision and introduced a system of checks and balances which has rendered it almost impossible to make any decision that favours an individual against the rest of his colleagues. Thus in a so-called merit system it becomes less and less easy for those in positions of responsibility to recognize merit. The decision is so masked as to appear to emanate impartially as part of the daily routine of the department. In seeking to protect the individual against the arbitrary decisions of authority the staff themselves have reinforced the inhuman impartiality of the machine which is already an almost unavoidable outcome of the growth of organization. Inside the Civil Service as in the wider world the apotheosis of equality can mean the elimination of any outstanding virtue. In this effect we have one of the most pointed examples of 'entropy', or levelling down, which the late Frank Pick, in an illuminating address[1] singled out as one of the fatal proclivities of large-scale organization.

We must accept the inevitability in the modern world of the tendency of administration to expand in scale, the desirability that in such circumstances favouritism shall be eliminated by routine procedures and that the interests of the general body of participants shall be protected through representatives; all tendencies calculated to reduce the status of the individual in relation to the system. The problem is to discover ways of restoring initiative to the individual, imposing real merit tests and encouraging thought without sacrificing the safeguards

[1] Published in *Public Administration*, Vol. XIII (1935), pp. 135–45, under the title 'Some Reflections on the Administration of a Public Utility Undertaking'.

that have been laboriously built up or doing injustice to the vast majority. Some may say straight away that this objective is unattainable. If they are right then the future of the world is indeed dim. Dictatorship, whether it emanates from the whim of a power-holder or the over-routinization of a system, cannot be self-regulating for long. All human advance emanates from the minds and initiative of individuals. A system that seeks to legislate these out of existence in the interests of mediocrity is already doomed by its own state of mind.

SOME REFLECTIONS ON THE FAILINGS OF PRESENT PERSONNEL PROCEDURES

If we look back over the various personnel methods described in Part I of this study we shall be struck both by the good intentions behind them and by the general effectiveness of the system of personnel management that has been built up, while at the same time we are bound to recognize that the hoped for objectives have not always been achieved. It is proposed briefly to summarize and juxtapose some of the lessons here with special emphasis on the improvement of the individual's capacity to participate.

(i) *Recruitment*. At the recruitment stage, unless specific minimum technical requirements can be laid down, the overriding efficiency condition is equality of treatment and an educational standard at least sufficient to ensure potential suitability for the work. No better method to ensure this has yet been devised than the open competitive examination based upon a general educational test. This sort of test has the virtue of impartiality and of selecting, not necessarily all the best, but a fair sample that will include a reasonable proportion of the best and on the other hand will include few who will not measure up to the work assigned to them. The latter should be eliminated at the probation hurdle. The recent trend towards including a personal interview in such examinations seems to be based upon the idea that the purely written tests are ineffective (when there is in fact no proof that the oral tests have improved the quality of the successful candidates) and upon the assumption that among those who qualify through a purely written test there will not be a sufficient proportion of the personality type required by the new social administration. There seems to be little evidence of this.[1] Even in our much socialized administration the careful thinker is more valuable as an administrator than the glib talker. The interview test is inevitably subjective and this introduces an incompatible element into the competition. The interviewers recruiting for general Civil Service grades usually have not even the advantage of

[1] See, for example, R. K. Kelsall *Higher Civil Servants in Britain* (1955), Chapter Four.

knowing what type of work the candidate will be called upon to perform and therefore of being able to match him to his job, as is the case with outside selection boards who are usually filling specific posts. Members of interview boards bring to the table the image of an ideal type which will inevitably prejudice them against anyone who does not conform to pattern. But more serious is the effect that, however impartially and honestly they may act, the unsuccessful candidate is more likely to attribute his failure to their bias than to his own shortcomings. It is less usual for those who fail in a written examination to blame anyone but themselves. It is rather interesting to note that the popularity of the interview test as part of open competition coincides with the broadening of the basis of our general educational system and the breaking down of class monopolies at the public schools and universities after the First World War. It is as though somewhere a subconscious idea had arisen that the unadulterated battle of brains in the examination room might well let some through who were not *personae gratae* with the powers-that-be and that since education was no longer a final bar some other test had become socially necessary. The personality test is unavoidably subjective and unless personality is one of the essential requirements of a particular job (and this is not the case with the general Treasury classes of the Civil Service) it should not be imposed as part of the generalized entrance test. Where personality requires to be tested the personality test then becomes a technical requirement and the situation is quite different. This is the case, for example, with the specialist inspectorate classes and certainly with the diplomatist.

The reader should here be reminded of the incorrectness of the general impression that the Civil Service has since 1870 been recruited mainly through a system of open competition. Even in normal circumstances large sections were recruited on the basis of nomination or by limited competition and open competition applied particularly to the more strictly office or Treasury classes. Furthermore, even in these classes the vicissitudes of war and social upheaval have brought in large numbers in other ways. The vast majority of the present Clerical Officers have not sat strictly competitive examinations and only a minority of them have been subjected to an educational test commensurate with the work of the class. This is also true of large numbers of the Executive and Administrative Classes, a case indeed of the best laid plans not being achievable in actual practice. There can be no doubt whatever that if the present Treasury classes had been consistently subjected to the sieve of open competition, as was the intention of the original reformers, we should today have a vastly more efficient Civil Service. In these ideal but in fact historically impossible circumstances we should no doubt have had a smaller Civil Service, and it would almost certainly have been better paid. There is nothing to be said in favour of dispensing with open competition and all excuses to weaken it should be subjected to the most rigorous examination.

(ii) *Allocation.* Usually when the general educational type of test is adopted at the recruitment stage the precise kind of work to which the candidate will be assigned is not known and indeed cannot be known by the examining body. The general Civil Service classes are organized upon this assumption. The Civil Service Commissioners do ask successful competitors to indicate their preferences, but it seems that at this stage there is more scope for aptitude tests, and even for the use of the interview to assess personality, than at the earlier competitive stage. In the larger departments which have a wide range of different posts available, and therefore a frequent flow of suitable vacancies, the aptitude sieve could be left to them. There is no doubt that much of the present action at this stage is very haphazard and that much more could be done to make the most of the talents made available to the departments through the examinations. On the other hand the practical difficulties are considerable. The recruiting and appointing authorities find it difficult to meet the mere numerical needs of the various geographical areas. In some there are too few candidates and for them successful candidates may be unwilling to opt. (A number of accepted candidates do in fact relinquish appointments rather than take up posts in areas they do not like.) The result is that establishment branches are primarily concerned to plug gaps in their staffing plan with whatever bodies that are placed at their disposal. They are in the position often of the beggars who cannot choose and are not very inclined to ensure that the round pegs do go into the round holes. The present over-generalized type of classification certainly does assist in ironing out these difficulties, but only at the expense of long-term efficiency. The only cure seems to lie in the direction of making these posts more attractive to newcomers.

(iii) *Probation.* This is a brief but important stage in the new official's career. This is when his training begins. He has to learn his new work and this takes place mainly on the job. The problem is to get a really valuable report on his potentialities within a brief period of one or two years. Probation has been widely recognized as important by all the authorities, but despite the serious attention given to it latterly there are grave doubts as to its effectiveness. However, it is only in a minority of cases that any real problem arises, for the majority of examination entrants can be vouched for with confidence by the supervisor by the end of the probation period. If this were not the case the examinations themselves would be suspect, and they are not. It is the few borderline cases that get through, to the disadvantage of the individual himself as much as to the public service as an institution. At this stage the natural tendency of kindly supervisors (whose sympathies it must be remembered cost them nothing in this case) means that only the obviously ineffective are rejected. Some way must be found to hold such supervisors responsible for blatantly bad choices and all participants in the process must be made clearly aware of the reason why a good choice is important to all, not least to the unsatisfactory candidate himself who will be more happy in life if he finds at this early stage something more compatible with his real aptitudes. For this stage definite tests should be devised and impartially applied, and the rejected candidate should be positively assisted to find a more appropriate occupation. He could even be financially indemnified for the loss of a right earned by virtue of his success in the examination. Such resettlement money would be well spent.

There are particular difficulties with temporary officials who today are subject to a very brief probation and not subsequently to any positive reports. The supervisor must make an adverse report if the officer becomes woefully incapable, but the system is irksome and so designed as to protect the official reported upon, and because of this is often evaded by kindly or lethargic supervisors. Periodical efficiency reports should be called for upon all officers and the services of temporary officers should be subject to periodical renewal and controlled by some kind of aptitude test. It is possible today for a temporary governmental clerk to be quite deficient in the capacity to write the Queen's English and to cypher, and yet eventually to manage to sidestep into a full-blown permanency without having been subjected to adequate tests of competence in clerkship.

(iv) *Training*. Civil Service training is largely practical. It is obvious that a newcomer has to be made competent on his work as soon as possible and the least percipient supervisor will have to ensure this even if left to his own devices. In our detailed description of what is being done it was shown that at its best Civil Service staff training has reached a high standard, although this is an achievement that is very variable if the Service is considered as a whole. It is less in the devising of new schemes and methods than in the more widespread dissemination of a more dynamic vision that advancement in this sphere is to be sought. The development of this proposition is so close to the theme of the following chapter that it is not proposed to discuss it further at this stage.

(v) *Internal Selection and Rewards*. A member of a graded service is paid according to the work of his grade and not for his actual services. Jobs assigned to a grade vary in interest and degree of difficulty and the executive allocates his staff accordingly, but they are not specifically rewarded for their personal efforts. The actual value of a job to the community will vary considerably according to the efficiency with which it is performed by the individual who will not receive a commensurate reward except through promotion to a higher grade (for which he may be assessed on quite a different basis). This situation is usual and to some degree inevitable in a graded service. But it can be carried too far; for example, by the automatic application of the long salary scale. Such a scale that provides for remuneration over a long period of years cannot possibly apply with any accuracy to the merits of a number of officials, each of whom will have had differing experiences and will have developed differently in the meantime. Once a reasonable standard of payment has been assured further advances should in some way depend upon merit. A long scale may be broken into sections by the imposition of efficiency bars (as in the case of the Clerical Class), but the tendency is for the passing of these bars to become a matter of routine. More attention should be given to this operation, definitely impartial tests being devised. Even the annual increment should only be awarded upon a certificate of satisfactory performance from the supervisor. One way out of the general difficulty would be to have a larger number of grades, within which salary increases were more or less automatic, but advancement from a lower to a higher grade was subject to the most stringent promotion tests.

One well-known phenomenon in graded services is the recognized existence in all grades of officers who are obviously of poor calibre and not up to their current tasks. This is one of the most potent reasons why supervisors and managers are notoriously unwilling to be even moderately strict in their judgments. It is always possible to look round and find someone in the higher grade who is obviously less competent than the officer under consideration. The only cure for this situation is the use of demotion which prevents an officer from holding on to any post incompetently or with obvious lack of interest. The disgruntled officer who asks why he should care and makes it clear that he does not intend to pull his weight in future should be given a reason for caring. This would not indeed be easy: a radically new outlook would be called for. Nevertheless, the problem must be faced. The idea that injustice will be done to conscientious officers can be exaggerated. The present system of equal pay for unequal effort and unequal interest is even more unjust and insidiously fatal in its effects. The Treasury's subtle cure of grade inflation which permits the Civil Service grade gradually to lose importance and rebalances the system by bringing in new grade levels to which promotion selection acts as a kind of sieving process is even more unjust to a large number of above average officers who fail to get promotion because the outlet has become restricted.

Other ways of rewarding merit outside the promotion line need to be discovered. It has to be recognized that promotion to a higher grade may call for qualities and capacities that a very good official may not have. It is wrong that his special aptitudes on his present work should be ignored. There is a wide efficiency margin between the normal situation of the job satisfactorily performed and the situation in which every worker does his job with added enthusiasm and skill. A system that gets the best out of its participants will reach a standard of efficiency beyond the dreams of those who have to struggle to achieve administrative satisfaction with mediocre talents.

The difficulty here is to devise a system of merit payments that will not depend upon some degree of favour. One way is to assign allowances to posts within a grade which have special responsibilities or call for special aptitudes. Thus members of the Executive Class may be given managerial control of a local office. Assignment to such a post is not promotion and may not in fact prove to be a very good avenue to promotion. An allowance system would not only be just to the individual, it would also attract officers to such positions in preference to the more specialist or 'staff' jobs at Regional Office and Headquarters. It might be answered that this problem could be met by dividing the two categories into separate grades, but in practice it is desirable to have an interchange between the two types of work in a large department. Also there are specialist jobs in such departments requiring experience on the general grade to which it is desirable to attract special talent, but not on a permanent basis: staff training for example. These, too, could be allowance posts. The idea is not new but it could be widely extended in the circumstances mentioned with considerable advantage to the general efficiency. Another method would be to make special allowances to officers obtaining academic or professional qualifications recognized as of particular value to the Service in general or the department in particular. This could be met by a system of additional increments over and above the existing scale. Such a system already exists, for example, where competence in languages is required. Another method, which would have to be carefully safeguarded, would be the granting of personal increments for special experience to officers who have reached their maximum.[1]

In the field of promotion, as we have seen in Chapter VI, chance is still an important factor even in such a closely regulated service and the problem of comparing the practical competence and actual performance of individuals in a large organization becomes more and more difficult. This is an argument against the generalized grade and the service-wide basis of personnel organization. Much more, however, could be done to improve the working of the present system. The important tasks of reporting and interviewing for promotion are given to members of the appropriate grade often with very little training. It is too lightly assumed

[1] A method widely adopted in other fields.

that these are accomplishments that the senior acquires as he goes along. On the contrary they are highly skilled operations for which much more conscious preparation is needed than is usually at present provided. But this is not the only reason for variable standards. It is recognized that the reporting officers are not usually speaking the same language. Furthermore, the test imposed by the promotion boards need to be more objective than at present and where the selection board method is adopted there is much to be said for the appointment of an independent chairman from outside the promotional unit. In the case of higher posts it might even be desirable to subject short list candidates to a practical test on the lines of the house party system or French 'concours'. Confirmation of promotion should only follow a very rigorous investigation of the promotee's actual achievement on the new work. This could, of course, be much more effectively implemented if the method of demotion had ensured that the level of competence in the higher grade was unchallengeably above that of the grade from which the promotee came. A system needs to be devised whereby more responsibility is attributed to reporting officers who make obvious bad choices.

The promotion process must cease to create the impression that the individual is a passive actor who, having done his best on his job, must supinely await judgment from above. Although it would probably negative the value of the report if its contents were communicated to the reportee, as much information as possible should be given to him and his own comments on his work should be invited rather than treated with suspicion. On appeal an officer who wants to state his case personally should be entitled to do so and there should be well-defined grounds for appeal to a higher court (at least in the case of a class not confined to service in one department). The general feeling in the Civil Service today is that one should be good and await one's turn and do nothing likely to 'blot one's copybook'; although just what this involves no one really knows. It is, for example, widely held that although one may appeal in writing under existing rules it is not really very wise to do so. In this case it is not so much the bureaucratic machine as particular individuals working in establishment sections at the time who do not like to be answered back.

(vi) *Staff Participation*. The present Whitley system is built on sound lines, but it could be more effective if its participants so willed. More attention should be given to participation in administration and this would depend upon the interest and quality of those who accept office. One trouble is that the system is based upon association activity and association office is apt to attract members of a particular type, admirable enough in themselves, often prepared to give unbounded service to their fellows, but not by any means characteristic of their grade. Somehow a more truly representative basis needs to be evolved and this might be found in the direction of allowing some representation to minority groups inside the associations or direct representation by members selected by the grade on the basis of personal character and ideas. The present association and Whitley spokesmen are not called upon to state minority views, but it is by no means obvious that these are unimportant to the administration. This is not a matter in which majority opinion is necessarily right or in which minority opinion has no constructive contribution to make.

INDIVIDUAL OR AUTOMATON?

In the foregoing it has been argued that the individual must somehow be brought into focus. Something must be done to encourage and to reward genuine initiative. This will clearly call for a more dynamic system of personnel management, and one conclusion to be drawn is that as never in the past, establishment staff will have to be specially coached for their work. It is not good enough that they should just pick it up as they go along as is too frequently the practice at present. The same method applied to the medical man would be seen to be both disastrous and criminal. It is hardly less serious in the present connexion if we bear in mind what damage bad staff management can do to the body bureaucratic. It is not that the Civil Service is inefficient in this respect, but that it is far from perfect and the future will call for even greater efficiency. We cannot expect to muddle into it as we muddle into so many things. It is a national characteristic of which we are unwarrantably proud. More effective forethought and preparation are called for. It is not only that human beings are concerned, but the supremacy in the State of civil service over bureaucracy is at issue.

It is one of the virtues of the smaller staff unit that the internal personnel system can be more coherent because the personal touch is still retained and the participants have been brought up together. In a large-scale organization the mere flow of individuals from one branch to another gives them wider horizons and places them in a better position to make comparisons. They easily detect discrepancies in treatment and if these are to their own disadvantage they have a greater excuse for feeling disgruntled. Thus the vices of large-scale organization are apt to be cumulative. This could be an argument against excessive flow between staff in different promotional fields. So long, however, as the general Service class exists transfers will be both desirable and expedient and it will be important that similar levels of opportunity shall be maintained as far as possible. In *The Civil Service: Its Problems and Future* the present author proposed the establishment of a Personnel Organization Board[1] to exercise an oversight of the staffing patterns of the

The Civil Service: Its Problems and Future [1] (2nd Edn. 1948), pp. 131 and 140.

various departments and to control the flow of transfers according to needs and with the object of maintaining the general level of opportunity throughout the Service. Since then the system of promotion pools has greatly facilitated this sort of adjustment, but there should still be ample scope for an impartial board to exercise a general oversight and make adjustments when necessary. It is absurd that an excess either of abilities or special talents should be retained in a stagnant backwater, while in other more dynamic spheres there is a dearth of skills. Of course, there are limits to the way in which human beings can be moved about and it would be the object not only to improve the general efficiency of the administration, but also to maximize the satisfaction of the individual. For example, an officer who feels that his present branch is not using his particular experience and qualifications to the full on his present work (possibly because any special assets he may have are of no particular value there) should be able to put his case to the Board and be entitled to a considered answer.

All such designs to improve efficiency have to steer round one important rock. This is the insistent call upon the State to find billets for 'lame ducks'. Members of the armed forces, and the war-wounded in particular, are usually deemed to be entitled to special privileges. The Americans have paid special attention to this problem and legislation in the United States has ensured that the Civil Service there shall suffer an appreciable margin of incompetency on account of preferences to war veterans in selection and remuneration. Obviously the nation has obligations in this sphere and the incidence of two world wars in the course of one lifetime was bound to affect adversely the efficiency of the Civil Service. The policy of full employment and the State's tendency to use the Civil Service as a means of giving a lead to outside employers both encourage inefficiency. The present policy of encouraging the employment of married women whose home responsibilities detract from their mobility, or older people whose advanced years make them less suitable for work requiring the quick if not very well-stocked mind of the school leaver is bound to render the efficiency problem more difficult.

It may well be that one looming development, namely automation in the office and the replacement of the large-scale routine office by the electronic computer, will frustrate this tendency to find jobs for the mediocre. It is easy to see that these new scientific and technological advances are leading to ways of doing quickly and effectively what large administrative structures have been evolved to do laboriously. They may in fact give a further fillip to large-scale organization in administration merely as a prelude to its diminution. One must bring so much routine work together in one place as to ensure that it can be done there economically by the substitution of an expensive electronic device for the many human workers who are to be largely replaced. But both the manufacture of these intricate machines and their operation and servicing will call for much higher talents and skills than those replaced. Whether humanity has sufficient intellectual resources in reserve to meet this challenge is for the philosopher and educationist to consider and decide. On the threshold of such remarkable changes it would be unrealistic to ignore the possibilities, even if we know too little yet to forecast their effect on our main problems.

There is one thing about which we can be certain. The theses of this chapter will not be disproved by the new advance: rather will they be further emphasized. The encouragement of greater interest and the perfection of greater skills will continue to be a vital administrative requirement. Having done something to put the individual official back into the picture may we now try to see what sort of contribution he should himself set out to make?

CHAPTER XII

NEEDED – A NEW PROFESSIONAL CONSCIOUSNESS

The work of the Civil Service is so varied, encompassing as it does the activities of many occupational groups, that it is not easy to visualize the Service as a single profession. Indeed, there is a strong tendency for certain homogeneous occupational groups inside the central departments to develop their separate identities. The Foreign Service has since the war consolidated into a completely independent professional group, and there is much to be said for regarding the government scientists as a separate professional service very much as are the teachers and members of the armed forces. Their function is research and not administration. Certain other specialist groups, such as medical men and lawyers, have special loyalties outside the public service and it seems desirable that they should normally be birds of passage in the Civil Service, bringing to it the invaluable advantage of their outside experience and passing on later to adventure in the wider fields of their vocation. Specialist work in a public department cannot usually have such a broadening influence as experience in the more general reaches of the profession and it seems desirable that the number of professionals who become permanent civil servants should be reduced to a minimum. On the other hand there are those specialist groups, like the engineers of the Post Office and the naval architects of the Admiralty, whose life's work must mainly lie inside the government service: they can properly be integrated into the Civil Service.

The distinctive mark of the civil servant as a member of a profession rests upon his special expertness in government administration. His job is administration and his normal field of operations an office, whether he be a typist or the skilled adviser on top policy. It has certainly been suggested in this study that various departments or groups of departments have sufficiently differentiated techniques to justify the creation of separate functional services (on the lines of the Foreign Service), but there is no reason why such a development into more manageable occupational groups should preclude their broader integration into a main administration service.

It is doubtful whether in his notable address, *Portrait of a Profession*, Sir Edward Bridges had any such broadly based profession in mind. It is the custom to regard the Administrative Class as the Civil Service profession *par excellence* and there is not much evidence that members of the other Civil Service classes set any great store by their professional status. There is, of course, and rightly so, a touch of selectness about the membership of any profession which lends itself to the normal outlook of an *élite*. The Civil Service in its wider guise has little sense of professionship. In fact the pervasion of the rank and file by the spirit of trade unionism, which places a premium upon equalitarianism and levelling out, is against the growth of a true professional *esprit*. For example, the staff associations are more intent upon obtaining equality of pay and conditions for temporary members on the score of justice than of ensuring that such members should first be as fully qualified and competent as their permanent colleagues. The general effect of all this, as well as of the drawbacks discussed in the preceding chapter, is to place mediocrity on a pinnacle and to depress any special competence to the level of the mass. It is the existence of the *élite* that prevents this trend from moving to its ultimate conclusion. The abolition of the *élite* therefore presupposes the abolition of the mediocrity complex, otherwise the last condition will be much worse than the first.

A one class, or classless, system presupposes a scheme in which there is equality of opportunity, a scheme in which in fact the individual has had his individualism restored. Somehow the civil servant must have his initiative given back to him. Otherwise the Civil Service of the future will be peopled by born slaves who have no wish to think for themselves. Such a slave mentality is a preconditioning factor of bureaucracy, for in the making of your bureaucrat freedom of thought has no place. How then shall the individuality of the civil servant be restored?

THE TASK OF STAFF TRAINING

In the first place the general attitude to staff training must be radically altered and not least on the part of the individual civil servant. The time has passed when the new entrant, successful at a competitive examination of high academic standard, could be considered sufficiently trained in his profession by the mere process of doing his job. This proposition would be true in any case in face of the rapid advance of administrative techniques and the heightened demand made upon the individual practitioner by the more complex requirements of modern administration; but the shocking truth, not generally recognized, is that the average civil servant today is less well equipped educationally than his forebears. Only a small proportion of the present office grades have qualified at an educational level commensurate with the needs of their profession and the principle of open competition has been watered down for reasons that have little connection with the real needs of the State service.

It has to be recognized that the saving of money on training, an easy way for the economizer to earn applause under our system of national finance, is as much a false economy as is a similar attitude to education in the national sphere. The recent recession from the Assheton summit would have been less possible had it not been for the apathy inside the Civil Service, an apathy considerably strengthened by the general experience of so many civil servants, which infuses them with a definite prejudice against training. The lazy and the mediocre combine to form a majority band always sufficiently vocal to cry down those who support more constructive views. A national trend against examinations (which of course are so anti-egalitarian in effect!) helps to give the attitude inside the Civil Service an appearance of respectable realism which is basically unsound and indeed against the long term interests of the civil servants themselves.

The departments are fully alive to the need for equipping their recruits with a sound experience and knowledge of their own particular functions and can be depended upon to do what is necessary both by the time-honoured method of training at the desk or bench, which is indeed still the most valuable method of training in all professions, and by some formal training at training centres through lectures and discussion. They are less likely to bother about training their staffs in general office procedures, i.e. the basic methods of administration, or to spend much time on background training which is concerned with general Civil Service practice as well as the relationships of the departments with other sectors of the national administration. The neglect of the former is even more serious today when the Civil Service has absorbed so many who are deficient in penmanship and literary skills: the virtual ignoring of the latter fails completely to recognize that the official knowledgeable on the wider government environment is *ipso facto* a better public servant than his narrowly self-centred colleague. A knowledge and understanding of the wider reasons surrounding his work will at a minimum have the great advantage of instilling interest in work that is often of a routine nature. The good official must be interested in what he is doing. The outstanding lesson of the Crichel Down case[1] is surely that the inefficient self-centred official is as much a threat to public freedom as any deficiency in the constitutional system that may have been revealed by this sad sequence of events.

There is scope for more co-operation between the departments in training matters that are of general concern. There is also a case for the setting up of a Civil Service Staff Training College. It is true that the provision of general courses is to a large extent within the present province of the Treasury's Training and Education Division, but recent experience suggests that this branch should be confined to general advice and administration, and that the Civil Service training organization should be separated under an independent director, advised by an expert committee representative of both the official and staff interests.

[1] See R. D. Brown *The Battle of Crichel Down* (1955).

The proposed college should have a separate budget and be responsible for the provision of training common to the Civil Service, in such subjects as Civil Service History and Procedures, Official Correspondence and the Handling of Files, Establishment Work, Public Relations, Teaching Techniques, Conduct of Public Business, and so forth. While such a college should make full use of outside assistance, its teaching staff should come mainly from inside the departments and have practical experience of how the machine works: its methods should be soundly based upon the best practices of the Civil Service. In the interests of economy courses could be provided in the regions except where small numbers or other reasons rendered a national basis desirable.

The civil servant is entitled to a minimum service of this sort to fit him into his profession, but the general nature of his pre-entry education (except where he is recruited as a specialist) places upon him the responsibility of taking a more active part than at present in pursuing this objective.

THE NEED FOR PROFESSIONAL STUDIES

Beyond the normal confines of staff training, which is the responsibility of the authorities themselves, covering both the techniques peculiar to the individual departments and the general practical subjects appropriate to the proposed Civil Service Staff Training College, there is the academic field of public administration in which all officials, as public servants should be actively interested. Unfortunately the lack of any such accepted professional discipline[1] has greatly reinforced the antipathy to specialized professional study to which the natural apathy of the civil servants themselves has contributed. It is not merely that the majority have failed to recognize that the present situation is to their disadvantage, reducing their status through the lack of accepted professional expertise, but that the minority who hold more active views individually find themselves confronted by a vacuum in the educational system that cannot be filled in any short term period.

There is little common ground between Civil Service staff training as it is at present and the academic study of public administration in so far as it exists at all in this country. In the universities in Britain, public administration, with rare exceptions, consists of a conglomeration of studies in political science, economics and sociology, all very useful as basic introductory disciplines for the study of public administration, as

[1] There is in consequence a dearth of suitable books on the subject, unless one goes to America, where the political and social background is sufficiently different to reduce considerably the value to us of their many authoritative works. In order to introduce students to the subject the present author has written two books, both published by Staples Press Ltd., namely, *An Introduction to Public Administration* and *The Essentials of Public Administration*.

a practical art and science, rather than the real live subject itself. It is mainly controlled by specialists in other academic fields who have little live realization of what public administration means (and even those who have had practical experience themselves, mainly in wartime, are obviously too involved in other important fields merely to maintain much less to extend their practical knowledge of the public administration field). But the real reason why the subject has not developed as far as it should have done, and in fact has done in the United States and elsewhere, lies in the lack of demand. Nobody really wants to study public administration.

The competitors at the Civil Service examinations are not required to undertake such studies before they enter the Service: they are not encouraged to do so afterwards. The administrative *élite* are in the same position and if by the very nature of their work they do become life-long students and practitioners in the subject there is little urge among them to participate in its general advancement.[1] In fact the very nature of their assignment may well suggest to them that no one but themselves has any real reason to be interested in such studies. For the member of a less august class to show such interest is to some extent a presumption, albeit a presumption that in the existing situation can be safely ignored.

A first step to breaking the vicious circle and to creating a demand of the right sort would be official recognition that the study of public administration was a desirable activity on the part of any civil servant, and the assignment of a recognized status to the existing diplomas and certificates in the subject. The obvious mode of recognition would be the granting of a special increment or increments to holders of accredited qualifications. This would give due encouragement, as is provided in other professional spheres, without creating any claim to advancement purely on the strength of success in such examinations. Such study obviously would not necessarily demonstrate a particular individual's competence for a higher grade although, other things being equal, it would naturally be one of the factors entering into the decision. On the other hand the definite advantage to the Civil Service as a whole of having a more professionally knowledgeable membership could fairly be paid for by additional remuneration without doing anyone an injustice.

In time, however, the situation might well change. With the extension

[1] Although the Royal Institute of Public Administration does not publish a breakdown of its membership figures it is clear that support from the Administrative Class for the only organization in this country that exists to advance the study and practice of Public Administration is not very widespread. Of the Institute's total individual membership in this country during 1955, of 2,210, about 1,000 are stationed in London where most of the Administrative Class is employed. This exiguous total not only covers all classes of the Civil Service but also officials in Local Government and the Public Corporations. The reader can easily draw his own conclusions!

of such studies and their consequent improvement it might well be possible to devise certain minimum professional qualifications, the holding of which would give an officer a definite right to consideration for higher administrative posts. As a result of increased demand for public administration studies, a considerable improvement in the present academic facilities could be anticipated, as well as the development of the subject itself as a more effective discipline. More teachers skilled in the subject would gradually become available; more satisfactory texts would begin to flow from the printing houses. There is so much leeway to be made up that the smallest change in outlook could lead to almost spectacular results. Gradually the present gap between staff training and the academic world would be closed with mutual advantage, since in this subject as much as in any the marriage of practice with theory is essential. Neither the official training centres nor the schools can do the job on their own. They must co-operate by pooling their very different experiences.

Not the least practical advantage of such a development would be the weakening of the strong parochial tendencies of the departments. The exchange of ideas through common study would lead to the exploration of specialist problems common to a number of departments. For example, the inspectors of one department would gain access to the experience of inspectors elsewhere and this would enable them to examine and assess both the similarities and the differences in practice appropriate to different services and situations. There is today much experience and knowledge stultified in official backwaters for the want not merely of the machinery, but of the habit or impulse to exchange ideas which a truly professional outlook would encourage.

The general acceptance of public administration as a separate academic discipline and the formulation of professional standards, in terms of both theoretical qualification and practical experience, would make it possible to admit older persons to the Civil Service competitions, as in the case of other professions, upon the minimum requirement of holding such qualifications. It should become just as much an anachronism to give a novice, however highly placed, a high administrative job as to give the same individual a high medical or engineering post. It is certainly not generally realized how much present inefficiency is due to the placing in responsible positions of people who lack the right administrative talent and experience. In higher positions the policy of learning by doing is too expensive to be tolerated. The evil is masked by the fact that administration is a team job in which it is not easy to assign personal responsibility for results and the figurehead can easily hide his incompetence under a cloak of suavity and bluff, except of course to his immediate subordinates whose views are not usually called for.

WANTED, A NEW OUTLOOK

The trouble with the large-scale Civil Service organization is that the individual civil servant counts for nothing. There is nothing but his own morale and personal energy to impel him to do his best. Many of course do so, largely because they are made that way and have discovered the ultimate truth that a job well done is its own best reward, one of the highest rewards that anyone can obtain from life. But there are plenty of other types – the lazy, the timid, the unenterprising – who soon learn that the line of least resistance is the most congenial and rewarding and whose sense of public service is not highly developed. The lower standards and looser methods of recruitment during these latter years have greatly increased this element and it is a public necessity that the trend should be reversed.

The individual officer knows that he is not likely to receive full credit for what he does: sometimes those above him will not even be aware of the full implications of what he personally is doing. Some will do their utmost to take credit for his successes whilst leaving him to take the blame for any failure. And even when he receives due credit from his immediate superiors they will still have the task of pressing his case further up the line. There are many human reasons why they will sometimes fail in this. The official himself cannot do very much about it since he cannot in fact know what is going on behind the scenes. He is given few opportunities normally to make his own representations to high authority – though of course he may obtain publicity as a member of the departmental drama society or by acting the goat at the annual Christmas party.

Something must be done to put the individual official back into the picture. As a member of a nation-wide profession the civil servant must have the means to make representations to a central body if he feels at any time that the most is not being made of his capacity and experience in the service of the State. At the moment he is bound constitutionally within the confines of the department in which he serves. There is no avenue of appeal beyond the head of the department. Obviously this is least important to a member of the Administrative Class who may well find it less difficult to drop a word in the right quarter without breaking the rules.

A PROFESSIONAL COUNCIL FOR THE CIVIL SERVICE

What is wanted is a new sort of Professional Council for the Civil Service. At present the civil servant's professional interests are the responsibility of a diversity of authorities. First, there is the Treasury, both as the main staff agency of the central departments, promulgating the internal law of the Civil Service, and as the place in which the informal general staff of the Service meets under the leadership of the Head of the Civil Service, the place in fact where the ruling *élite*, in the persons of senior members of the Administrative Class, foregather to formulate whatever professional policy is at present formulated. This latter is a clandestine arrangement when compared with the various statutory councils authorized for the other major professions. Second, there is the National Whitley Council on which leaders of both Official and Staff elements in the Civil Service come together. But, although by its constitution this Council is entitled to deal with many matters that are of professional import, in practice it has to devote most of its time to problems that fall within the normal sphere of trade unionism. It is indeed not practicable to draw a precise line between trade union and professional functions, particularly as in other fields there are bodies that concern themselves with both types of function. Third, there are the Civil Service staff associations themselves, some of which take a greater interest than others in matters of a broadly professional character. In the main, however, the interest of these associations in the general standards and advancement of their profession has been little more than sporadic. Fourth, there is the Royal Institute of Public Administration, which, covering as it does all branches of public administration, cannot give special attention to the professional interests of the Civil Service, although it is indeed an organization that has an important contribution to make in this sphere. Fifth, and last, there is the Civil Service Council for Further Education, a representative Whitley organization, which is concerned with the civil servant's spare time craft and cultural activities, but is precluded by its general policy from placing greater emphasis on professional studies than on any other educational activities.

With such a plethora of overlapping authorities, each with its own essential functions, it is hardly surprising that little concentrated attention has been given to the development of a Civil Service professional consciousness on a broad basis. It might have been hoped that the National Whitley Council would have given a lead in this direction, but on past showing one can hardly be optimistic on the possibility of a more active approach in the future. Presumably the Official Side are quite satisfied with things as they are, while the Staff Side is too heterogeneous to be able to give a professional council the initial support that it would require.

The main hope is that a few of the leading associations will come together to form such a Council, on which the various interested bodies and individual civil servants would be represented. Its broad objects might be:

(i) to maintain the morale and general standards of the Civil Service profession, by discussion of and inquiry into cases where standards and practices applied are alleged to be below the level that the public has a right to expect from its servants;

(ii) to explore ways and means of improving the professional efficiency of present members of the Civil Service;

(iii) to support measures aiming at raising the civil servants' *esprit de corps*;

(iv) to encourage the advancement of Civil Service learning and aid the exchange of information that has a particular professional relevance;

(v) to undertake research into subjects that have a close bearing upon the efficiency of the Civil Service; and

(vi) to handle public relations with a view to making the public more aware of the Civil Service's aims and activities and to protect its good name from ill-considered and unjust criticism.

Such an organization would need to be established on a voluntary basis, and would require the support of a small group of staff associations as independent bodies, but its aim should be to represent all sections of the Civil Service both corporately and as individuals who support the ideal of professionalism as applicable to their occupation.

The greatest advantage of the establishment of a Professional Council of the Civil Service would centre in its provision of a forum in which civil servants could freely and frankly discuss all matters relating to their conduct and efficiency as members of the profession and to which they could being fresh ideas for ensuring the maximum professional contribution to the general well-being. Through such a Council the Civil Service could participate in bringing informed criticism to bear on the evils of bureaucracy without sacrificing their present virtue of impersonality in public affairs. It is certain that if reforms are ever undertaken in the Civil Service with a view to introducing a real incentives system and bringing the individual official back into the picture as a live agent and human being the existence of such a Council would be invaluable in facilitating changes that are long overdue.

CHAPTER XIII

THE PUBLIC'S PART

It may very well be that in the long run the public gets the Civil Service it deserves. In the recent historical circumstances of Britain, however, there is a good deal of evidence to support the proposition that the British public have for long had a better Civil Service than it is entitled to. Certainly it has always tempered a general respect for its servants' good intentions with a strong inclination to believe the worst of their competence. Today the situation that cradled the old Civil Service is so quickly disintegrating that it is doubtful whether the public will long continue to rejoice in its bureaucratic good fortune. Since the middle of the last century the nation has been able at modest cost to tap off from the national fund of human talent rather a larger proportion of talent for the public services than they really needed. Now the position is being rapidly reversed. With much greater needs, created by the growing complexity of the public administrative sectors of the national economy, the Civil Service is being heavily pressed by the demands on this fund which are being made by other sectors of the economy, and despite the improved supplies made available by an advancing educational system there is grave doubt whether the Civil Service manages to maintain its ground. It will certainly not do so at the prices that the Treasury, as the nation's careful watchdog, has so far been prepared to pay.

Today – many would say unfortunately – the nation's choice is not between bureaucracy and no bureaucracy: it is between bureaucracy by design and bureaucracy by default; the bureaucracy of efficiency and the bureaucracy of incompetence. The former has its dangers and needs careful safeguards; the latter spells inevitable disaster. When Rome declined, its bureaucracy did not disappear; it became an increasing burden upon a dwindling eminence. From an efficient service it declined into an inefficient bureaucracy, a cancer absorbing the dwindling nourishment of a dying civilization. Today's symptoms are not so dissimilar as to encourage complacency.

The virtue of civil service, a Victorian invention, was that it emphasized the element of service and depreciated the bureaucratic element. The spirit of the aristocracy was subtly absorbed into the new democratic system of government, and while the functions of the State remained simple enough for personal ministerial manipulation the subordination of the Civil Service could be understood by the makers of governments. But as the tasks of administration became more complex and the makers of government both more numerous and in general less well-informed, the direct link of understanding between governors and officials became more tenuous. It happened too that the Civil Service itself, largely by reason of historical causes, expanded in a way least likely to maintain its general standards of efficiency and it failed to develop a wide professional consciousness and techniques of administration commensurate with its responsibilities.

The very method of policy-making in a democracy by amateurs rather than experts assumed the existence of a body of experts competent to work out the administrative means for the policy's effective implementation. The failure of social reformers to appreciate the need to ascertain in practice whether their theoretical schemes are in fact viable administratively, constitutes one of the most startling criticisms of the wisdom of our political and academic leaders. It was an outstanding characteristic of the grand social plan adopted under popular inspiration by the Labour Government of 1945–50 that, generally speaking, the administrative necessities of the accepted schemes had not been adequately considered before the administrators were given the order to go ahead with the job. Politicians were often compelled to pursue objectives that were far beyond the capacity of existing institutions. It is a remarkable tribute to the Civil Service that, despite this, its part of the task was so effectively undertaken. How much more effective might have been the results if the social reformers and their political co-partners had in the earlier discussion stages given more thought to the administrative implications of their schemes!

But it must not be forgotten that, in a democracy, the social reformers have to sell their ideas to the people, who are certainly not likely to be interested in administration as such, or to thank those who attempt to explain to them why something they would like very much from the State cannot immediately be provided. Their views on the Administration are based partly on their personal experiences of officialdom, partly upon the interpretation of official, or bureaucratic, activities conveyed to them by the Press. As agents whose duty it often is to prevent evasion by the citizen of his legal responsibilities and particularly to obtain from him monies due in taxation the Civil Service has to stand the inevitable brunt of the citizen's dislike of officialdom throughout the ages. The fact that in the Welfare State by far the major part of the official's activities are directed to the advantage of the individual citizen has not yet been sufficiently widely recognized to outweigh the normal reaction of the people to bureaucracy. They do not regard the Civil Service as their very good servants and there is little evidence that in their schooling in citizenship this fact is brought home to them with sufficient insistence.

THE PRESS'S PART

The Press is very much at fault. This is partly due to their own ignorance and partly due to the natural proclivity of publicists to play to the gallery. It may well be, too, that the immemorial attack upon the Civil Service for its alleged slacking and excessive capacity for tea drinking arise largely from a national guilt complex on these very matters. The ignorance of the Press on many subjects with which they are called upon to deal immediately and without much time for thought and research is widely attested by the garbled accounts that appear in the most responsible organs on matters of which one has sufficient expert knowledge to judge. This is, however, an inevitable risk of their profession, one that can only be reduced by improved professional education and training, a matter in which journalism is very similarly placed to public administration. The answer here is clearly a much closer and more sympathetic liaison between the Press and Public Administration with the object of ensuring not that the former should represent the views of the latter – that after all is the latter's own business – but to ensure that they get their facts right. After all these are both public services, resting on similar ideals but frequently adopting diametrically opposed methods. The former's job is to disseminate news and views, the latter's to carry out their functions impartially and without shouting.

Since the ultimate effectiveness of democratic government depends largely upon the understanding of the people, it follows that the Press in misrepresenting public administration to the people is knowingly obstructing the advance in effectiveness of popular government. It is true that today public affairs have become so complex that it is impossible even for the student or the professor to be expert in more than a limited field. If, therefore, democracy depends upon popular understanding it is clear that the prospects for democracy become less and less as the years pass. There are, however, broad principles of citizenship which it is the duty of both the educational system and the Press to disseminate and it is within the framework of such knowledge that the position of the Civil Service, as the people's professional agency, should be understood. That it is not generally understood is proof that the job of popular instruction is not being effectively performed. It would be better if the political 'scientists' paid a little more attention to this important subject, even at the expense of some of the very erudite, philosophic, and occasionally impractical problems on which they delight to exercise their reasoning capacities.

Effective popular government depends upon an enlightened citizenship, well schooled in political knowledge and capable of discussing practical problems without undue emphasis upon emotional and sentimental factors. No such community has ever yet existed. When it does the hour of human regeneration will be at hand. In the meantime we must accept the quite considerable mercies we already have in the functioning of our parliamentary system and seek by every means to improve upon them.

THE REPRESENTATIVE'S PART

Here then is the saving institution – the representative council in both central and local government. If the people show sufficient interest in their own political affairs to choose responsible representatives and give support to politicians who, if eventually called to ministerial positions, will demonstrate the considerable administrative capacity needed to fulfil their responsibilities effectively, all will be well. It would seem therefore that, apart from the need for the people to be knowledgeable as well as interested in the general processes of self-government and for the civil servants to be better skilled professionally, as discussed in the last chapter, it is equally necessary that the practical politicians should be well enough informed to act as the executive agents of the former *vis-à-vis* the latter. They must be able both to illuminate the administrative situation to the people and to control the administrative activities of the civil servants, altogether an exceedingly exhausting requirement when one takes into account the wide range of the statesman's responsibilities. Old hands at the game, with whom the country is fortunate to be well endowed, through long service and assiduous labour will in time have achieved some perfection in this, but the question to be asked is whether the newcomer should continue to be recruited as a carefree amateur whose knowledge of administration may amount to little or nothing.

The intensive study of public administration should clearly not be confined to the professional administrator. Every council member in the country, whether at Westminster or Little Muddleton, should be well informed on this subject. That many are not, both personal pronouncement and public achievement too frequently bear witness. The practical man will of course resent any such proposal as being academic and one can sympathize with the simple soul who has a leaning towards a simple world. Most of us have this in our hearts even when we do not admit it! Unfortunately all that has gone with the achievements of science. Atomic energy as the common man's new servant would never have been released if practice had been unsupported by much brilliant theorizing. The amateur, we must hope, will still have his place – it is the supreme ideal of democracy that he should – but it is no longer practicable for him to occupy effectively the positions of political control. In a scientific world the policy of setting the blind to lead the blind can only lead to disaster. Inevitably, too, the professional administrator will gain the upper hand and the people will find themselves the slaves of their erstwhile servants. Thus the professional advance considered essential in our last chapter can only be safeguarded by a corresponding advance on the part of the people and the politicians.

The crux of the whole problem rests within the four walls of Parliament. Here is represented the sovereign power of the people. Even if the centre of gravity has, particularly since the turn of the century, moved inexorably towards the Executive it is still inside Parliament that the final authority lies. It is there that the ministerial administrator can be called to account and it is a good thing that responsibility for administration should be concentrated upon the shoulders of such administrators. There would be no surer way than the creation of close day-to-day contacts between the legislature and the administration of causing the Civil Service to sacrifice its professional attitudes to politics and to become an intriguing bureaucracy. The present doctrine of ministerial responsibility is a powerful dam against the growth of bureaucracy.

On the other hand Parliament needs to be well informed about the administration, and it is doubtful whether it can be sufficiently well informed if it depends mainly upon the information provided by aggrieved members of the public or through the interested statements of ministers. Of course, it also has the informed reports of occasional committees and royal commissions, but a more continuous court of reference seems to be needed under modern conditions. The existence of a vigorous school of public administration would be a greater advantage to no one than to the legislator who, as an individual, would have access to an important centre of impartial information.

However, there seems to be no valid reason why Parliament should not have its own standing committee on the Civil Service to keep it up to date on the current practices of public administration inside the departments. Proposals have been made from time to time that a series of parliamentary committees should be established to cover, in an advisory-exploratory capacity, specific State departments or series of departments. Such a system has certainly had well-informed advocates and equally well-informed opponents, but this is largely a political problem that it is not appropriate to discuss here. From the administrative viewpoint there appears to be no more objection to the setting up of an expert Select Committee on the Civil Service, on the lines suggested by the National Expenditure Committee in 1942[1], than there is to the existence of the Public Accounts Committee, which has proved so valuable in keeping Parliament informed on the financial activities of the departments. The proposed committee would not have the disadvantage of the suggested multiple committee system of adding greatly to the burden of Parliament by the drawing off of so many members or

[1] Sixteenth Report from the Select Committee on National Expenditure. Session 1941–2, pp. 38–9.

of interfering with the policy responsibilities of ministers. Its job would be to conduct a continuing review of the machinery of government with particular emphasis on administrative efficiency and personnel problems, and to report periodically to Parliament. The wartime Committee's suggestion that it should have the assistance of a professionally appointed Assessor and small expert staff would appear to be essential to the success of such a scheme.

It is true that this proposal was rejected by the Government-of-the-day. There is nothing surprising in the fact that ministers should find much to object to in the setting up of a committee entitled to animadvert upon their administrative activities or that in this they should receive enthusiastic support from their professional advisers, but clearly the interests of Parliament and people must be paramount. Such a committee seems to be a necessity if in future Parliament is effectively to exercise its critical functions in relation to public administration, which is very much a closed book to outsiders. The effective interpretation of the administration to the country is surely one of the important outstanding problems of statecraft, and any means for improving the position should not be rejected in the guise of mere theory. If the Public Accounts Committee had never been instituted, or no senior civil servant had ever been appointed Accounting Officer for his department directly responsible to Parliament, the conventional political theorists would find no difficulty in proving them incompatible with the spirit of the constitution. In both cases theory stands confounded by effective practice. And so no doubt would have been the case of the wartime proposal for a standing Civil Service Parliamentary Committee had it been adopted.

DANGERS OF SPOILS

There is one final problem to be touched upon: namely, the tendency of all communities, and particularly democratic communities, to regard the public service as an incomparable dumping ground for those to whom the State owes a debt, a cheap way of meeting the nation's obligations to individuals. It is this tendency that has elsewhere greatly assisted the development of spoils methods of meeting old party debts, with a consequent grave devaluation of public office and depreciation in public efficiency. For the individual patronage of oligarchy is substituted the group patronage of democracy.

After a war there is always a powerful demand from diverse interests for places to be found for them in the public service. Obviously disabled ex-Service people receive special consideration and there is no doubt that office work provides suitable posts for such deserving members of the community. But even for these the Civil Service should not become a dumping ground for the incompetent. The State's debt to the individual is best paid by means of an adequate pensions system, work then being found on a competitive basis, the disabled recruit being remunerated for these services competitively according to his capacities. In this way the individual debt is adequately met and the public interest adequately protected. There are almost certain to be sufficient suitable candidates among the disabled to render it unnecessary to reduce the normal standards of the profession on their behalf. Any such reduction, if it be agreed to, is bound to lead to a general all-round lowering of efficiency, with considerable loss to the community. This situation undoubtedly arose in the British Civil Service after the First World War. After the Second, the ex-Service element seems to have been treated on a surer basis of personal equity, compatible with the maintenance of professional competence. On the other hand government policy of using the Civil Service as an example in other directions, e.g. the employment of married women and of older-aged workers, may have serious effects in reducing the general competence of the Civil Service. It is important for the people to understand how far their interests rest upon the maintenance of the highest possible levels of Civil Service efficiency and how far it is against their interests to permit the State Service to be used as a vehicle for a new sort of group patronage.

Whether or not in the long run the people get the Civil Service they deserve, it is to their advantage to deserve the best they can get. Bureaucracy in any of its guises is too expensive a luxury for any community to be willing to support it. Despite the criticisms of this book – all of which are put forward in a constructive spirit – the British Civil Service is still essentially anti-bureaucratic in outlook. Its development towards a more effective professional ideal is an objective greatly to be desired and needing very much to be encouraged.

CHAPTER XIV

POSTSCRIPT: A CHANGING SERVICE IN A CHANGING WORLD

The publication, since the completion of the preceding chapters, of the Report of the Royal Commission on the Civil Service, makes a postscript desirable to bring the reader up to date. It also marks a further stage in the history of the Civil Service. Certainly the limited nature of its content emphasizes the importance of facing up to the approaching crisis of the Civil Service, the threat of which does not appear to have worried the Commissioners sufficiently, if indeed they recognized its existence.

RECAPITULATION

The Civil Service today still embodies the principles and ideas of the notable report signed by Trevelyan and Northcote in 1853. It took a long time for the new pattern to cover the whole Civil Service and it was not really before the end of the first decade of the twentieth century that the main principles of impartial selection, open competition, and classification on the basis of a service-wide division of labour had been substantially accepted. Even then pockets of patronage still survived; many departments still continued to maintain their separate grade patterns; while generally the bipartite division was becoming somewhat too simple for an administrative situation growing more complicated with the steadily spreading responsibilities of the central government.

After the hectic interlude of the First World War, which at least acclimatized the Civil Service to the acceptance of women as officials and demonstrated to some outside administrators that public administration was less simple than they had in their freer world imagined, the Civil Service returned thankfully to its former line of development. The Reorganization of 1920 brought the system up to date by placing the general classification on a tripartite instead of a bipartite basis. But while this greatly increased the uniformity of the Civil Service structure by extending the sphere of the general Treasury classes, some departments continued to maintain their own grading patterns in order to meet their specialized functional requirements. Despite greatly improved central direction through the Treasury, departmentalization still continued vigorously in the sphere of day-to-day personnel management. This was, of course, very desirable in such a large-scale organization provided it was not pressed to extremes. One notable change at that time, certainly not visualized in the age of Trevelyan and Northcote was the tempering of paternal leadership by the introduction of an effective system of joint consultation in the guise of Whitleyism. In future the rank and file, through their representatives, were to be able to participate in moulding their own conditions of service and the methods of staff management employed by the administration. For example, notable improvements were made in the promotion system which, however, continued on a strictly departmental basis.

By the eve of the Second World War there had not occurred any radical change in the situation. Outwardly the Civil Service not only appeared to be the legitimate child of 1853 but obviously embodied the spirit of the early reformers and had the capacities needed to measure up to the developing situation. Only one aspect was calculated to worry the forward-looking administrator; namely, the radical dislocation of the Civil Service's age grouping brought about by the post-war recruitment of older ex-Servicemen, but even this was now being gradually readjusted by the full return to open competitive recruitment at school-leaving levels. Despite the lowering of recruitment standards during the early post-war period, the existing and potential capacities of the highly educated direct entrants were still sufficient in the aggregate to outweigh the amount of intellectual dilution that the Civil Service had then suffered.

The catalytic effect of the Second World War and the impact of the subsequent peace which, unlike the former peace, did not presume the resumption of a world that had passed away, altered the whole outlook. The new Civil Service had to be expanded to meet the increasing demands of an accelerated process of socialization and thus the degree of impersonality which we have shown in earlier chapters to be the biggest stumbling block of effective staff management, was further accentuated. At the same time the work of the Civil Service was growing more complex with the introduction of new methods and machines and this called for greater rather than lesser skills on the part of officials. One important aspect of this development, namely the increase in direct contacts between members of the Civil Service and the public, was having a considerable influence upon the nature of the civil servant's daily tasks. Furthermore, the greater variety of the State's responsibilities called for the services of many experts whose primary function as civil servants was centred in some professional specialization instead of in administration as such. Their work, instead of being solely advisory, was in many directions taking on more and more an executive slant. The most notable post-war development in the Civil Service was the reorganization of these professional experts, hitherto recruited and employed on a purely departmental basis, into all-service hierarchies on patterns similar to the administrative-clerical sectors of the Civil

Service. The principles of 1853 were still at work in a situation that would have been incomprehensible to their originators.

During this time the external situation had changed so much that even a Civil Service gradually developed in peacetime on the old assumptions, would have found it difficult to gear itself successfully to its new tasks. The growth of socialization, the spread of large-scale organization, and the continuing advances of science and invention – speeded up beyond all expectations, except perhaps in the novels of H. G. Wells, by the exigencies of war, which has always been the most effective midwife to administrative revolution – add up to a challenge that only a most resilient and farsighted administration was likely to cope with. Not only does the nation in general require more of the administrative and other resources that the Civil Service needs, but the diminished attractiveness in the new situation of the Civil Service as a career was bound to place it in an inferior position in the labour world. Such a situation calls for a policy of making the Civil Service more attractive to the potential recruit not merely in terms of standard of living, which can be over-emphasized, but in terms of prestige and inspiration. The Press and the people, or at least some of them, have vied in depreciating the work of officialdom and indeed official policy, in two not entirely compatible ways, has contributed further to worsen the position.

The first of these is the policy adopted during the war of using the Civil Service as an example to lead the country into ways desired by the Government. Thus the Civil Service, willingly indeed, but against a just promise of post-war restoration, was led to give up certain advantages in hours and leave and other conditions. This policy has been since continued, e.g. in introducing into the service the employment of married women, the principle of equal pay and latterly the recruitment of the elderly. All these changes may be desirable, and indeed in our present national situation inevitable, but this does not mean that administratively they can be accommodated in the existing system without radical adjustments and in some directions undesirable repercussions. The second policy in question is the trend to assimilate the Civil Service's conditions of service with those of the rest of the employed classes. Where this means worsening the conditions, it obviously makes the job of recruitment more difficult.

The Civil Service has shared with the rest of the middle group the losses in status and purchasing power inevitable in a period of wartime expense and working class advance, but the striking aspect of the situation is that in comparison with analogous occupations, such as bank clerks, local government officers and teachers, the Civil Service's position has become relatively less attractive[1]. It is therefore hardly a

[1] See, for example, two articles in *The Economist* (January 1956), Vol. CLXXVIII, pp. 184 and 278.

matter for surprise that the post-war Civil Service is finding it increasingly difficult to recruit sufficient persons of the type it requires and that this position was badly deteriorating even while the Priestley Commission was sitting.

But there is another factor that can hardly be exaggerated in assessing the probable impact of the approaching crisis: namely, the dislocation of the age grouping of the Civil Service. The failure to bring in a full quota of young open competition entrants during the 'twenties and later is now showing up seriously, and of course the evil is being intensified by the wartime gap from 1939 to 1945, followed by the failure of post-war recruitment to restore the flow to the required level. It is important to the efficiency of a service based upon a life career that the age groupings should be evenly balanced, with rather larger groups at the base of the pyramid to deal with routine work and provide for normal wastage. Recruitment at higher ages not only dislocates the system and renders staff management more difficult but (except where such late age entrants bring in with them an experience for which the Service has a special need) it also, by shortening the average official life of the civil servant, reduces the aggregate of the valuable skills that depend largely upon the accumulation of experience in public administration.

Reference to Table VI on page 206 will show how the age banding of the present Civil Service has grown top heavy. Unless more younger recruits can be attracted this position will worsen and the aggregate of available experience decrease.

It may be suggested that the disappearance during the next few years from the active scene of a large body of older civil servants, as is certainly foreshadowed by the table, will be a good thing if only because the older officials tend to be the most hidebound and least resilient in meeting new situations. This, of course, is true, but cannot be considered independently of the prospects of replacing the experienced by an equally large band of youthful officials of the right calibre and potentialities. Table VI shows that a large number of civil servants are now being retained after the hitherto normal retiring age of sixty, a system which greatly increases the conservatism of the Civil Service at a time when increased resilience is the great need.

There is, however, another side of the picture. The top age groups at present include a large number who were recruited under the old conditions. Many of them carry forward the traditions of the Civil Service of the 1914 period. When they go a tradition will have ended. What have their successors to put in its place?

This is a leading question. The Civil Service does not encourage its middle grades to think about their professional responsibilities. It is to be feared that only a minority of the existing middle band of civil servants have been brought up to face the grave responsibilities that lie ahead of them. There is no suggestion here that they will fall short of their task when the day comes, but unlike their predecessors they will not have the skilled assistance below them which they themselves have been providing for the present seniors. With the diminution of recruitment at the base the task of the leaders becomes more difficult. It could easily be that the new leaders of the Civil Service in a few years' time will find their resources inadequate to the even more complex situation by which they will inevitably be faced. This is the shadow of the grave crisis by which the Civil Service is today faced.

TABLE VI

Age Distribution in the Civil Service (Established Non-Industrial Staff) on January 1st, 1955

Age	Administrative	Executive	All grades
Under 20	—	179	17,836
20–24	92	2,589	34,426
25–29	307	3,126	41,309
30–34	415	8,975	65,758
35–39	595	8,641	58,166
40–44	531	7,531	59,193
45–49	402	5,453	53,989
50–54	311	7,031	53,165
55–59	446	15,474	71,270
Over 60	201	4,614	34,577
Totals	3,300	63,613	489,689

THE PRIESTLEY COMMISSION, 1953–5

The Royal Commission's report[1] was published in November 1955, just two years after their inquiry had been put in hand. The most significant, and unusual, sections of the report will be found in the brief Chapter III[2] which, with a calmness that no doubts masks a good deal of feeling, refers to the limitations placed upon the inquiry by the narrowness of its terms of reference.

[1] *Royal Commission on the Civil Service* 1953–5; *Report* (Cmd 9613). See also above.
[2] op. cit., pp. 13–14.

In seeking a new comprehensive principle of pay to replace the Tomlin formula[1] the Commissioners' objective is described as 'an efficient service fairly remunerated'[2] and one 'recognized as efficient and staffed by members whose remuneration and conditions of service are thought fair both by themselves and by the community they serve'.[3] This objective, they consider, can be met by the principle of 'fair comparison' with the current remuneration of outside staffs employed on broadly comparable work, taking account of differences in other conditions of service. In applying this principle internal relativities between classes and between grades would have to be taken into account. More attention would necessarily be given to the short-term changes which the Tomlin formula excluded.

The difficulty of discovering the actual levels of remuneration outside the Service is admitted and the present practice of the two sides each putting forward its own somewhat partial information in controversies about remuneration is condemned. To overcome an undoubted difficulty the Royal Commission make what is perhaps their most radical proposal. They recommend the setting up of a fact-finding branch, separate from those divisions of the Treasury responsible for establishment matters, with the task of collecting the information about the outside situation on which negotiations in future should be based. The staff are to be enabled to participate in this work, which might possibly be attached to the Ministry of Labour and National Service.

The pay scales actually recommended in the Report, and based upon the assumption that the present Civil Service is efficient and would stand up to outside comparisons, do not include any substantial alterations except for the higher grades of the Administrative Class and equivalent ranks. For the top posts advances of £1,000 to £1,500 a year are recommended, but generally the increases suggested go no further than to offset the payments at present due for permanent overtime, the continuance of which is rightly condemned by the Commission. In fact for the Clerical Officers the proposals represent a small decrease in the pay packet.

Reference to Diagram II on page 45 will suggest how much of the working sector of the administration is massed below the £1,000 salary line. Full acceptance of the Royal Commission's proposals would not begin to affect the picture given by the diagram until that level had been reached, and then not very much, below the £2,000 level. No real effort was made to restore the differentials of the middle grades. To sum up on the question of remuneration: it cannot be considered that the Commission's proposals have done anything to encourage recruits, who

[1] See p. 52.
[2] op. cit., para. 67(i), p. 15.
[3] op. cit, para. 95, p. 24.

are little likely to be influenced by the higher rewards for the few top posts which on the most optimistic assessment they are not likely to reach in any case for twenty-five to thirty years.

The Commission accept the system of provincial differentiation, proposing even to widen the gap at the lower end of the salary scale, but they state a preference for a system which takes the provincial rate as the standard and makes an addition for the higher costs of living in the Metropolis. They advocate a 5-day week, to be reached through an intermediate stage of a 10½-day fortnight as previously proposed by the Treasury. Either method would be based upon a fortnight of 84 hours in London and 88 hours elsewhere. Cuts in the present annual leave allowances are also proposed. Only minor adjustments in the present Superannuation arrangements are contemplated.

The Report was generally received with a flourish in the Press, who apparently thought that the proposals represented an all-round advance in Civil Service pay. They were right only about the leaders who, everyone agreed, had long been poorly remunerated relatively to those with equal responsibilities in other spheres. The Civil Service itself was not enthusiastic, although reactions in the association journals were generally judicial in tone and indisposed to rant. Obviously little had been expected and at this stage, with difficult negotiations with the Treasury ahead, the task of marshalling resources and arguments for battle was considered more important than polemics.

If we look at the detailed proposals in the Report there is very little that is new or that could not have been achieved through the existing consultative machinery. The general principles adumbrated may very well err on the side of underestimating the stress laid by the Tomlin Commission on the importance of the long-term factor in determining the conditions of employment appropriate to a life career. Such principles ought not, of course, to ignore the need for a good deal of flexibility at a time when changes in the value of money are almost daily invalidating the terms of the contract of service into which State and servant have entered. Quite apart from the difficulty of obtaining the objective information on which comparisons may be based – a process that certainly should be made more effective by the setting up of an impartial fact-finding agency – there is still the difficulty of assessing those other factors outside the normal pay scales referred to in the phrase 'differences in other conditions of service'.[1] These differences are imponderable. At one time security of tenure was an important attraction of Civil Service employment, more than sufficient to outweigh the manifest disadvantages of the restriction of opportunity which State service inevitably imposes. How are these to be valued except by returning to the Anderson Committee's principle of paying rates that

[1] op. cit., para. 96, p. 25.

will be sufficient to attract suitable recruits and maintain an efficient service? And this would burke the whole issue.

The proposed deterioriation in annual leave allowances would make the Service less attractive, as would also the perpetuation of the relatively longer working day introduced under the exigencies of war. It is true that a five-day week would to some extent offset these drawbacks, but service to the public may require the attendance of such large skeleton staffs on Saturdays that this principle will in some departments be only partially attainable. The overriding importance of service to the public in the public services raises the question here whether this is not a condition in which civil service itself presupposes that officials will not in many cases be able to share an advantage available to large sectors of the community. In this case the longer leave allowances, maintained in much less favourable past times, would appear to be fully justified. On the question of superannuation the Royal Commission literally refuse to tidy up certain inconsistencies,[1] although it must be recollected that in this sphere no radical proposals were put forward.

Only rarely does the Report adopt viewpoints proffered by the civil servants' own representatives. The most notable exception is in the proposed pay advances for the holders of the top positions, obviously fully supported by the staff associations concerned. Little has been proposed to restore the lost differentials of the middle grades, whose importance as supervisors and managers has advanced inversely with their standards of remuneration. In conceding considerable but not unreasonable advances for the leaders it could be argued that neither trade union pressures nor common equity had much to do with it. Apart from the obvious financial point that large increases for the leaders are cumulatively less expensive than modest increases for all the rest, there is the sociological and ideological factor that the present policy everywhere of ensuring that the leadership group has standards of remuneration far above those of the rest of the working hierarchy is really determined by the new ruling class themselves. This is certainly a symptom of the much heralded 'Managerial Revolution', which in this country at least is largely negatived by the highly Gilbertian method of taking most of it back through progressive Income Tax and Surtax.

The Royal Commission, then, have produced a document that frequently endorses the Treasury viewpoint. Despite its restricted terms of reference this seems to be a pity and from a reading of its day-to-day examination of witnesses this does not appear to have been inevitable. The impartiality of the chair stands out brilliantly, even when compared with the Royal Commissioners' illustrious predecessors. The probing

[1] Such as, for example, the existing rule that a long serving civil servant who completes forty years established service before reaching his sixtieth birthday can neither retire on full pension straight away nor receive further addition to his pension except for service after 60.

nature of questions put by members, coupled with fairness and balance in argument suggests a very high standard of inquiry. If the results are therefore disappointing the reasons must be sought elsewhere. It may perhaps be found in the very nature and methods of such investigatory bodies, or perhaps in the environment in which the investigations took place. The Treasury viewpoint is important largely because it is only at that important administrative focus that the whole problem of Civil Service is under constant and expert review, and subjected to an overriding policy based upon an assessment of the nation's needs and financial situation. Alternative viewpoints are amateur in comparison and the Royal Commission could not be expected in two short years to make up for such a grave defect in the nation's information.

It is certain, therefore, that the Report of the Royal Commission of 1953–5 will not rank with its great predecessors. Its findings are ephemeral, almost inevitably destined to be superseded in subsequent negotiations, but for this the Royal Commission deserves little blame. Its scope was inadequate to a great task that remains still to be performed.

* * * *

Events have been unfolding at breakneck speed even as this final chapter is being completed. The Government having accepted the Royal Commission's advice, negotiations with the Civil Service through its associations and Whitley Council culminated in an agreement which was formally ratified on June 18th, 1956. Rarely, surely, has a Royal Commission Report been so quickly and totally implemented; and never, certainly, one dealing with the Civil Service.

The official offer, though embodying substantially the Royal Commission's proposals, was presented to the staffs through Whitley channels as a comprehensive solution to be accepted or rejected as a whole – the so-called 'package' offer. This included *inter alia* (i) the acceptance of the principle of basing pay on 'fair comparisons'; (ii) the abandonment of permanent overtime (which had been worked since the war) and standardization of the working week at 42 hours in London, 44 in the provinces (inclusive of one hour's lunch break); (iii) the adoption of the 5-day week as widely as the full maintenance of current standards of public service would permit; (iv) the basing of annual leave allowances on length of service as well as salary maxima, and involving a reduction in the allowance during an officer's earlier years of service; (v) revision of pay scales on the lines proposed by the Royal Commission, modified by awards on account of increases in the cost of living which had in the meantime been given; and (vi) parity of conditions of service for temporary staff.

The staffs had reservations to make under certain of the headings, but after discussion, sometimes heated, the acceptance of the 'package' was approved one by one at the annual conferences of the several staff associations. It will be noted that the change to the 5-day week was adopted without the intermediate step of a 10½-day fortnight which the Royal Commission had visualized. It was also agreed to set up the proposed fact-finding organization, called the Civil Service Pay Research Unit, under the general control of a Committee of the Civil Service National Whitley Council, with a Civil Service staff under a director appointed by the Prime Minister. Its functions will involve two processes:

(i) 'establishing job comparability, due allowance being made for differences in grading structure'; and

(ii) 'the discovery of the pay and conditions of service that attach to jobs regarded as comparable'.

Thus the Priestley Commission passes into history with an admirably effective piece of tidying up by H.M. Treasury and the civil servants through their negotiating machinery. The introduction of the 5-day week should certainly have the effect of improving the Civil Service's attractiveness to the recruit, although other factors in the settlement may well offset this obvious advantage.

THE CRISIS AND ITS SOLUTION

If the appointment of the Priestley Commission clearly indicated the recognition of the existence of a crisis in the Civil Service, the restriction of its terms of reference certainly suggests that as late as the autumn of 1953 the gravity of that crisis was not fully recognized even in the most influential circles. We have argued that the spirit of civil service is essential to an efficient democracy; equally an efficient public service is essential to a Welfare State based upon the degree of socialization already operating in Britain. But the large-scale administrative organization in which the Civil Service is now involved renders it difficult to preserve the civil service spirit and to prevent the encroachment of bureaucracy. The Civil Service is in peril because no real attempt is being made to resolve the opposition between two apparently incompatible tendencies.

The general policy of both using the Civil Service as a general pattern in implementing policies which it is considered desirable that the rest of the working population should adopt and at the same time of assimilating Civil Service conditions of employment to those of the wider community is undoubtedly adding to a crisis that would have arisen in any case. The modern state may have a Civil Service; if not, it must have a Bureaucracy, and in either case it cannot afford inefficiency. An efficient Civil Service is therefore, by definition, a *sine qua non*, and if this be accepted the whole idea of assimilating official and non-official sectors of the community is suspect, except in a completely socialized community. If we accept this proposition it will be seen that the assumptions on which the Royal Commission's principles of remuneration are based, are wrong and it may well be that the community's most vital interest rests in recognizing this. The real danger lies in the fact that the effects of a declining Civil Service are insidious. The crisis is no less serious for being unspectacular. The cure if too long delayed may come too late to reverse a trend that has gone too far. In any case it will take a long time to operate effectively. There is little margin for further delay.

CONCLUSION

It is not claimed that this book propounds a cure for the crisis of the Civil Service. The situation is much too complicated for any such claim to be proffered, nor are all the factors that need attention confined within the administrative sphere of the central government. This particular crisis is merely part of a larger crisis of national inspiration.

What is urgently needed is a change of attitude not only in the public mind but within the Civil Service itself, as discussed in the early chapters of the present Part. Specific proposals of the type scattered throughout this book are merely examples of some of the detailed changes that need to be introduced to make the Civil Service into a dynamic organization; there are many equally valid alternatives to be considered. The point to be pressed is that complacent acceptance of existing methods will not assist us in grappling with the tasks ahead. The myopic obstruction of existing interests must not be allowed to prevent alterations essential to an emergency situation which those who are implicated are rarely able to comprehend in advance.

The nation needs more than ever before a Civil Service capable of the highest devotion and sacrifice to its service and this presupposes an esteem on the part of those served much higher than exists today. We need a body of civil servants even more efficient than those of a past age and this presupposes professional standards far above anything visualized before. The officials of the future will need higher qualifications to deal with much more difficult tasks and situations. They will need to combine a sense of political impartiality as high as ever with an awareness of the world only achievable through the maintenance of a living interest in all that goes on in life in the broadest sense. Such ends can no longer be achieved through a narrow oligarchic system admirably suited to a Platonic world. In the new Civil Service there will have to be embodied the principle of equal opportunity towards which the wider community is gradually moving. The community will not get its new Civil Service on the cheap, but from its efficiency it will derive an economy that mediocrity will never produce. Bureaucracy, whether of the efficient or the inefficient variety, will be dear at any price, as all history shows. Above all the New Civil Service, like the New World, will only emerge on the wings of a more liberal understanding.

SELECT BIBLIOGRAPHY

This list includes only books and pamphlets dealing with the British Civil Service which have been published since 1939. Other writings have been mentioned in footnotes to the text. References to the Civil Service and allied topics will also be found in works on the British Constitution, in books on public administration in a general sense and in the biographical writings of statesmen and officials. The files of *Public Administration*, published quarterly by the Royal Institute of Public Administration, and of the periodicals of the various Civil Service staff organizations also contain a store of basic information on the subject. The list is divided into Non-Official and Official sections and arranged generally according to the date of publication.

NON-OFFICIAL

1941 **The Growth of the British Civil Service, 1780-1939,** by Emmeline W. Cohen. 221 pp. (Allen & Unwin)
A brief history of the Civil Service; the only one so far available.

1941 **The Higher Civil Service of Great Britain,** by H. E. Dale. xiv+232 pp. (Oxford University Press)
A valuable examination of the manners and quality of the highest ranks of the Civil Service between the wars.

1942 **Passed to You Please,** by J. P. W. Mallalieu. 160 pp. (Victor Gollancz)
Mainly a polemic against officialdom to a popular recipe, with a characteristic 'Introduction' by the late Prof. H. J. Laski.

1942 **Civil Service Reform,** by the Liberal Party. 16 pp. (Liberal Publication Dept.)
The interim report of a sub-committee on the Reform of the Civil Service appointed by the Party's Industrial and Social Reconstruction Committee.

1943 **So Far . . .,** by W. J. Brown. 295 pp. (Allen & Unwin)
The informative autobiography of a prominent Civil Service trade union leader.

1943 **The Civil Service: Retrospect and Prospect,** by W. J. Brown. 80 pp. With a 'Foreword' by Sir N. F. Warren Fisher. (Published by the Author)
A brief description of the Civil Service with reference to wartime developments.

1943 **Civil Service Staff Relationships,** by E. N. Gladden. xi+184 pp. With a 'Foreword' by Sir Horace Wilson (William Hodge & Co.)
Discusses the rise of staff associations and the Whitley system of joint consultation.

1943 **The Personnel and Problems of the Higher Civil Service,** by H. E. Dale. 16 pp. (Oxford University Press)
Text of the Sydney Ball lecture, to the Association of Barnett House, Oxford.

1944 **Post-War Reconstruction,** by the Institution of Professional Civil Servants. 15 pp. (Published by the Institute)
Deals with the professional, scientific and technical branches of the Civil Service.

1944 **The Professional Civil Servant's Handbook,** by L. A. C. Herbert. 352 pp. (Institution of Professional Civil Servants)
A later edition is available of this useful compendium which covers a wide range of Civil Service topics.

1944 **Representative Bureaucracy,** by J. D. Kingsley. 324 pp. (Antioch Press, U.S.A.)
A stimulating survey of the development of the British Civil Service which, nevertheless, loses by leaning too much on a preconceived class interpretation of administrative history.

1945 **The Civil Service and the People,** by R. W. Rawlings. 162 pp. (Lawrence & Wishart)
An interesting account based upon a class interpretation of Civil Service development.

1945 **The Civil Service: Its Problems and Future,** by E. N. Gladden. 187 pp. (Staples Press)
A survey of development, structure and internal problems, together with a proposed scheme of reform. A second edition appeared in 1948.

1945 **Law and Orders,** C. K. Allen. xvi+385 pp. (Stevens & Sons)
A general study of the relations between the Executive and other branches of government, with numerous references to the position of the Civil Service and the delegation of powers. Follows the tradition of Lord Hewart's famous polemical study, 'The New Despotism'.

1945 **A Modern Guide to the Civil Service,** by L. C. White. 78 pp. With a 'Foreword' by the late Prof. H. J. Laski. (University of London Press)
A practical description of the Civil Service at that time.

1947 **Officials and the Public,** by Sir Henry Bunbury. 19 pp. (*Current Affairs,* issued by the Bureau of Current Affairs)
A general survey of civil servants and their work, for discussion purposes.

1947 **The Civil Service and the Changing State,** by H. R. G. Greaves. 240 pp. (G. Harrap & Co.)
A controversial discussion of the higher Civil Service, supplemented by chapters on the public corporations and the machinery of government.

1947 **The Crisis of the Bureaucracy,** by L. Skevington. 14 pp. (The Pilot Press)
A stimulating essay by a wartime civil servant contributed to Pilot Papers, *Vol.* 2, *No.* 2.

1947 **Recruiting Civil Servants,** in *Planning,* No. 266. 19 pp. (P.E.P.)
Continues a discussion launched by P.E.P. during the war on the political aspects of the machinery of central government in Planning *No.* 173 *'The Machinery of Government, and No.* 214 *'A Civil General Staff'.*

1947 **The Experience of a University Teacher in the Civil Service,** by Sir Oliver S. Franks. 17 pp. (Oxford University Press)
Text of the Sydney Ball lecture to the Association of Barnett House, Oxford.

1947 **The Reform of the Higher Civil Service.** 60 pp. (Fabian Society)
For a Fabian report this document displays an unusual degree of upper-class consciousness and a tendency to overstress the parallel between the Civil Service and the Armed Forces.

1950 **Master of the Offices,** by H. Legge-Bourke. 41 pp. (Falcon Press)
A polemic on the control of the Civil Service.

1950 **Portrait of a Profession,** by Sir Edward Bridges. 33 pp. (Cambridge University Press)
The Rede Lecture, 1950, *by the Head of the Civil Service.*

1951 **Staff Reporting,** by I. E. P. Menzies and E. Anstey. 95 pp. (Allen & Unwin)
A useful survey of Civil Service practice, which does not, however, presume to delve far below the surface. Has a Foreword by Sir Horace Wilson.

1951 **The Civil Service Today,** by T. A. Critchley. 150 pp. (Victor Gollancz)
Pays special attention to the work of civil servants of different grades.

1952 **Le Civil Service Britannique,** by Paul-Marie Gaudemet. 172 pp. (Libraire Armand Colin, Paris)
A comprehensive and detached survey on legalist lines by an eminent French scholar.

1952 **How the Civil Service Works,** by Bosworth Monck. 258 pp. (Phoenix House)
A brief account not only of the Civil Service but of the Central Government. The second half of the book is devoted to a summary of the work of the individual departments.

1952 **Modern Staff Training,** by F. J. Tickner. 159 pp. (University of London Press)

Although dealing with the wider aspects of its subject this book, by a former Director of Training and Education at H.M. Treasury, is undoubtedly based largely upon the author's experience of Civil Service training.

1952 **The Fountains in Trafalgar Square,** by C. K. Munro. x+202 pp. (William Heinemann)

Personal recollections and opinions of a retired civil servant who is also well known as a dramatist.

1952 **The C.S.C.S. Compendium.** xvi+556 pp. (Civil Service Clerical Association)

The latest edition of a work first compiled before the war, bringing together a budget of official information relevant to personnel management of the Civil Service.

1953 **Yours for Action,** by Bernard Newman. viii+196 pp. (Civil Service Clerical Association)

A well-illustrated commemorative volume describing the development of the largest staff association of office workers in the Civil Service.

1953 **Whitleyism,** by James Callaghan. Fabian Research Series, No. 159. 40 pp. (Fabian Society)

A study of joint consultation in the Civil Service written from a Labour standpoint.

1954 **The Civil Service in the Constitution,** by K. C. Wheare. 34 pp. (The Athlone Press)

A lecture delivered before the University of London to commemorate the centenary of the Trevelyan-Northcote Report.

1955 **The Battle of Crichel Down,** by R. Douglas Brown. 192 pp. (The Bodley Head)

A balanced survey of an occurrence that caused a considerable stir at the time.

1955 **Higher Civil Servants in Britain,** by R. K. Kelsall. xvi+233 pp. (Routledge & Kegan Paul)

A study of the origins and social background of members of the higher ranks of the Civil Service from 1870 *onwards.*

1955 **A History of Red Tape,** by Sir John Craig. ix+211 pp. (Macdonald & Evans)

A broad general survey of the development of the central departments, their officials and their work.

1955 **The Civil Service in Great Britain,** by G. A. Campbell. 383 pp. (Pelican)

Covers the whole machinery of the central administration; a readable and reliable if somewhat mixed up budget of information.

1955 **The Foreign Office,** by Lord Strang. 226 pp. (Allen & Unwin)
A valuable contribution to the New Whitehall Series. Provides an excellent account of the staff and functions of the Foreign Service.

1955 **The Real Rulers of Our Country,** by Elijah Wilkes. 16 pp. (Routledge & Kegan Paul)
A provocative essay in a pamphlet series, entitled 'Passport to Survival'.

1956 **The Civil Service; Some Human Aspects,** by Frank Dunnill. vi+226 pp. (George Allen & Unwin)
A valuable account of the Service which places the chief emphasis on the human element.

1956 **The Civil Service in Britain and France.** Edited by William A. Robson. vii+191 pp. (The Hogarth Press)
A series of instructive essays by a number of well-known experts on the subject, extended from a special issue of 'The Political Quarterly', *originally published at the end of* 1954.

OFFICIAL

1942 Report from the Select Committee on **Offices or Places of Profit under the Crown.** 55 pp.
Deals 'inter alia' with the position of civil servants.

1942 Sixteenth Report from the Select Committee on National Expenditure (session 1941–2) on **Organization and Control of the Civil Service.** 55 pp.
This report led to the development of O & M and Staff Training in the central administration.

1943 Proposals for the **Reform of the Foreign Service** (Cmd. 6420). 10 pp.
Summary of the Government's proposals for reform following the Foreign Minister's statement in the House of Commons on June 11th, 1941.

1944 Report of the Committee on the **Training of Civil Servants** (Cmd. 6525). 34 pp.
The Assheton Report on which the present system of training is based.

1944 **Recruitment to Established Posts in the Civil Service during the Reconstruction Period** (Cmd. 6567). 23 pp.
A Statement of Government policy and Report by the Civil Service National Whitley Council.

1945 **The Scientific Civil Service** (Cmd. 6679). 16 pp.
A White Paper stating the Government's plans for reorganization. Includes as Annexe, 'Report of the Barlow Committee on Scientific Staff'.

1945 **Post-War Prospects for the Established Civil Servant.** 16 pp.
A pamphlet addressed by H.M. Treasury to serving civil servants, especially members of H.M. Forces.

1945 **The Administrative Class of the Civil Service** (Cmd. 6680). 2 pp.
This briefest of all White Papers, covers an organizational change and announces revised salaries for the whole class.

1946 **Marriage Bar in the Civil Service** (Cmd. 6886). 24 pp.
Report of a Committee of the Civil Service National Whitley Council.

1947 Fifth Report from the Select Committee on Estimates (session 1946–7) on **Organization and Methods and its Effect on the Staffing of Government Departments.** xxv+111 pp.
Includes a brief appendix listing the functions of Treasury and Departmental O & M.

1947 **Working Conditions in the Civil Service.** 164 pp. and appendices.
A comprehensive survey by a Study Group appointed by H.M. Treasury.

1948 Ninth Report from the Select Committee on Estimates (session 1947–8) on **The Civil Service Commission.** xiii+43 pp.
Includes an examination of the work of the Civil Service Selection Board.

1949 **Staff Relations in the Civil Service.** 38 pp.
A valuable survey issued by the Treasury; up-to-date editions are published from time to time.

1949 Report of the Tribunal to inquire into **Allegations reflecting on the Official Conduct of Ministers of the Crown and other Public Servants** (Cmd. 7616). 82 pp.
Known as the Lynskey Report, it exonerates the Civil Servants involved in the Inquiry.

1949 Report of the Committee on **Higher Civil Service Remuneration** (Cmd. 7635). 14 pp.
Known as the Chorley Report, it recommends improvement for the higher posts.

1949 Report of the Committee on the **Political Activities of Civil Servants** (Cmd. 7718). 42 pp.
The Masterman Report.

1950 Report of the Committee on **Intermediaries** (Cmd. 7904). 92 pp.
An inquiry into 'how far persons are making a business of acting as specialists in the submission of applications for licences or permits, or otherwise as intermediaries between Government Departments; and to report whether the activities of such persons are liable to give rise to abuses; and to make recommendations.

1951 Seventh Report from the Select Committee on Estimates (session 1950–1) on **the Foreign Service.** xxx+284 pp.
Contains useful information about the establishments abroad.

1951 Memorandum by the Civil Service Commissioners on the Use of the **Civil Service Selection Board in the Reconstruction Competitions.** 46 pp.
An authoritative account of the 'house-party' experiment.

1951 Report of the Committee on the **Organization, Structure and Remuneration of the Works Group of Professional Civil Servants.** 28 pp.
An investigation carried out in accordance with recommendations of the Chorley Committee (Cmd. 7635).

1952 **Digest of Pension Law and Regulations of the Civil Service.** 382 pp.
A comprehensive collection of extracts, etc., from Superannuation Acts, and Rules, Regulations and Orders issued in connexion therewith, compiled by H.M. Treasury.

1952 Report of the Committee on the **Organization, Structure and Remuneration of the Professional Accountant Class in the Civil Service.** 22 pp.
Discusses 'inter alia' the question whether the scope of the class should be extended to cover accounting work habitually carried out by members of the Executive Class.

1954 **Public Inquiry ordered by the Minister of Agriculture into the disposal of land at Crichel Down** (Cmd. 9176). 34 pp.

1954 Report of a **Committee appointed by the Prime Minister to consider whether certain Civil Servants should be transferred to other duties** (Cmd. 9220). 4 pp.
A footnote to the Inquiry into the Crichel Down affair (Cmd. 9176).

1954 **The British Civil Service, 1854–1954,** by Wyn Griffith. 32 pp.
A brief history officially published on the occasion of the centenary of the publication of the Trevelyan-Northcote Report.

1954 **Royal Commission on the Civil Service (1953).** Introductory Factual Memorandum on the Civil Service. 184 pp.
Royal Commission on the Civil Service (1953): Supplement to Introductory Factual Memorandum on the Civil Service (Medical and Legal Staffs). 13 pp.
Information compiled by H.M. Treasury for the guidance of the Royal Commission.

1954/55 **Royal Commission on the Civil Service:** Minutes of Evidence 1–28. 1,176 pp. in twenty-four separate issues.

1954 **Royal Commission on the Civil Service:** Appendix I to Minutes of Evidence: First Selection of Supplementary Statements from Witnesses. 57 pp.

1955 **Royal Commission on the Civil Service:** Appendix II to Minutes of Evidence: Second Selection of Supplementary Statements from Witnesses. 89 pp.

1955 **Royal Commission on the Civil Service, 1953–5: Report.** 239 pp.
The Report of the Priestley Commission on the Civil Service.

1955 Report concerning the **Disappearance of Two Foreign Office Officials.** 8 pp.

White Paper on the case of Burgess and Maclean who disappeared behind the Iron Curtain in 1951.

1956 **Statement on the Findings of the Conference of Privy Councillors on Security.** 5 pp.

A White Paper following an inquiry into the lessons of the Burgess-Maclean affair.

Choice of Careers. Up-to-date information on situations in the Civil Service is published in pamphlets in this series, provided by the Central Youth Employment Executive and revised from time to time.

N.B.—All the above Official publications are issued and sold by H.M. Stationery Office. Question papers from previous examinations are also purchasable from the Stationery Office. Information about the examinations for entry into the Civil Service may be obtained from the Civil Service Commission, 6 Burlington Gardens, London, W.1.

INDEX

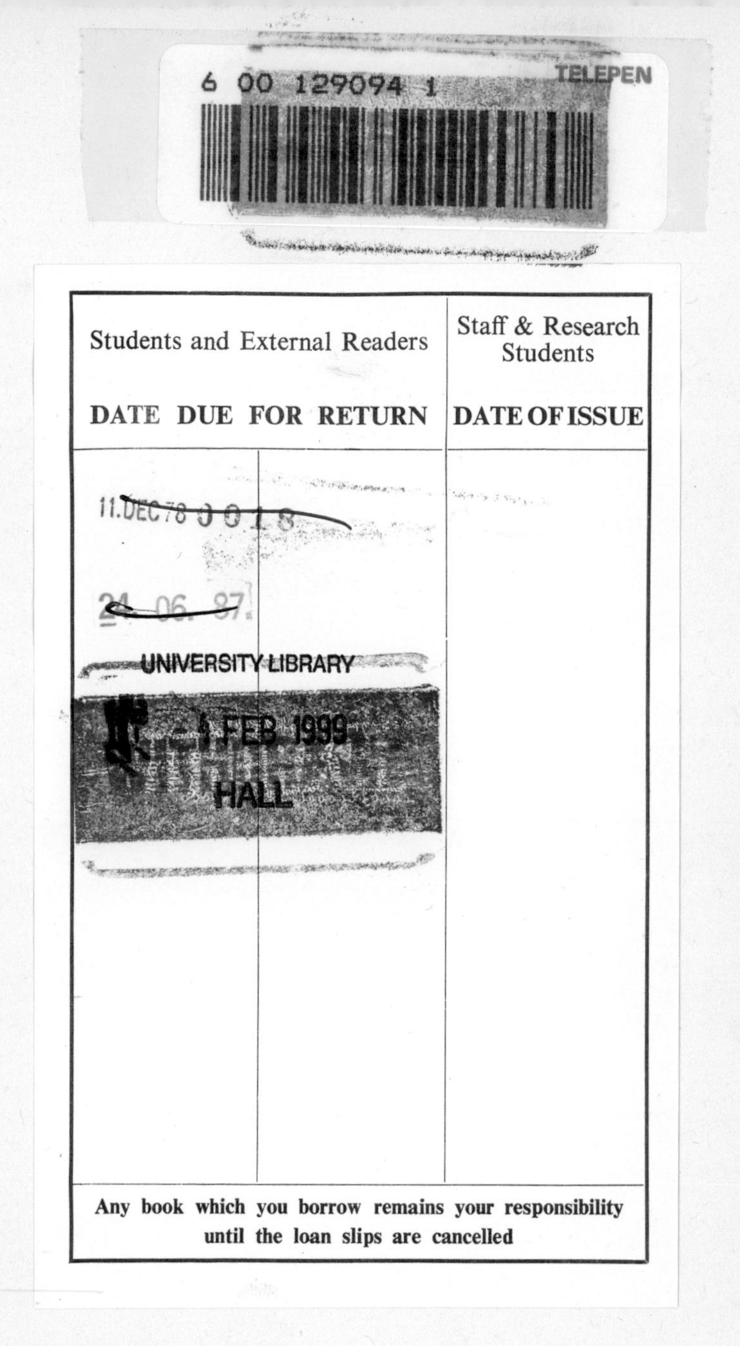